What you need to know about Improving Basic English Skills

SECOND EDITION

Jerry D. Reynolds
Educational Consultant

Marion L. Steet

National Textbook Company
a division of NTC/CONTEMPORARY PUBLISHING GROUP
Lincolnwood, Illinois USA

ISBN: 0-8442-5967-5

Published by National Textbook Company,
a division of NTC/Contemporary Publishing Group, Inc.
4255 West Touhy Avenue,
Lincolnwood (Chicago), Illinois 60712-1975 U.S.A.
© 1998 by NTC/Contemporary Publishing Group, Inc.

6 7 8 9 10 11 12 13 14 15 MER 15 14 13 12 11

Library of Congress Cataloging-in-Publication Data

Reynolds, Jerry D.
    What you need to know about improving basic English skills — 2nd
ed.
      p.   cm. — (NTC skill builders)
   Summary: Uses activities to develop proficiency in grammar,
punctuation, spelling, vocabulary, sentence and paragraph
development, and letter writing.
    ISBN 0-8442-5967-5
    1. English language—Grammar—Problems, exercises, etc.
[1. English language—Grammar—Problems, exercises, etc.]
I. Steet, Marion L. II. Series.
PE1112.R39   1997
428.2—dc21   97-12336
                           CIP
                            AC

TABLE OF CONTENTS

Using the Right Words   49

UNIT 3   Mastering the Mechanics   113

Improving Spelling Skills   147

Building Vocabulary   177

Applying Writing Skills   207

Combining Sentences   229

PREFACE

The goal of this worktext is, as the title states, to help you improve your English skills. There is always room for improvement of one's English skills. Regardless of age, education, or occupation, most everyone has problems using the English language as effectively as it could be used.

Spoken and Written English

Many, if not most, of your problems with English develop when you forget that there are two closely related but essentially different kinds of English—*spoken* English and *written* English. To use our language effectively, you must be able to adapt easily from one of its forms to the other. If these two forms of English were identical, you could simply apply one set of rules to both, and many of your problems would disappear. But, unfortunately, spoken English and written English are *not* the same. You simply can't ignore their differences.

In speaking and in writing, your ideas are only as effective as the manner in which you express them. When you speak, you don't have to worry about spelling, punctuation, and capitalization. But when you write, these skills become very important. When you speak, you can correct yourself immediately if your listener doesn't understand. When you write, however, your writing must stand alone. When you speak, your words vanish in the air; but when you write, they remain on paper for everyone to see. Small wonder that others are more critical of the way you write than of the way you speak.

Rules for Good English

Because people from different parts of the country and from different backgrounds speak English differently, it is very difficult, if not impossible, to establish hard and fast rules for a standard spoken English. But while people may expect varieties of spoken English to "sound" different, they expect written English to "look right" on paper. That is why fairly rigid and universal standards for written English have been established and why these standards are taught. In fact, the sort of "good" English an educated person is expected to use is called Standard English—or, more accurately, Standard Written English. This worktext will help you improve your Standard Written English.

How to Use This Book to Improve Your Performance

Each of the seven units in the book is organized in the same manner, beginning with a Pretest to help you determine what you already know about the skills in that unit. You can then record your Pretest score on the Progress and Performance Chart, which follows this preface. Following the Pretest is a series of lessons, each of which includes clear explanations of rules—followed with opportunities for Practice and Application of these skills. For further reinforcement, you can use your own writing to see if you can locate and correct errors and, thus, to apply what you have learned.

At the close of each unit is a Posttest—similar to the Pretest—designed to help you assess your performance in mastering the skills in the unit. Set a high standard for yourself in each unit, and strive to achieve that standard. By charting *both* your Pretest and Posttest scores on the Progress and Performance Chart, you can easily see the *growth* you have made in each unit. Hopefully, you will see this same improvement in your own writing of reports, letters, and papers.

To be successful in the technological age we live in, you must have a strong command of basic English skills. The seven units in this worktext—supported by guided practice and frequent application throughout the book—will give you the tools to become a better writer and speaker of English.

Recording Your Test Scores

This chart is designed for you to determine your progress and to assess your performance on the Pretest and Posttest for each of the seven units.

1. After taking the Pretest at the beginning of the unit, fill in the bar graph of that unit with your Pretest score.

2. Follow the same procedure for the Posttest by filling in the appropriate column of the bar graph with your score.

3. The bar graph for the Example illustrates that the student correctly answered eleven out of a possible twenty on the Pretest: 55 percent of the answers were correct. The student's performance on the Posttest shows significant progress: all twenty answers (100 percent) were correct.

4. By following this procedure for each of the seven units, you can easily see the progress you have made between the Pretest and Posttest for each unit, as well as your overall performance on all tests.

Percentage	Example		Unit 1		Unit 2		Unit 3		Unit 4		Unit 5		Unit 6		Unit 7	
	Pretest	Posttest	Pretest	Posttest	Pretest	Posttest	Pretest	Posttest	Pretest	Posttest	Pretest	Posttest	Pretest	Posttest	Pretest	Posttest
100	20		20		50		20		50		20		20		10	
90	18		18		45		18		45		18		18		9	
80	16		16		40		16		40		16		16		8	
70	14		14		35		14		35		14		14		7	
60	12		12		30		12		30		12		12		6	
50	10		10		25		10		25		10		10		5	
40	8		8		20		8		20		8		8		4	
30	6		6		15		6		15		6		6		3	
20	4		4		10		4		10		4		4		2	
10	2		2		5		2		5		2		2		1	
0	0		0		0		0		0		0		0		0	

Name _____   Number Correct × 5 = ☐

Three choices follow each numbered sentence. Two of these choices represent different ways of rewriting the original sentence. Circle the letter of the choice (B or C) that represents the better rewriting. If you feel that the original sentence does not need to be rewritten, circle A, *no change*.

1. Carlos said that the gym will be closed next week. For repairs and painting.
   A. no change
   B. Carlos said that the gym will be closed next week; for repairs and painting.
   C. Carlos said that the gym will be closed next week for repairs and painting.

2. The heir to the Singer fortune married Isadora Duncan. A dancer whose performances shocked some.
   A. no change
   B. The heir to the Singer fortune married Isadora Duncan, a dancer whose performances shocked some.
   C. The heir to the Singer fortune married Isadora Duncan a dancer whose performances shocked some.

3. Paula feeds the dogs. Before leaving for school.
   A. no change
   B. Paula feeds the dogs before leaving for school.
   C. Paula feeds the dogs; before leaving for school.

4. I bought the bike. Which has twenty-four gears.
   A. no change
   B. I bought the bike, which has twenty-four gears.
   C. I bought the bike it has twenty-four gears.

5. Just when I thought he had finished. He began talking again.
   A. no change
   B. Just when I thought he had finished, he began talking again.
   C. Just when I thought he had finished he began talking again.

6. Epoxy glue dries almost on contact, therefore, you must be sure not to get any on your fingers.
   A. no change
   B. Epoxy glue dries almost on contact, therefore your must be sure not to get any on your fingers.
   C. Epoxy glue dries almost on contact; therefore, you must be sure not to get any on your fingers.

7. Josh is a Leo, he's supposed to have an outgoing personality.
   A. no change
   B. Josh is a Leo he's supposed to have an outgoing personality.
   C. Because Josh is a Leo, he's supposed to have an outgoing personality.

8. Mr. Owens presented the award. The award was a check. The check was for five hundred dollars. The winner was Kevin.
   A. no change
   B. Mr. Owens presented the award and it was a five-hundred-dollar check and the winner was Kevin.
   C. Mr. Owens presented the award, a check for five hundred dollars, to the winner, Kevin.

9. Eddie Rickenbacker became a millionaire as president of Eastern Airlines, and he was an ace fighter pilot in World War I.
   A. no change
   B. Eddie Rickenbacker became a millionaire as president of Eastern Airlines; and he was an ace fighter pilot in World War I.
   C. Eddie Rickenbacker, who was an ace fighter pilot in World War I, became a millionaire as president of Eastern Airlines.

10. The storm came suddenly. It came from the west. It brought hailstones. They were the size of golf balls.
    A. no change
    B. The storm came suddenly; it came from the west; it brought hailstones; they were the size of golf balls.
    C. The storm came suddenly from the west, bringing hailstones the size of golf balls.

11. We ordered new furniture, and it's for the lawn, and it's wrought iron, and the table has a striped umbrella.
    A. no change
    B. We ordered new furniture. It's for the lawn and it's wrought iron. The table has a striped umbrella.
    C. We ordered new wrought-iron lawn furniture. The table has a striped umbrella.

12. Because you cannot have a table, every one is reserved.
    A. no change   B. You cannot have a table. Because every one is reserved.
    C. You cannot have a table because every one is reserved.

13. The Atlanta police officer riding the horse he helped us understand which streets were one-way.
    A. no change
    B. The Atlanta police officer riding the horse helped us understand which streets were one-way.
    C. The Atlanta police officer riding the horse. He helped us understand which streets were one-way.

14. Lynn proudly hung the painting on the wall that she had bought at the thrift shop.
    A. no change
    B. Lynn proudly hung the painting on the wall. That she had bought at the thrift shop.
    C. Lynn proudly hung on the wall the painting that she had bought at the thrift shop.

15. Transcribing his shorthand quickly, the letter was finished before five o'clock by him.
    A. no change
    B. After transcribing his shorthand quickly, the letter was finished before five o'clock.
    C. Transcribing his shorthand quickly, he finished the letter before five o'clock.

16. Karen told me that she had given up eating junk food over the phone.
    A. no change
    B. Karen told me over the phone that she had given up eating junk food.
    C. Karen told me that she had given up eating funk food. Over the phone.

17. The couple who had been arguing foolishly vowed they would never speak to each other again.
    A. no change
    B. The couple who had been arguing foolishly vowed. They would never speak to each other again.
    C. The couple who had been foolishly arguing vowed they would never speak to each other again.

18. The auctioneer required buyers to pay cash and that they should make their own shipping arrangements.
    A. no change
    B. The auctioneer required buyers to pay cash. And make their own shipping arrangements.
    C. The auctioneer required buyers to pay cash and to make their own shipping arrangements.

19. If one does not participate, you cannot expect to be paid.
    A. no change   B. If you do not participate, you cannot expect to be paid.
    C. If you do not participate, one cannot expect to be paid.

20. In many novels, detective work seems fun, but actually it was dull and routine.
    A. no change
    B. In many novels, detective work seems fun, but actually it is dull and routine.
    C. In many novels, detective work seemed fun, but actually it is dull and routine.

Sentence Fragments: Prepositional Phrases

Name _____ Possible Score | 10 | My Score | |

A sentence expresses a complete thought and consists of a subject and a predicate that are not introduced by a subordinating word. A sentence fragment is a part of a sentence that cannot stand alone. Fragments are often phrases and clauses that have been incorrectly written as complete sentences. The next five lessons explain sentence fragments and how to correct them.

A prepositional phrase begins with a preposition and ends with a noun or a pronoun as in *on the road* or *for him*. Sometimes, a prepositional phrase is incorrectly punctuated as a complete sentence. Then it is a sentence fragment, an incomplete sentence. One way to correct such a fragment is to join it to a sentence.

> We walked home in the rain. **After the track meet.** [fragment]
>
> We walked home in the rain **after the track meet.**

Practice

Correct the sentence fragment in each of the following items by joining it to the sentence.

1. Mr. Martinez found a parking space. Near the supermarket. _____

   _____

2. The ice on the river has melted. Under the bridge. _____

   _____

3. Nobody laughed at our team. After the win Saturday. _____

   _____

4. Sophath left her book. Beside the bike rack. _____

   _____

5. Mr. Russo will divide the prize. Between you and me. _____

   _____

6. We hid the money. Behind the cereal boxes. _____

   _____

7. The keys were left under the doormat. For my brother and me. _____

   _____

8. Make a left turn. By the gas station. _____

   _____

9. The printer spewed out the report. In a flash. _____

   _____

10. The ship lay hidden. Behind a screen of fog. _____

    _____

Sentence Fragments: Appositives

Name _____   Possible Score [7]   My Score [ ]

Appositives identify, explain, or restate other words in sentences. When an appositive is incorrectly punctuated as a complete sentence, it is a fragment. Such a fragment may be corrected by joining it to a sentence.

Marty met Mr. Berman. **The new swimming coach.** [fragment]

Marty met Mr. Berman, **the new swimming coach.**

Practice

Correct the sentence fragment in each of the following items by joining it to the sentence. For clarity, use a comma to separate the appositive from the rest of the sentence.

1. Dave's new friend is Titan. A gigantic two-year-old Saint Bernard. _____

_____

_____

2. Beth ordered grapefruit juice. Her favorite drink. _____

_____

_____

3. That truck belongs to the Thompsons. The family next-door. _____

_____

_____

4. The rotary engine is named for its inventor. Felix Wankel. _____

_____

_____

5. Duke Ellington wrote "Mood Indigo." A great blues tune. _____

_____

_____

6. Niles won first prize. A new mountain bike. _____

_____

_____

7. The country's best-known cat was Morris. A star of TV commercials. _____

_____

_____

UNIT 1 Solving Sentence Problems

Name _____

Possible Score | 14 | My Score

Participial, gerund, and infinitive phrases are verbal phrases containing verb forms that are not part of the main verb of a sentence. When one of these verbal phrases is punctuated as a complete sentence, it is a fragment.

> Pete worked late. **Finishing his report at twelve.** [fragment]
>
> Laura's duties are many. **From drawing up contracts to issuing statements.** [fragment]
>
> We checked the old newspapers. **To find the article about Marie.** [fragment]

One way to correct such fragments is to join them to sentences.

> Pete worked late, **finishing his report at twelve.**
>
> Laura's duties are many, **from drawing up contracts to issuing statements.**
>
> We checked the old newspapers **to find the article about Marie.**

Another way to correct participial and gerund phrases written as sentences is to turn them into complete sentences.

> Pete worked late. **He finished his report at twelve.**
>
> Laura's duties are many. **They range from drawing up contracts to issuing statements.**

Practice 1

Correct the sentence fragment in each of the following items by joining the verbal fragment to the sentence that precedes it. Use a comma before the fragment in items 1 and 5.

1. Tom walked home slowly. Discouraged after failing the exam. _____

_____

_____

2. B.J. left early. To catch up with you. _____

_____

_____

3. The scientist worked frantically. To assemble the monster. _____

_____

_____

4. Everyone encouraged Tanya. To try out for the team. _____

_____

_____

5. My brother ate some yogurt. Thinking it was pudding. _____

_____

_____

Practice 2

Correct the sentence fragment in each of the following items by making it a complete sentence.

1. Carol decided to see the movie. After hearing us talk about it. _____

    _____

    _____

2. I couldn't answer. Not having understood the question. _____

    _____

    _____

3. Kevin couldn't find the path. Covered with drifting snow. _____

    _____

    _____

4. We stood around Ms. Garcia's desk. Watching the experiment. _____

    _____

    _____

5. Thousands lined State Street. Waiting for the mayor and her family. _____

    _____

    _____

6. A new sport is freestyle skiing. Commonly called "hotdogging." _____

    _____

    _____

7. Diane waited until five. Fearing the worst. _____

    _____

    _____

8. On weekends we earned money. By washing cars and baby-sitting. _____

    _____

    _____

9. Michelle wants to practice more. Before trying out for the team. _____

    _____

    _____

Sentence Fragments: Compound Verbs

Name _____   Possible Score | 15 | My Score | |

A compound verb consists of two verbs joined by a connecting word as in *tripped and stumbled, is failing but is continuing,* and *accept or reject.* When the connecting word and the second verb are incorrectly punctuated as a complete sentence, the result is a fragment.

Tom looked all over for his gloves. **And finally found them in his pocket.** [fragment]

One way to correct a fragment like this is to join both the connecting word and the second verb to a sentence.

Tom looked all over for his gloves **and finally found them in his pocket.**

Another way to correct this kind of fragment is to make it into a complete sentence.

Tom looked all over for his gloves. **He finally found them in his pocket.**

Practice 1

Correct the fragment in each of the following items by joining it to the preceding sentence.

1. Roberto and Carol entered the three-legged race. And won it. _____

_____

_____

2. We flushed out the radiator. But forgot to replace the radiator cap. _____

_____

_____

3. Luisa asked for quiet. And called the meeting to order. _____

_____

_____

4. Karen is on the stage crew. And also plays in the band. _____

_____

_____

5. The bus skidded on the wet pavement. And slid into a ditch. _____

_____

_____

6. The speaker talked for thirty minutes. And then answered questions. _____

_____

_____

Practice 2

Correct the fragment in each of the following items by making it into a complete sentence.

1. Henry Aaron tied the home-run record on April 4, 1974. And broke it four days later. _____

_____

_____

2. Raoul is good at biology. But has a hard time with math. _____

_____

_____

3. Diane grabbed her books. But left her lunch on the table. _____

_____

_____

4. Bárbara collects the money. And also pays the bills. _____

_____

_____

5. I dived into the water. And swam across the river. _____

_____

_____

6. Our teacher has a doctor's degree. But never mentions the fact. _____

_____

_____

7. Sally found your glasses. And turned them in to the office. _____

_____

_____

8. The ground crew dragged the infield. And put down the bases. _____

_____

_____

9. Marcia paid the bill. And left a tip for the waiter. _____

_____

_____

Sentence Fragments: Adjective Clauses

Name _____

Possible Score | 15 | My Score

An adjective clause is part of a sentence. Usually, it is introduced by a connecting word as in *who was late, which was broken,* and *that was noticed.* Even though an adjective clause may begin with a word like *who, whom, whose,* or *which,* it is not a question. When an adjective clause is incorrectly punctuated as a complete sentence, it is a fragment.

Pat came with a key. **Which didn't fit any of the locks.** [fragment]

There are two ways to correct a fragment like this. You can join the adjective clause to a sentence, or you can make it into a complete sentence.

Pat came with a key, **which didn't fit any of the locks.**

Pat came with a key. **It didn't fit any of the locks.**

Practice 1

Correct the fragment in each of the following items by joining it to the preceding sentence. Use a comma before the fragments in items 3, 4, and 6.

1. Dad will test-drive the motorcycle. That Russ wants to buy. _____

    _____

    _____

2. Kimson interviewed the student. Whose photo won first prize. _____ _____

    _____

    _____

3. Interest here is growing in soccer. Which is the world's most popular sport. _____

    _____

    _____

4. Try to avoid making loud noises. Which will wake the baby. _____

    _____

    _____

5. He wouldn't wait on the customer. Who had pushed to the head of the line. _____

    _____

    _____

6. At the Grand Ole Opry I saw the Friday-night show. Which was terrific. _____

    _____

    _____

Practice 2

Correct the fragment in each of the following items by making it into a complete sentence.

1. These baseballs are made in Taiwan. Which is ninety miles off the coast of China. _____

   _____

   _____

2. Everyone wanted to see Olga Korbut. Who had won three gold medals. _____

   _____

   _____

3. I bought an old car. That gets very good gas mileage. _____

   _____

   _____

4. I sat next to Mrs. Tuchman. Who has written a best-seller. _____

   _____

   _____

5. I should clean the garage. Which hasn't been cleaned in months. _____

   _____

   _____

6. They chose a student. Whose academic record was good. _____

   _____

   _____

7. We are going to visit Akron. Which is the tire capital of the world. _____

   _____

   _____

8. The road led to Wood Dale. Which is a pretty town. _____

   _____

   _____

9. We found a rusty anchor. Which had been buried six feet under the ground. _____

   _____

   _____

Application

Name _____   Possible Score [24]   My Score [ ]

A. Rewrite the following sentences, correcting each fragment. Make the fragment a complete sentence or join it to a sentence, whichever seems more effective.

1. Ms. Judy Lee is going to cross the country. In a hot-air balloon. _____

_____

_____

2. Matt is noted for the tricks he does. With a hacky sack. _____

_____

_____

3. The one with the largest circulation is the *Tribune*. A morning paper. _____

_____

_____

4. Our class sent get-well cards to Sydney. The sick elephant. _____

_____

_____

5. In the front yard sat a huge dog. Growling at passersby. _____

_____

_____

6. You need a passport. To travel in most foreign countries. _____

_____

_____

7. I'd need an hour. To explain the process to you. _____

_____

_____

8. They replaced the battery. And checked the electrical system. _____

_____

_____

9. Linda's always entering contests. And always losing. _____

_____

_____

10. You must file a claim. Or forget your loss. _____

_____

_____

11. We bought some pasta. That was made fresh today. _____

_____

_____

12. *Casablanca* is a great movie. That can be rented at the video store. _____

_____

_____

13. The tornado destroyed the homes. That lay in its path. _____

_____

_____

14. Emily collects coins. And sometimes sells them. _____

_____

_____

15. Jane gave her reasons. Which were good enough for me. _____

_____

_____

16. A Porsche is one car. That I've never driven. _____

_____

_____

B. On a separate sheet of paper, rewrite the following paragraphs, correcting each fragment. Make the fragment a complete sentence or join it to a sentence, whichever is more effective.

No one has yet solved the mystery of the Bermuda Triangle. An area off the coast of Florida. This area covers about 440,000 square miles. From Florida to Bermuda to Puerto Rico and back to Florida. Within this triangle over fifty ships and planes have disappeared. In most cases without leaving a trace.

One of the strangest incidents occurred in 1945. Five U.S. bombers disappeared. On a training mission. A seaplane also vanished. Carrying an experienced crew. The seaplane had taken off. To search for the bombers.

There is no good explanation for these events. Most of which occurred in fair weather. Some scientists think that unexpected storms or downward air currents caused the accidents. And speculate that ocean currents carried the wreckage away.

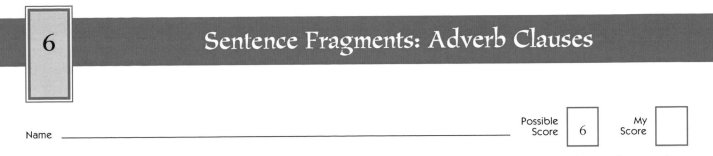
Name _____ Possible Score [6] My Score [ ]

An adverb clause usually begins with a connecting word like *because, if, when,* or *although* as in *because I want to, if you say so, when the lights went on,* and *although it rained.* An adverb clause is part of a sentence. When an adverb clause is incorrectly punctuated as a complete sentence, it is a fragment. One way to correct such a fragment is to join it to a sentence.

Lee takes his camera with him. **Wherever he goes.** [fragment]

Lee takes his camera with him **wherever he goes.**

When Jo arrived. Her cousins and aunts were waiting for her. [fragment]

When Jo arrived, her cousins and aunts were waiting for her.

Practice

Correct the fragment in each of the following items by joining it to a sentence. Use a comma after the fragments in items 2, 3, and 6.

1. You can repair this toaster. If you want to. _____

    _____

    _____

2. Just as the band started. Miguel slipped into his seat. _____

    _____

    _____

3. Since no one understood it the first time. Al explained the solution again. _____

    _____

    _____

4. Linda plays volleyball. Because she enjoys the game. _____

    _____

    _____

5. We decided to wear raincoats. After we heard the forecast. _____

    _____

    _____

6. Whenever he gets the chance. Gene practices his guitar. _____

    _____

Application

Name _____

Possible Score | 4 | My Score |

Rewrite the following paragraphs, correcting each fragment. Join the fragment to a sentence. Use commas where they are needed.

When a million dollars worth of jewels went on display in Stockholm. Officials picked the deadliest guards they could find. As visitors crowded into the embassy. They saw three of the most poisonous snakes in the world. The snakes were nestled behind glass, where the diamonds and the sapphires were kept.

Snake expert Olle Rosenqvist said, "I starved these vipers for about a week. So that they would be full of poison. If thieves should try to steal the jewels. They would be bitten and die."

Name _____

Possible Score 19   My Score [ ]

When no punctuation or only a comma is used between two sentences, the result is a run-on sentence. One sentence "runs on" into the other.

The kindling was damp the fire would not catch. [run-on]

The kindling was damp, the fire would not catch. [run-on]

There are several ways to correct a run-on sentence. If you feel that the ideas in a run-on sentence are really separate, make them into two sentences.

The kindling was damp. **T**he fire would not catch.

However, if you feel that the ideas are closely related, you should join them. You could join them with a semicolon or with a semicolon plus a connecting word. Notice that a comma follows the connecting word.

The kindling was damp; the fire would not catch.

The kindling was damp; **therefore,** the fire would not catch.

Still another way to join these ideas is to use a comma and a conjunction like *and, but,* or *or.*

The kindling was damp, **and** the fire would not catch.

Practice 1

Write *C* before those sentences that are correct, write *RO* before those that are run-on.

_____ 1. The jury voted to acquit the defendant was jubilant.

_____ 2. Lynn plays racquetball twice a week at the Y, she runs three miles every morning.

_____ 3. The wind shifted, but the smog remained.

_____ 4. The morning passed quickly however the afternoon dragged on—and on.

Practice 2

The following are run-on sentences. Rewrite each one, separating the ideas into two sentences.

1. Backpacking is fun, in most parks the trails are well marked. _____

_____

2. June is the best month for fishing, July is the worst. _____

_____

3. A bale of hay weighs three hundred pounds a bale of cotton weighs four hundred pounds. _____

_____

4. Do you know Jill's remedy it's to eat a spoonful of peanut butter. _____

_____

UNIT 1 Solving Sentence Problems

Practice 3

The following are run-on sentences. Correct them by adding semicolons in the appropriate places.

1. I bought a recording of Beethoven's Ninth it's played by the Boston Philharmonic.

2. Work when it's time to work play when it's time to play.

3. Track events involve running field events involve jumping and throwing.

4. His den was lined with handsomely bound books the trouble was that he never read any of them.

Practice 4

The following are run-on sentences. Rewrite each one, adding a comma and an appropriate coordinating conjunction.

1. A slogan is not a solution a catchy phrase is not an insight. _____

_____

_____

2. Wrench the bolt firmly don't force it. _____

_____

_____

3. Sam double-parked he didn't get a traffic violation. _____

_____

_____

4. You should oil your mitt regularly the leather will crack. _____

_____

_____

5. You had better start now you will never finish in time. _____

_____

_____

6. We counted the cash we came up short. _____

_____

_____

7. Stacie isn't home now I'll be glad to take a message. _____

_____

_____

Name _____

Possible Score | 7 | My Score | ☐

One idea in a run-on sentence may be less important than the other. You may correct the run-on sentence by rewriting the less important idea as a subordinate clause.

> The kindling was damp, the fire would not catch. [run-on]
>
> **Because the kindling was damp,** the fire would not catch. [subordinate clause]
>
> The kindling was **so** damp **that the fire would not catch.** [subordinate clause]

Practice

The following are run-on sentences. In each, rewrite one of the ideas to make it into a subordinate clause.

1. The undertow below the dam is strong, we shouldn't swim there. _____

_____

_____

2. The bricks aren't here, we can't lay the patio. _____

_____

_____

3. I was jogging, I heard a wood thrush singing. _____

_____

_____

4. You enter the city, the smell of the refineries hits you. _____

_____

_____

5. You're going sailing, remember to wear a life jacket. _____

_____

_____

6. Chad lost the election, he received a large vote. _____

_____

_____

7. The shirt comes in red, I will buy it. _____

_____

_____

17

Application

Name _____

The following paragraph has been written incorrectly as a single run-on sentence. Rewrite the paragraph, using as many different methods for correcting run-on sentences as you can.

In Houston there's a surprise awaiting potential home buyers you can still buy a ten-room house for $30,000 the house has parquet floors, hand-stained wall paneling, and working fireplaces it's built with wood from seventeen countries, the doorknobs and hinges are solid brass now here's the catch to live in this house, you have to be five inches tall this house is a dollhouse the real-estate agent is a famous Texas department store.

_____
_____
_____
_____
_____
_____
_____
_____
_____
_____
_____
_____
_____
_____
_____
_____
_____
_____
_____
_____

Name _____

Possible Score | 14 | My Score | |

To avoid a string of short, choppy sentences, examine your writing for sentences that are closely related and then combine them. Two closely related sentences that seem equal in importance may be combined in one of three ways: you may combine them with a comma and a coordinating conjunction, with a semicolon, or with a semicolon plus a connecting word followed by a comma.

> The concert was scheduled to begin at eight. The conductor was delayed. [two short, choppy sentences]
>
> The concert was scheduled to begin at eight, **but** the conductor was delayed.
>
> The concert was scheduled to begin at eight; the conductor was delayed.
>
> The concert was scheduled to begin at eight; **however,** the conductor was delayed.

On the other hand, if a pair of closely related sentences seem unequal in importance, you can make the less important sentence into a subordinated clause. One way to do this is to begin or end that sentence with a subordinating conjunction like *after, although, as, because, if, when,* or *while.*

> The detective questioned the girl. She was changing a tire.
>
> The detective questioned the girl **as she was changing a tire.** [subordinate clause]

Another way to change the less important sentence into a subordinate clause is to begin it with a relative pronoun like *who, which,* or *that.*

> The detective questioned the girl **who was changing a tire.** [subordinate clause]

In both versions the more important sentence stands as the main clause.

Practice 1
Combine the first three pairs of sentences with a comma and a coordinating conjunction; combine the second three pairs with either a semicolon or a semicolon plus a connecting word.

1. The band played early. The fireworks went off late. _____

   _____

2. The tapestry was beautiful. It was too expensive. _____

   _____

3. His income is modest. He enjoys teaching. _____

   _____

4. Kathy nominated Maria. Maria declined the nomination. _____

   _____

5. Grandma is seventy-five. She acts much younger. _____

   _____

6. Some went skiing. The rest stayed indoors. _____

   _____

Practice 2

Combine each of the following pairs of sentences into a single sentence. Make one sentence in each pair into a subordinate clause. Use either a subordinating conjunction or a relative pronoun.

1. The wind died down. The boat still capsized. _____

   _____

   _____

2. The sheriff bought a horse named Elmer. The horse had a bad leg. _____

   _____

   _____

3. Cynthia plays pool. She enjoys the game. _____

   _____

   _____

4. Elaina lived in Spain. She spoke fluent Spanish. _____

   _____

   _____

5. A summons came for Charlie. He was surprised. _____

   _____

   _____

6. We like New York. It's a port city. _____

   _____

   _____

7. They bought a house. It has no garage. _____

   _____

   _____

8. The weather was threatening. The weather bureau issued a tornado watch. _____

   _____

   _____

Name _____ Possible Score | 6 | My Score | |

To avoid choppy writing, you should combine sentences that are closely related. When the closely related sentences are unequal in importance, you can often reduce the less important sentences to phrases or to single words. Then insert these phrases or words into a more important sentence as appositives or modifiers.

The media class took over a radio station for one afternoon. The station was WFYC.

The media class took over a radio station, **WFYC,** for one afternoon. [appositive]

Snow fell throughout the day. It was heavy. It was accompanied by high winds.

Heavy snow, **accompanied by high winds,** fell throughout the day. [modifiers]

Practice

Combine each of the following sets of sentences into a single sentence. Reduce one or two sentences in each set to a phrase or to a single word. Then insert the phrase or the word into the remaining sentence as an appositive or a modifier.

1. Croquet is a lawn game. It is a polite, leisurely game. _____

_____

_____

2. The writer spoke at the meeting. She is the founder of the new arts magazine. ___ _____

_____

_____

3. I watched the horse. It was grazing. It was in the lower meadow. _____

_____

_____

4. Pennants flapped in the breeze. They were multicolored. They were vinyl. _____

_____

_____

5. Hundreds of people came. They came by car. They came by bike. They came on foot. _____

_____

_____

6. Alligators are now a menace in Florida. They were once almost extinct. _____

_____

_____

Application

Name _____

The following paragraph has been written as a string of short, choppy sentences. Rewrite this paragraph, combining sentences whenever appropriate. Try to reduce the number of sentences to five. Use as many methods of combining sentences as you can.

An automobile accident may be unavoidable. You can still take certain maneuvers. These maneuvers will lessen car damage. They will lessen personal injuries. For example, to avoid a crash head-on, make a turn. The turn should be sharp. The turn should be to the right. Then the oncoming car will hit you in the side. You might lose control of your car. Don't worry. Anything is better than this. This is a head-on crash!

_____

_____

_____

_____

_____

_____

_____

_____

_____

_____

_____

_____

_____

_____

_____

_____

_____

_____

_____

_____

Name _____

Possible Score | 12 | My Score | |

Coordination means connecting ideas that are equal in importance. When ideas of unequal importance are connected, the result is faulty coordination.

> **The team left the huddle,** but **the school mascot, a goat, ran onto the field**. [faulty coordination]

Connecting the two clauses in this sentence with *but*—that is, coordinating them—means that the ideas they express are equally important, but they aren't. The important idea is that the goat ran onto the field. That the team left the huddle is only a detail telling when the goat ran out. To revise this kind of faulty coordination, put the less important idea in the form of a subordinate clause beginning with *as, if, when, since, while, because, after, before,* or *although.*

> **As the team left the huddle,** the school mascot, a goat, ran onto the field.

In the following sentence, *and* is used to connect, or coordinate, two clauses that are not equal in importance.

> **Joe Simpson won the million-dollar lottery,** and **he is a cattle rancher**. [faulty coordination]

That Joe Simpson won a million dollars is more important than the fact he is a cattle rancher. To revise this kind of faulty coordination, put the less important idea in the form of a subordinate clause beginning with *who, which,* or *that.*

> Joe Simpson, **who is a cattle rancher,** won the million-dollar lottery.

Practice 1

Rewrite the following sentences, putting the less important idea in the form of a subordinate clause. Begin the subordinate clause with *as, if, when, since, while, because, after, before,* or *although.*

1. The senator rose to speak, and the television set went blank. _____

   _____

   _____

2. I like to work outdoors, and I wish I lived on a farm. _____

   _____

   _____

3. The runners were on the course, but the storm struck. _____

   _____

   _____

4. Gas prices went up, and public transit became popular. _____

   _____

   _____

5. John knows little about mechanics, and I fixed the pump. _____

_____

_____

6. She could not go, but she had to practice the cello. _____

_____

_____

Practice 2

Rewrite the following sentences, putting the less important idea in the form of a subordinate clause. Begin the subordinate clause with *who, which,* or *that.*

1. Ms. Grant has a pilot's license, and she is my math teacher. _____

_____

_____

2. Whitey Ford won 236 games, and he was a pitcher for the Yankees. _____

_____

_____

3. The books lay on the table, and they were bound in leather. _____

_____

_____

4. The fittings withstood the pressure, and the pressure exceeded fifty pounds per square inch. _____

_____

_____

5. Neolithic people were farmers, and they made tools from flint and bone. _____

_____

_____

6. Oona's car is for sale, and it needs a new clutch. _____

_____

_____

Name _____

	Possible Score	5	My Score	

Connecting a string of clauses with *and*'s usually results in faulty coordination.

> The committee investigated the agencies, and **it wrote a report,** and **the report was suppressed,** and **that was unfortunate.** [faulty coordination]

To revise such a sentence, change some of the clauses to phrases or to single words. If necessary, break the sentence into two shorter sentences.

> The committee investigated the agencies and **wrote a report. Unfortunately**, the report was suppressed.

Practice

Rewrite the following sentences, correcting the faulty coordination. Change clauses into phrases or into single words. Where appropriate, break the sentence into two sentences.

1. Mother worked in the garden, and she pulled weeds, and she thinned the beets, and she dusted the tomato

   plants. _____

   _____

   _____

2. Our group rehearsed the play, and it was a "whodunit," and it was by Agatha Christie. _____

   _____

   _____

3. The columns still stood, but they were gray, and they were flecked with moss. _____

   _____

   _____

4. It was a quiet night, and I sat alone, and I watched the fireflies, and they were winking at each other. _____

   _____

   _____

5. The meal was beans and onions, and there was also rice, and coffee and tea were served afterward. _____

   _____

Application

Name _____ Possible Score [5] My Score [ ]

Read the following paragraphs. The numbers show where sentences have been left out.

    LeRoi Anderson was playing in his first golf tournament. **(1)** As Anderson approached the first tee, there were perhaps fifty spectators standing about. Now to those accustomed to jammed freeways and packed beaches, fifty people standing around a golf course might seem like a small enough crowd. To Anderson, however, fifty people were far too many—perhaps forty-eight or forty-nine too many. **(2)**

    Anderson bent over to place his ball on a tee. As he addressed the ball, he waggled his club and peeked out at the fairway winding through the trees.

    (3) There was a shocked gasp from the crowd, then silence. **(4)** The silence that followed his gaffe was oppressive. Sweating hard now, Anderson prepared to attack the ball yet a third time. Just then, a voice broke through the silence, "Tough course, isn't it, Mac?"

    A few hesitant giggles flowed quickly into a burst of laughter. **(5)** Then, with the tension broken, he took up his stance, swung smoothly, and stroked the ball onto the center of the fairway.

    The sentences that follow were removed from the paragraphs. Each sentence contains faulty coordination. Rewrite each sentence to get rid of the faulty coordination.

1. He was a good golfer, and he was a nervous individual, and his game often fell apart under stress. _____

_____

_____

2. They stood far back from the tee, but Anderson could feel their breath on his back, and their breath was heavy.

_____

_____

3. One hundred eyes were burning holes into him, and Anderson took a mighty swing, and he missed the ball.

_____

_____

4. Anderson readdressed the ball, and he jerked the club back, and he swung, and again he missed the ball. ___

_____

_____

5. Anderson stepped back from the ball, and he sighed, but he offered a weak smile. _____

_____

Name _____   Possible Score | 19 | My Score | |

You use subordination whenever you connect two clauses that are unequal in importance. The less important clause may begin with a subordinating conjunction like *after, although, because, before, in order that, just as, since,* or *when* or with a relative pronoun like *who, which,* or *that.*

> **Unless** the rain stops, [subordinate clause] the picnic will be held in the pavilion. [main clause]

> We returned the book [main clause] **that** was overdue. [subordinate clause]

When you connect clauses, be sure to subordinate the less important one. Otherwise, the result will be upside-down subordination.

> **Just as** the explosion occurred, **Martha put out the cat.** [faulty subordination]

You can usually correct upside-down subordination by switching the subordinating conjunction to the beginning of the other clause.

> The explosion occurred **just as** Martha put out the cat.

Notice that when a subordinate clause precedes a main clause, the two are separated by a comma.

Faulty subordination also occurs if you place *and* or *but* between a main clause and a subordinate clause beginning with *which* or *who.*

> The band needs new uniforms **but which** cannot be purchased until the money for them is raised. [faulty subordination]

> The school board hired a new English teacher **and who** will also coach track. [faulty subordination]

To correct this kind of faulty subordination, simply remove the word *and* or *but.*

> The band needs new uniforms, **which** cannot be purchased until the money for them is raised.

> The school board hired a new English teacher, **who** will also coach track.

Practice 1

Rewrite the following sentences, turning upside-down subordination right side up. That is, switch the subordinating conjunction to the beginning of the other clause. Remember to add a comma if the subordinate clause comes first.

1. The sun went down when the farmer planted by the tractor headlights. _____

   _____

   _____

2. When we sat down to rest, our legs grew tired. _____

   _____

   _____

3. Because you cannot be seated, the show has started. _____

   _____

   _____

4. Before the water level must be raised, the skiff will float. _____

_____

_____

5. Debbie could reach the door before the phone rang. _____

_____

_____

6. The director pleaded with Tina although she refused the part. _____

_____

_____

7. Because we can't go surfing today, the water is calm. _____

_____

_____

8. The first days of school are hectic although old friendships are renewed. _____

_____

_____

9. The herd calms down unless the cowhands will be up all night. _____

_____

_____

Practice 2

Read the following sentences and draw a line through *and* or *but* whenever it is used between a main clause and a subordinate clause beginning with *which* or *who*. Add commas where necessary.

1. The batter hit a foul ball and which was caught by a boy in the stands.

2. Pollution is a contemporary problem and which has no easy solutions.

3. *My Mother, the Doctor* was written by Joy Singer and who is also a physician.

4. The team showed spirit at first but which soon vanished as the score mounted against them.

5. It is a comfortable, roomy tent and which you will enjoy camping in with your family.

6. She was a singer of great talent but who never came up with a hit CD.

7. Jogging is a strenuous exercise but which many people find boring.

8. "The Love Song of J. Alfred Prufrock" is a dramatic monologue and which was written by T. S. Eliot.

9. Amelia Earhart was a renowned aviator but who vanished over the Pacific in 1937.

10. There's a new swimming instructor at the Y and who was the AAU one hundred-meter backstroke champion.

More about Faulty Subordination

Name _____

Possible Score | 5 | My Score | ☐

When you add too many details to a main clause, the result is often oversubordination, a string of subordinate clauses in which each clause refers to an element in a previous clause.

Babe Didrikson Zaharias ranks as a great athlete who **won** two gold medals in the 1932 Olympics, **which** were held in Los Angeles **where** the Babe's appearance drew large crowds **that** broke previous attendance records. [faulty subordination]

To revise this kind of faulty subordination, leave out unnecessary details and change clauses to phrases or to single words. If possible, break up the oversubordinated sentence into two sentences.

Babe Didrikson Zaharias, winner of two Olympic gold medals, ranks as a great athlete. The Babe's appearance in the 1932 Olympics in Los Angeles drew record-breaking crowds.

Practice

Rewrite the following sentences, correcting the oversubordination.

1. After she left college, she taught school in Madison, which is the capital and which is where she met James West, who became her husband. _____

   _____

   _____

2. Those toys, which were made in Taiwan, where the labor costs are low, are very durable. _____

   _____

   _____

3. There is the man who feeds the pigeons nuts which he buys from the vending machine that stands in the lobby.

   _____

   _____

4. This book was written by Helen MacInnes, who has written many spy novels that are exciting and that are set in foreign lands. _____

   _____

   _____

5. That's the mountain bike that I bought from the woman who manages the store that is across the street from the high school. _____

   _____

   _____

Application

Name _____

Complete each of the following sentences by supplying either a main clause or a subordinate clause as indicated in parentheses. Use appropriate capitalization and punctuation. To begin a subordinate clause, choose an appropriate subordinating conjunction from the following list.

  Time: after, as, before, when, while

  Condition: although, because, if, since, unless

  Identification: who, which, that

1. The winner was Jean-Paul, _____

_____

_____ (subordinate clause: identification)

2. Since most auto accidents are caused by speeding, _____

_____

_____ (main clause)

3. (subordinate clause: condition) _____

_____

_____ ticket prices in pro football are being raised again.

4. Although we ordered the material months ago, _____

_____

_____ (main clause)

5. (main clause) _____

_____

_____ unless the fog lifts.

6. (subordinate clause: time) _____

_____

_____ Holly enlisted in the army.

7. (subordinate clause: time) _____

_____

_____ the roof fell in.

Double Subjects

Name _____   Possible Score [22]   My Score [ ]

A sentence must have a subject. Sometimes, the subject is understood; sometimes, it is compound—two subjects joined by a conjunction like *and*.

> (You) Turn left at the intersection. [understood subject: **you**]
>
> Ben and I are running for office. [compound subject: **Ben and I**]

A sentence, however, should not have a double subject—that is, a subject noun followed by a pronoun. Such a sentence may be corrected by eliminating the unnecessary pronoun.

> The airplanes **they** have been inspected. [double subject]   The package **it** is on the table. [double subject]
>
> The airplanes have been inspected.   The package is on the table.

Practice 1

Write *C* before the sentences that are correct; write *DS* before those with double subjects.

_____ 1. Paul he worked on his uncle's farm last summer.

_____ 2. Tell Marion that I called her.

_____ 3. The James boys and I have developed an interest in banking.

_____ 4. This faucet needs a new gasket.

_____ 5. Rona went waterskiing, and, afterward, she swam.

_____ 6. The rain it came down steadily, washing out the ball game.

_____ 7. Both my sisters they went to Florida State University.

_____ 8. As the treasurer, she is responsible for balancing the books.

_____ 9. Coretta she signed up for graphic design.

_____ 10. William he wanted a tie to wear with that suit.

Practice 2

The following sentences contain double subjects. Find and eliminate the unnecessary pronouns, drawing lines through them.

1. The song it went on and on.

2. Three of the girls they forgot to bring water bottles.

3. The state trooper he asked to see my driver's license.

4. The passengers they accepted the delay with good humor.

5. The woman with the gavel she is the auctioneer.

6. Several of the players they protested the umpire's decision.

7. Because the humidity was low, the heat it did not bother me.

8. The gym it was decorated for the prom.

9. That mechanic with the long hair he fixed our car.

10. My brother he stood up for us.

11. Our friends they came to our rescue.

12. In this part of the country, the weather it is worst in February.

Application

Name _____ Possible Score [24] My Score [ ]

On a separate sheet of paper, complete each of the following sentences by supplying a subject.

1. _____ wore jeans with a yellow sweater.

2. _____ ordered a large pizza with olives and mushrooms.

3. Before noon _____ was dry.

4. _____ collapsed with a loud roar.

5. Swinging through the trees, _____ overtook the safari.

6. _____ cried softly in the moonlight.

7. _____ and _____ prevented a catastrophe.

8. _____ proofread my term paper, staying up till twelve o'clock to finish.

9. _____ was my big goal, my dream.

10. Because of the response, _____ played another song.

11. If you hurry, _____ can catch the last plane.

12. _____ and _____ couldn't stay to see the end of the show.

13. That _____ is always breaking down.

14. Right from the beginning, _____ thought you were kidding.

15. _____ went to see the soccer game at Busch Stadium.

16. _____ wearing a green jacket helped us with our luggage.

17. Before visiting that country, _____ need to get some shots.

18. _____ found happiness in collecting matchbook covers.

19. Without hesitation, _____ said that she would volunteer for the mission.

20. Beyond doubt, _____ and _____ are the funniest students in our class.

21. _____ signed up for a course in theater.

22. Several of the _____ protested the umpire's decision.

23. When asking Kim to dance, _____ blushed.

24. _____ and _____ can't stop laughing once they get started.

Misplaced Modifiers

Name _____ Possible Score [21] My Score [ ]

Modifiers are used to describe, qualify, or identify other words in sentences. A modifier may be a single word, a phrase, or a clause as in the following sentences:

The foundation was laid **quickly.** [a single word modifying a verb]

Arguments **about the rules** delayed the match. [a phrase modifying a noun]

This story is about a woman **who flies balloons.** [a clause modifying a noun]

Be careful where you place a modifier in a sentence. Generally, it should be as close as possible to the word it modifies. Otherwise, the modifier may confuse rather than clarify your meaning. Such a modifier is called a *misplaced modifier.*

She wrapped the scarf around her throat **that she bought at the garage sale.** [misplaced modifier]

Because of its position, the clause *which she bought at the garage sale* seems to modify the word *throat.* Modifying clauses beginning with *who, which,* and *that* should be placed immediately after the words they modify.

She wrapped the scarf **that she bought at the garage sale** around her throat.

Single-word modifiers like *almost, also, ever, hardly, just, merely, nearly, often,* and *only* should be placed before the words they modify. However, notice that shifting such a modifier may change the entire meaning of a sentence. Consider the following sentences:

We **even** could not budge the fallen limb. [misplaced modifier]

We could not **even** budge the fallen limb.

Even we could not budge the fallen limb.

Practice 1

Read the following sentences. If a modifier in bold type is correctly placed, write *C* in the blank. If a modifier is misplaced, write *M*.

_____ 1. The television picture was relayed by a satellite **that orbited the earth.**

_____ 2. Jan polished her boots until they looked new **almost.**

_____ 3. Corinne read a book about President Truman **who is writing a term paper on the Cold War.**

_____ 4. I put the chair in the bedroom **that I bought at the garage sale.**

_____ 5. Austin **nearly** swam a mile.

_____ 6. Every part must pass a thorough test **that goes into our stereo receiver.**

_____ 7. The spy **who called himself Cicero** was never caught.

_____ 8. **Even** Jaime couldn't guess what the solution was.

_____ 9. Jessica couldn't **even** guess what the solution was.

_____ 10. The car spun out in the number three turn **that had been leading in the race.**

_____ 11. The boat **that he started to build** will never be finished.

_____ 12. Jeff bought some flowers for his mother **that wilted.**

Practice 2

The following sentences contain misplaced modifiers, which are in bold type. Rewrite each sentence, placing the modifier correctly.

1. Herb's jacket has a zip-out lining and a hood, **which is newer than mine.** _____

   _____

   _____

2. I **hardly** had enough money to pay for the gasoline. _____

   _____

   _____

3. Corey sent Leah a rose and his thanks, **which she put in a vase.** _____

   _____

   _____

4. The beagle belongs to Mr. Granados **that is on a leash.** _____

   _____

   _____

5. The farmer was **only** willing to sell part of her land. _____

   _____

   _____

6. The audience enjoyed the concerto **that sat on the grass.** _____

   _____

   _____

7. Twenty dollars is **nearly** not enough for this original painting. _____

   _____

   _____

8. I visit **often** my uncle who lives in Kansas City. _____

   _____

   _____

9. We saw the sheep grazing on the lawn **that had been sheared.** _____

   _____

   _____

Name _____ Possible Score [6] My Score [ ]

The modifying phrase in the following sentence is misplaced:

> The guidebook says that one can visit the Mormon Tabernacle **on page 37.**

The phrase *on page 37* is intended to modify *says*. Yet, because of its position, this phrase seems to modify *Mormon Tabernacle* or possibly even *visit*. Moving the phrase closer to the word it modifies would make the meaning of the sentence clearer. Note, however, that phrases and clauses that tell *where, when,* and *how* may also be placed at the beginnings of sentences, even though this may separate them from the words they modify. Consider the following examples:

> The guidebook says **on page 37** that one can visit the Mormon Tabernacle.

> **On page 37,** the guidebook says that one can visit the Mormon Tabernacle.

Practice

The following sentences contain misplaced modifiers, which are in bold type. Rewrite each sentence, placing the modifier correctly.

1. The game began just as we arrived **with "The Star-Spangled Banner."** _____

_____

_____

2. Several debates occurred during the convention **about procedures.** _____

_____

_____

3. The commuters failed to notice the old man selling flowers **in their hurry.** _____

_____

_____

4. Marsha wrote her books during business flights **on scrap paper.** _____

_____

_____

5. I read an article in a magazine **about forest fires.** _____

_____

_____

6. Many old warehouses are being made in our city **into loft condominiums.** _____

_____

_____

Application

Name _____

Possible Score [10]   My Score [ ]

Rewrite the following sentences, correctly placing the misplaced modifier in each.

1. My sister's wedding was in June, which was formal. _____
_____
_____

2. Most kids are afraid of heights slightly. _____
_____
_____

3. Glasses should be discarded with chips and cracks. _____
_____
_____

4. Everyone in the class nearly contributed something. _____
_____
_____

5. Julia decided to become a lawyer in junior high. _____
_____
_____

6. Juanita said she would tell the truth at the start of her report. _____
_____
_____

7. Yuta barely could reach the top shelf. _____
_____
_____

8. Hurricane Bob veered north, which was near Key West. _____
_____
_____

9. You should stay at home in bed with a cold like that. _____
_____
_____

10. To leave the boat, Ralph fell into the water in a hurry. _____
_____
_____

Dangling Modifiers

Name _____

Possible Score 15   My Score

Modifiers are words that qualify the meaning of other words. When a modifier seems to qualify a word that it cannot logically qualify, then the modifier is dangling as in the following example:

Unscrewing the radiator cap, a blast of steam shot up. [dangling]

The modifying phrase *unscrewing the radiator cap* seems to qualify the word *blast*. Yet, logically, a blast cannot unscrew a radiator cap. The modifier in this sentence is dangling. One way to correct this dangling modifier is to add a word to the sentence that the modifier can logically qualify. Note that adding such a word may involve recasting the sentence.

Unscrewing the radiator cap, *I* released a blast of steam.

Another way to correct this dangling modifier is to add a subject and make the phrase a clause.

As *I* was unscrewing the radiator cap, a blast of steam shot up.

Here are two pairs of sentences. The first sentence in each pair has a dangling modifier. The second sentence shows how to correct the dangling modifier.

Sitting in the last row, the stage could hardly be seen. [dangling]
Sitting in the last row, *I* could hardly see the stage.

While delivering papers, a dog bit her ankle. [dangling]
While *she* was delivering papers, a dog bit her ankle.

Practice

Rewrite each of the following sentences to correct the dangling modifiers printed in bold type.

1. **Writing in a frenzy,** the deadline was met. _____

_____

2. **When sliced,** I like mushrooms. _____

_____

3. **On opening the rear door**, the alarm sounded. _____

_____

4. **While singing my song,** our dog began to howl. _____

_____

5. **Being very expensive,** I did not buy a ticket. _____

_____

6. **While standing on the balcony,** the sun went down. _____

_____

7. **Peering through the binoculars,** a black-throated green warbler was sighted. _____

_____

_____

8. The waiter seated us **after standing in line for thirty minutes.** _____

_____

_____

9. **Driving on nearly bald tires,** the highway was slippery. _____

_____

_____

10. **After graduating from high school,** my father will help me find a job. _____

_____

_____

11. **After swimming all morning,** the hamburgers smelled good. _____

_____

_____

12. **While shopping downtown,** Rodney's wallet was stolen. _____

_____

_____

13. **Huffing and puffing,** the top of the hill was finally reached. _____

_____

_____

14. **Crossing the goal line,** the ball slipped from Gene's grasp. _____

_____

_____

15. **While waiting in line for tickets,** the movie started. _____

_____

_____

Name _____

Possible Score: 6   My Score: ☐

If a modifier can modify either of two words in a sentence, then the modifier is squinting. A squinting modifier is one that looks in two directions at the same time as in the following example:

Donna said **during the meeting** Jim phoned her. [squinting]

Because of its position, the phrase *during the meeting* could modify either *said* or *phoned*. Did Donna say this during the meeting, or did Jim phone during the meeting? You can't be sure. So the modifier should be moved to give the sentence one meaning or the other.

During the meeting, Donna said Jim phoned her.

Donna said Jim phoned her **during the meeting.**

Practice

The following sentences contain squinting modifiers. These are printed in bold type. Rewrite each of these sentences so that the modifier qualifies only one word.

1. The board of health asked **after ten days** to be informed. _____

_____

_____

2. Spectators who cry out **rudely** disturb the performers. _____

_____

_____

3. The reduced fares on weekends **only** are for senior citizens. _____

_____

_____

4. Students who cut classes **often** fall behind in their work. _____

_____

_____

5. The cattle that had been inoculated **soon** recovered. _____

_____

_____

6. Ms. Wilson told them **when they finished painting** to let her know. _____

_____

Name _____

Possible Score [12]   My Score [ ]

Use each of the following modifiers to make a complete sentence. Then check your sentences to be sure that none of the modifiers is dangling.

1. Having grown up during the 1980s, _____

    _____

2. _____

    _____ after watching our team lose again.

3. To receive permission for a field trip, _____

    _____

4. If properly frozen, _____

    _____

5. _____

    _____ when riding in a plane.

6. _____

    _____ leaning against the rear wall of the garage.

7. Before I graduate, _____

    _____

8. Even though it was midnight, _____

    _____

9. During the tour of the White House, _____

    _____

10. Properly prepared, _____

    _____

11. In order to vote, _____

    _____

12. When buying a car, _____

Name _____

Possible Score | 13 | My Score | □

When two or more elements in a sentence have the same function, they should have the same form. That is, they should have parallel structure. In the following sentence, the elements in bold type are not parallel:

> I have always liked **swimming, fishing,** and **to lie** in the sun.

The words in bold type all have the same function, but the writer has used different forms. The writer has used two gerunds, *swimming* and *fishing,* and then shifted to an infinitive, *to lie.* The faulty parallelism of this sentence could be corrected in two ways: either make all the elements gerunds or make them all infinitives.

> I have always liked **swimming, fishing,** and **lying** in the sun.

> I have always liked **to swim, to fish,** and **to lie** in the sun.

Here are two pairs of sentences. The first sentence in each pair lacks parallelism. The second sentence shows how to correct the faulty parallelism.

> Kayaking requires **strength, courage,** and **the paddler must be experienced.** [not parallel: shift from nouns to a clause]

> Kayaking requires **strength, courage,** and **experience.** [parallel: three nouns]

> Neither **speed** nor **being elusive** was enough to earn Dan the starting slot. [not parallel: shift from noun to participle]

> Neither **speed** nor **elusiveness** was enough to earn Dan the starting slot. [parallel: two nouns]

Practice

Rewrite the following sentences, correcting the faulty parallelism.

1. Jackson promised to be more careful and that he would work more slowly. _____

   _____

   _____

2. No one enjoyed the haying, the milking, or to plow except Bill. _____

   _____

   _____

3. Mark is not only talented as a pianist but also at acting. _____

   _____

   _____

4. I'd rather go skiing than to sightsee. _____

   _____

   _____

5. Kim is easygoing, soft-spoken, and has patience. _____

_____

_____

6. To sing with a rock group and making lots of money was her big dream. _____

_____

_____

7. Tomás will either enlist in the navy or learning computer programming. _____

_____

_____

8. These melons are ripe, juicy, and have a sweet taste. _____

_____

_____

9. The ranger warned us to dress warmly and that we should keep dry. _____

_____

_____

10. Making a decision and to stick to it was something Bob couldn't do. _____

_____

_____

11. Laurie worked quickly, carefully, and was efficient. _____

_____

_____

12. Everyone complained about the heat and how humid it was. _____

_____

_____

13. Nealy's aunt was either very tired or a very sick person. _____

_____

_____

Shifts in Person and Voice

Name _____   Possible Score 13   My Score ☐

Shifts in pronoun reference often result in faulty parallelism. For example, it is faulty parallelism to shift from the third person to the second person as in the following example:

> If **one** wants an application, **you** should ask the principal.

This lack of parallelism can be corrected by making the pronouns the same person.

> If **you** want an application, **you** should ask the principal.

> If **one** wants an application, **one** should ask the principal.

Shifts in voice may also result in faulty parallelism. In English, a verb may have two voices—active, in which the subject does the action, and passive, in which the subject is acted upon. Note the difference between verb forms in the sentences that follow. Note, too, that the subject and the object in the active sentence switch positions in the passive sentence.

> A reporter **saw** the accident. [active voice—subject does the action]

> The accident **was seen** by a reporter. [passive voice—subject is acted upon]

By knowing the difference between the active voice and the passive voice, you can avoid shifting from one to the other, especially within a sentence.

> As the hikers **rounded** a curve, a peaceful valley **was seen** far below. [not parallel: <u>rounded</u> is active; <u>was seen</u> is passive]

A sentence like this may be corrected in two ways. You may change the passive verb to the active voice and add a subject. Or, you may recast the sentence to have a compound active verb.

> As the hikers **rounded** a curve, **they saw** a peaceful valley far below.

> The hikers **rounded** a curve and **saw** a peaceful valley far below.

Practice

Rewrite the following sentences to eliminate shifts in person and voice.

1. If one speaks Spanish, you should be able to understand Italian. _____

    _____

    _____

2. Although Al tried to get to the stadium on time, the kickoff was missed. _____

    _____

    _____

3. When you see an opportunity, one should take advantage of it. _____

    _____

    _____

4. The cyclists reached the river, and then the bridge was crossed. _____

    _____

5. Because Kyoto stopped for a newspaper, her train was missed. _____

_____

_____

6. If you want to be taken seriously, one should think before one speaks. _____

_____

_____

7. Jo jumped when the door slammed, and the tray of dishes was dropped. _____

_____

_____

8. When we visited the auto plant, a great deal about assembly-line techniques was learned. _____

_____

_____

9. Rosita kept the best items for her own collection, and the others were sold by her. _____

_____

_____

10. If one wants a quick refund, you should file your tax return early. _____

_____

_____

11. If you polish your CDs regularly, one can prevent them from skipping. _____

_____

_____

12. We painted the outside of the canoe blue, and the inside was painted white. _____

_____

_____

13. When Angie cleaned the attic, a valuable antique bottle was found. _____

_____

_____

Name _____   Possible Score [6]   My Score [ ]

Shifts in verb tense often result in faulty parallelism.

> When the game **ended,** the fans **rush** onto the field. [not parallel: <u>ended</u> is past tense; <u>rush</u> is present tense]

Since both actions described by these verbs take place at the same time, the tense of these verbs should be the same.

> When the game **ended,** the fans **rushed** onto the field. [parallel: both verbs are in past tense]

Practice

Rewrite the following sentences to eliminate shifts in tense.

1. Miguel prepared the sauce for the pasta and puts the bread in the oven. _____

    _____

    _____

2. Emily always wants to stay up for the late show but always fell asleep watching it. _____

    _____

    _____

3. His breakfast never varies: it consisted of yogurt and orange juice. _____

    _____

    _____

4. Joe didn't like the tacos but eats them anyway. _____

    _____

    _____

5. The horse reared in the starting gate and throws the jockey. _____

    _____

    _____

6. Sandra was upset and misses the free throw. _____

    _____

    _____

Application

Name _____

Possible Score 6

My Score ☐

Rewrite the following paragraph, revising it to eliminate shifts in the tense and voice of verbs.

      Harry Houdini was a famous magician who performs surprising feats of escape. To perform one trick, Houdini produced a length of rope, and a handkerchief was borrowed by him from the audience. Then Houdini asked for a volunteer from the audience who comes up on the stage, and the handkerchief was tied around Houdini's wrists by the volunteer. The volunteer next looped the rope through Houdini's arms, and both ends were held on to. Houdini made a quick move. The rope falls to the floor, and the handkerchief fluttered after it.

_____

_____

_____

_____

_____

_____

_____

_____

_____

_____

_____

_____

_____

_____

_____

_____

_____

_____

_____

Name _____   Number Correct × 5 = ☐

Three choices follow each numbered sentence. Two of these choices represent different ways of rewriting the original sentence. Circle the letter of the choice *(B or C)* that represents the better rewriting. If you feel that the original sentence does not need to be rewritten, circle *A, no change.*

1. We grew sweet corn in the field. Behind our house.

    A. no change   B. We grew sweet corn. In the field behind our house.

    C. We grew sweet corn in the field behind our house.

2. Many fans lamented the death of Arthur Ashe. The 1975 Wimbledon singles champion.

    A. no change

    B. Many fans lamented the death of the 1975 Wimbledon singles champion. Arthur Ashe.

    C. Many fans lamented the death of Arthur Ashe, the 1975 Wimbledon singles champion.

3. In art class, Neal sketched several designs for ceramic flowerpots. Finishing the sketches later at home.

    A. no change

    B. In art class, Neal sketched several designs for ceramic flowerpots finishing the sketches later at home.

    C. In art class, Neal sketched several designs for ceramic flowerpots, finishing the sketches later at home.

4. This is a can opener. That really works.

    A. no change   B. This is a can opener that really works.

    C. This is a can opener it really works.

5. If I were going camping in Minnesota. I would take a few warm sweaters.

    A. no change

    B. If I were going camping in Minnesota, I would take a few warm sweaters.

    C. If I were going camping in Minnesota I would take a few warm sweaters.

6. He asked them for food, however, they had none to give him.

    A. no change   B. He asked them for food; however, they had none to give him.

    C. He asked them for food, however they had none to give him.

7. You can afford the payments, don't buy a new car.

    A. no change   B. Unless you can afford the payments, don't buy a new car.

    C. You can afford the payments don't buy a new car.

8. Redheads get sunburned easily. They have less protective pigment. They should put on suntan oil.

    A. no change

    B. Redheads, who sunburn easily because they have less protective pigment, should put on suntan oil.

    C. Redheads get sunburned easily, and they have less protective pigment, and they should put on suntan oil.

9. The students formed a co-op. It was a nonprofit grocery. It was on Dell Street. Members could buy food there cheaply.

    A. no change

    B. The students formed a co-op, where members could buy food cheaply. The nonprofit grocery was on Dell Street.

    C. The students formed a co-op. Members could buy food there cheaply. It was a nonprofit grocery. It was on Dell Street.

10. John Steinbeck won the Nobel Prize for literature, and he was born in California.

    A. no change

    B. John Steinbeck won the Nobel Prize for literature; and he was born in California.

    C. John Steinbeck, who was born in California, won the Nobel Prize for literature.

11. My dog's named Mutt, and he's a cocker spaniel, and he's tan, and he likes to chew on old shoes.

    A. no change

    B. My dog's a tan cocker spaniel named Mutt. He likes to chew on old shoes.

    C. My dog's named Mutt, and he's a cocker spaniel. He's tan, and he likes to chew on old shoes.

12. The band began to play when everybody danced.

    A. no change

    B. The band began to play. When everybody danced.

    C. When the band began to play, everybody danced.

13. The custodian repairing the mailboxes he gave us an extra key.

    A. no change

    B. The custodian repairing the mailboxes gave us an extra key.

    C. The custodian repairing the mailboxes. He gave us an extra key.

14. Dawn parked the Model T in the driveway that she had bought at the antiques fair.

    A. no change

    B. Dawn parked the Model T in the driveway. That she had bought at the antiques fair.

    C. In the driveway, Dawn parked the Model T that she had bought at the antiques fair.

15. Finding no one at home, a note was left by Dave.

    A. no change

    B. After finding no one at home, a note was left by Dave.

    C. Finding no one at home, Dave left a note.

16. Lisa said that she enjoys barbecuing ribs when I asked her.

    A. no change

    B. Lisa said that she enjoys barbecuing ribs. When I asked her.

    C. When I asked her, Lisa said that she enjoys barbecuing ribs.

17. Joy said after a while the contest would begin.

    A. no change

    B. Joy said that the contest would begin. After a while.

    C. Joy said that the contest would begin after a while.

18. I expect the dancers to show up on time for practice and that they should replace their toe shoes monthly.

    A. no change

    B. I expect that the dancers show up on time for practice and to replace their toe shoes monthly.

    C. I expect the dancers to show up on time for practice and to replace their toe shoes monthly.

19. If one has little money, you should not look at expensive roller blades.

    A. no change

    B. If you have little money, one should not look at expensive roller blades.

    C. If you have little money, you should not look at expensive roller blades.

20. That nursery specializes in houseplants and grew many unusual orchids.

    A. no change

    B. That nursery specialized in houseplants and grows many unusual orchids.

    C. That nursery specializes in houseplants and grows many unusual orchids.

USING THE RIGHT WORDS

Pretest

Name _____ Number Correct × 2 = [ ]

Choose the word or phrase in parentheses that correctly completes each of the following sentences. Underline the word or words that correctly complete the sentence.

1. Don says that Rita and (he, him) are taking the 7:35 bus tomorrow morning.

2. I think it must have been (them, they) who planned the surprise party for Sharon.

3. The manager told Doug and (I, me) that work began promptly at eight.

4. Since Jan joined the company team, she plays softball as often as (us, we).

5. I think that with your black hair, that jacket suits you better than (he, him).

6. (Who, Whom) did you see when you went to the personnel office yesterday afternoon?

7. Maxine likes to guess (who, whom) the winners of the Emmy awards will be.

8. Did Anthony talk with the woman (which, who) wants to sell her car?

9. The last time we used the clubhouse, somebody left (her, their) parka in the coatroom.

10. If a volunteer isn't able to work, (he, they) should phone me immediately.

11. Neither the president nor the treasurer brought (her, their) report to the meeting.

12. Ruth often called her mother when (Ruth, she) was in the hospital last month.

13. The bus company has just raised its fares again. (This, This increase) has angered many commuters.

14. Skating is fun. I'd like to be (a skater, one).

15. Tung rolled up his sleeves, (stacked them on the counter, and washed the dishes, washed the dishes, and stacked them on the counter).

16. Sandy confessed that he has never enjoyed (that, those) sort of programs.

17. Sheila really loves (those, this) kind of weather.

18. We finally chose (them, those) striped shirts for Zachary's birthday present.

19. (Them, These) are the best hamburgers I've ever tasted!

20. That Brazilian soccer star (play, plays) with the North American Soccer League in New York.

21. These old cars (run, runs) best when the weather is mild and dry.

22. We (catch, catches) the 8:45 train on weekdays.

23. Did you know you (was, were) the last person to register for the photography contest?

24. The videocassettes (aren't, isn't) in the top drawer.

25. An umbrella and a raincoat (are, is) in the hall closet.

26. Perhaps the wheels on your car (need, needs) to be balanced.

27. Next to the fireplace (are, is) two bronze statues.

28. The news (start, starts) at ten o'clock.

29. Each of the walls (has, have) been painted a different color.

30. The last time we (saw, seen) the Silvermans, they were building a family room in the basement.

31. When Jody called at nine, Rosemary had already (gone, went) to work.

32. You have been (chose, chosen) to speak at the assembly.

33. If Joe (had, would have) arrived an hour earlier, he could have met Alan's brother.

34. Ms. Reilly should (have, of) told us sooner about the extra softball practice.

35. (Doesn't, Don't) Carmen need more time to practice for the bowling tournament?

36. Wayne and his sister (did, done) the dishes last night while listening to the ball game.

37. The doctor recommended that Mr. Simpson (begin, begins) a daily exercise program.

38. If Maggie (was, were) on the team, she could go with us to Springfield next weekend.

39. As we were walking home, Carol asked (did we like tacos, if we liked tacos).

40. Before unlocking the door, Don asked Jenny (where she was going, where was she going).

41. The cat has (laid, lain) on the porch in that patch of sunlight for an hour.

42. Uncle Brad told us to (leave, let) the puppies run loose when we got to the park.

43. After watching her practice all season, I wasn't surprised at (Barb, Barb's) winning so easily.

44. Many Americans still haven't found (anything, nothing) to equal denim clothing for leisure-time activities.

45. To start a car that has a dead battery, you must attach the jumper cables (correct, correctly).

46. Karl looked (unhappily, unhappy) when he heard that the concert had been canceled.

47. My sister Jane is a better hiker than (any, any other) member of her Scout troop.

48. Of the two speedboats, this one has the (more powerful, most powerful) engine.

49. Grandma says that she can't hear (good, well) now without her hearing aid.

50. The coach felt that the team played (bad, badly) yesterday, but we didn't agree.

Name _____ Possible Score | 37 | My Score | |

Use the personal pronouns *I, you, he, she, it, we,* and *they* as subjects for sentences. The pronouns in these sentences appear in typical subject positions:

> **I** am ready, and **he** is, too.   **We** hope that **you** will agree.
>
> **She** finished, but **they** didn't.   **He** and **I** saw the accident.

Use the personal pronouns *me, you, him, her, it, us,* and *them* as objects in sentences—that is, as direct objects, indirect objects, and objects of prepositions.

> Martha called **him.** [direct object]
>
> Tom gave **her** a present. [indirect object]
>
> This news is just between **you** and **me.** [objects of preposition]

Use the pronouns *I, you, he, she, it, we,* and *they* after forms of the verb *be* like *is, am, are, was, were, be,* and *been.*

> It **was she** who answered the telephone last night.

Practice 1

Underline the pronoun that correctly completes each sentence.

1. Elaine gave (we, us) the report.

2. We left Willis and (they, them) at the bus stop.

3. It must have been (she, her) who did that.

4. Either Bob or (he, him) will be the next captain.

5. (They, Them) are the ones Beth wants.

6. Just between you and (I, me), I don't believe it.

7. We sat next to Sally and (she, her) at the movie.

8. Mike thought (we, us) would arrive by ten.

9. Could it have been (he, him) at the door?

10. These books are for you and (they, them).

11. Is that package for (I, me)?

12. Jeff finally told (she, her) the whole story.

13. Paul and (I, me) are going to take the bus.

14. The message is from Tom and (he, him).

15. Do you think (she, her) will win the prize?

Practice 2

Underline the pronoun that correctly completes each sentence.

1. Joe called (they, them) about the game.

2. Ms. García talked with (he, him) on the bus.

3. No one can believe it was (we, us) who won.

4. Jane usually eats lunch with (she, her) and Barb.

5. John handed (he, him) the racket.

6. Kevin and Dick have challenged you and (I, me) to a game.

7. It is (they, them) who must take the responsibility.

8. Are you going with Judy or (I, me)?

9. Wes and (she, her) are leaving now.

10. Did you and (he, him) finish early?

11. (They, Them) and Al will buy the food.

12. Nobody understands Heather or (I, me).

13. Before you and (she, her) leave, call home.

14. Pete and (they, them) will help sell tickets.

15. Bill and (I, me) have something to tell you.

16. David made lasagna for Betsy and (he, him).

17. Do you think it was (she, her)?

Practice 3
Write sentences of your own, using the following phrases correctly.

1. Dave and I _____

   _____

2. Dave and me _____

   _____

3. you and her _____

   _____

4. you and she _____

   _____

5. Sue or him _____

   _____

24

Personal Pronouns after Than and As

Name _____ Possible Score **40**   My Score

Sentences with phrases like *than him* and *as he* often contain incomplete comparisons. That is, some unnecessary words in the comparison have been omitted. If you use a personal pronoun in such a comparison, choose the pronoun you would use if the comparison were fully stated. For example, in sentence 1 below, the pronoun *he* acts as a subject, even though the words *is strong* have been omitted. You can hear that *he* is the right choice; you wouldn't say *him is strong*. In sentence 2 below, the pronoun *him* acts as a direct object, even though the words *it fits* have been omitted.

1. Jerry is almost as strong **as he.** [as **he** is strong]
2. This jacket fits you better **than him.** [than it fits **him**]

Sometimes, either a subject pronoun or an object pronoun seems to fit. Your choice of pronouns will depend on the meaning you intend.

3. Anita helped Erik as much **as I.** [as **I** helped Erik]
4. Anita helped Erik as much **as me.** [as she helped **me**]

Practice 1

The following sentences have been written with the comparison fully stated. Underline the pronoun that correctly completes each sentence.

1. Joanne reads faster than (she, her) does.
2. Tim likes chili as much as (I, me) do.
3. Tim likes Sue as much as he likes (I, me).
4. Pat plays chess as well as (she, her) does.
5. Nobody works harder than (we, us) do.

6. Carl takes longer to eat lunch than (I, me) do.
7. Dad enjoys cooking as much as (we, us) do.
8. I liked that book more than (he, him) did.
9. Bob called you more than he called (I, me).
10. Bob called you more than (I, me) did.

Practice 2

Decide what word or words are missing from each comparison below. Then underline the pronoun that correctly completes each sentence.

1. Sometimes, you're as lazy as (I, me).
2. Skiing is easier for Mia than (he, him).
3. This color suits you better than (I, me).
4. Mr. Alves has a larger garden than (we, us).
5. Nobody knows Kim better than (I, me).
6. Doug felt worse than (they, them).
7. You were sick longer than (she, her).
8. Algebra is easier for Kathy than (he, him).
9. Bowling is harder for Joe than (we, us).
10. Jill plays tennis as often as (he, him).
11. Toni is as tired as (they, them).
12. Dad dives as well as (we, us).
13. You seem as popular as (she, her).
14. That girl is as athletic as (I, me).
15. History is harder for Stan than (she, her).

16. Nita runs as fast as (he, him).
17. That wrestler is stronger than (I, me).
18. Solving a math problem takes me longer than (she, her).
19. Kent is almost as tall as (she, her).
20. Those dancers are as talented as (he, him).
21. The photographers were as late as (we, us).
22. That hat fits you better than (she, her).
23. Chris seemed as enthusiastic as (they, them).
24. Casey was much slower than (we, us).
25. Joe types faster than (they, them).
26. Ms. Cheng golfs as often as (she, her).
27. You yelled much louder than (I, me).
28. The coach was as disappointed as (we, us).
29. Skating is more fun for Jane than (he, him).
30. Everyone laughed longer than (I, me).

Name _____ Possible Score | 30 | My Score | |

Underline the pronoun that correctly completes each sentence. If a sentence contains an incomplete comparison, choose the pronoun you would use if the comparison were fully stated.

1. Alec and (I, me) visited Iron City.

2. (They, Them) heated the blintzes.

3. Julie practices the guitar as much as (he, him).

4. Speaking in public is harder for Bill than (she, her).

5. That convertible belongs to Sharon and (I, me).

6. Those sky divers are braver than (we, us).

7. The lightning frightened Dave and (he, him).

8. It was (she, her) who surprised Rodney.

9. That scientist is more dedicated to the project than (we, us).

10. Rita Goldberg and (he, him) rowed across the lake.

11. That salesclerk charged Greg and (I, me) for the broken statues.

12. These fish sandwiches are for (they, them).

13. Her cousin is almost as shy as (she, her).

14. Doreen handed (we, us) a monkey wrench and two hammers.

15. Beth thought Tony and (I, me) had learned all the magic tricks.

16. Their host is as talkative as (they, them).

17. Skating is easier for Carol than (he, him).

18. Esteban and (she, her) invited the Casey twins to the barbecue.

19. Nobody understands our cat better than (I, me).

20. Jonah showed Aunt Mavis and (they, them) the trophy.

21. Jane Addams was more famous than (he, him).

22. Steve makes better salsa than (we, us).

23. Either Jerry or (she, her) is taking judo lessons.

24. Diane and (they, them) bought the bait over there.

25. That jogging suit looks better on you than (I, me).

26. Harley is as determined to win as (she, her).

27. Could the visitors have been Rona and (they, them)?

28. That T-shirt doesn't fit you as well as (I, me).

29. Is Brad going with Ellen or (he, him)?

30. Elena plays basketball more often than (we, us).

Who and Whom

Name _____

Possible Score 40 My Score ☐

Use the pronoun *who* as the subject of a question or a clause.

> **Who** finished? [subject of a question]
>
> Can you tell us **who** finished? [subject of the clause who finished]

Use *who* in questions and clauses with forms of the verb *be* like *is, am, are, was, were, be,* and *been.*

> **Who** is she? [with be in a question]
>
> I know **who** she is. [with be in the clause who she is]

Use the pronoun *whom* as a direct object or an object of a preposition in a question or a clause.

> **Whom** did you see? [direct object of see in a question: You did see whom?]
>
> Do you remember **whom** you saw? [direct object of saw in the clause whom you saw]
>
> To **whom** did you send it?
> **Whom** did you send it to? } [object of the preposition to in a question]
>
> We called the man to **whom** you sent it.
> We called the man **whom** you sent it to. } [object of the preposition to in the clause to whom you sent it]

The pronoun *whoever*, like *who*, is used as a subject and with forms of *be*. The pronoun *whomever*, like *whom*, is used as an object.

> Give this to **whoever** opens the door. [subject of the clause whoever opens the door]
>
> Give this to **whoever** is the winner. [with be in the clause whoever is the winner]
>
> Give this to **whomever** you choose. [direct object of choose in the clause whomever you choose]

Practice 1

Complete each question correctly with either *who* or *whom*.

1. _____ is that woman in the white lab coat?

2. _____ did you help?

3. _____ is going to bring the food?

4. _____ have you told about the contest?

5. _____ knows how to do this assignment?

6. _____ was the man in the leather jacket?

7. To _____ did you give the message?

8. _____ did he ask for directions?

9. _____ should I address this application to?

10. _____ are they going to hear at the conference?

11. _____ was at the rally?

12. _____ should be captain?

13. _____ did they mean?

14. _____ will finish first?

15. _____ have you met?

Practice 2

Underline the word that correctly completes the clause in each sentence below.

1. Matt met the woman (who, whom) will speak on the ozone layer.

2. Can you tell me (who, whom) he is?

3. You can go with (whoever, whomever) you like.

4. Did Judy tell you (who, whom) she photographed?

5. (Whoever, Whomever) did this will be sorry.

6. (Whoever, Whomever) they elect will be a very busy person.

7. Please tell me (who, whom) you have chosen.

8. Do you know with (who, whom) they are traveling?

9. This notebook should be returned to (whoever, whomever) owns it.

10. People (who, whom) live in glass houses shouldn't throw stones.

11. I can't imagine (who, whom) it could be.

12. Sharon will give the message to (whoever, whomever) answers the telephone.

13. The students (who, whom) Phil met yesterday are all seniors.

14. Have you heard (who, whom) will be at the party?

15. I have no idea (who, whom) they have invited.

16. Has anyone told Joe (who, whom) sent the mysterious package?

17. I don't know to (who, whom) I should report the accident.

18. (Whoever, Whomever) Dan appoints will be responsible for the tickets.

19. Helen can't remember (who, whom) told her that.

20. The woman (who, whom) Mary spoke to is her science teacher.

21. Leroy is the student (who, whom) I have already called.

22. Mom talked with the woman (who, whom) will probably be our next mayor.

23. Give the award to (whoever, whomever) has earned it.

24. We saw the same hikers (who, whom) you saw last week.

25. She is the one (who, whom) was an eyewitness.

Who, Which, and That

Name _____

Use the pronouns *who* and *whom* to refer to people.

The woman **who** is giving a speech is a state senator.

Will the swimmers **whom** you saw be competing in the meet?

Use the pronoun *which* to refer to animals or things.

The horses, **which** can start, stop, and turn quickly, are for sale.

The factory, **which** is empty, is being torn down.

Use the pronoun *that* to refer to animals, things, or people.

The cat **that** is sleeping on the porch belongs next door.

Has anyone seen the book **that** I was reading?

Have you met the basketball player **that** Tom knows?

Practice

Underline the pronoun that correctly completes each sentence.

1. Do you know the white-haired man (which, who) feeds the pigeons?

2. The bike (that, who) I was hoping to buy has been sold.

3. We all remember the dancers (which, who) performed in the park last summer.

4. Nobody understands the math assignment (that, who) is due tomorrow.

5. Wolves, (which, who) have strong family ties, travel in packs.

6. What did you think of the discussion (that, who) followed the meeting?

7. Will anyone (which, who) is interested please let me know?

8. Ice hockey, (which, who) developed in Canada, probably came form the older game of field hockey.

9. Did you see the people (which, who) gathered outside the mayor's office?

10. The Appalachian Trail, (which, who) extends from Maine to Georgia, passes through fourteen states.

11. The passengers (which, whom) the conductor helped from the train were not injured.

12. Customers (which, who) are barefoot are not allowed in the store.

13. The bald eagle, (which, who) is the national bird of the United States, is found only in North America.

14. The band members (which, whom) Carla telephoned will attend the rehearsal.

15. Did you like the pizza (that, who) Joe and Julian made?

16. The survivors (which, whom) the reporter interviewed were exhausted but glad to be alive.

17. The club was formed by ten students (which, who) like photography.

18. Buildings (that, who) are fire hazards should be demolished.

19. *ER* was the program (that, whom) Nina liked best.

20. Dogs, (which, who) are normally friendly, may bite when frightened.

Application

Name _____

Write sentences of your own, using the following phrases and choosing the appropriate pronoun from the words in parentheses.

1. the swimmer (who, whom) broke the record

   _____

   _____

2. the singer (who, whom) I like best

   _____

   _____

3. the teacher to (who, whom) you gave your report

   _____

   _____

4. (whoever, whomever) finishes first

   _____

   _____

5. (whoever, whomever) you choose

   _____

   _____

6. plants (that, who) need a lot of sunlight

   _____

   _____

7. school libraries, (which, who) are closed on weekends,

   _____

   _____

8. your friend (which, who) collects stamps

   _____

   _____

9. book reports (that, who) are handwritten

   _____

Pronoun Agreement

Name _____

Possible Score | 37 | My Score | ☐

The word that a pronoun refers to is called an *antecedent*. A pronoun should agree with its antecedent in number. That is, a pronoun should be singular if its antecedent is singular; it should be plural if its antecedent is plural.

I like **pizza** when **it** has anchovies. [singular]

Oranges are delicious when **they** are ripe. [plural]

Use a singular pronoun to refer to these types of antecedents: (1) nouns like *student, person, man,* and *woman* and (2) indefinite pronouns like *somebody, everyone, anybody,* and *nobody.*

If a **student** registers late, **he** (or **she**) has to pay a fine. [singular]

Does **everyone** understand what **she** (or **he**) is supposed to do? [singular]

Use a plural pronoun to refer to two singular antecedents joined by *and.* Use a singular pronoun to refer to two singular antecedents joined by *or* or *nor.*

We spoke to **Beth and Joe** as soon as **they** arrived.

Karen or Sara will give **her** report tomorrow.

Neither **Sam nor his brother** rode **his** bike today.

A pronoun should also agree with its antecedent in person. Avoid unnecessary shifts in person like this shift: If a **student** registers late, **you** have to pay a fine. Change either the antecedent or the pronoun to achieve pronoun-antecedent agreement.

If a **student** registers late, **he** (or **she**) has to pay a fine. [third person]

If **you** register late, **you** have to pay a fine. [second person]

Practice 1

Underline the pronoun or phrase in parentheses that agrees in number with the antecedent. In sentences where more than one answer is correct, choose just one answer.

1. A cat often purrs when (it is, they are) contented.

2. Have you tried the cranberry bread? Marty made (it, them).

3. Celia helped pick strawberries. (It was, They were) delicious.

4. All students should complete the assignment by Friday, or (he, she, they) will lose credit.

5. Unless drivers display parking permits on the rear window, (he, she, they) will be ticketed.

6. A student must use (her, his, their) ID card to be admitted.

7. If a person expects to play the guitar well, (he, she, they) must be willing to practice often.

8. If a junior wants to usher at graduation, (he, she, they) should see Ms. Reily.

9. When a child uses the wading pool, (he, she, they) must be accompanied by an adult.

10. Jo Ann has hunted everywhere for the badminton net. (It was, They were) in the attic.

Practice 2

Each of the following sentences contains an indefinite pronoun as an antecedent. Underline the pronoun in parentheses that agrees in number with the antecedent. In sentences where more than one answer is correct, choose just one answer.

1. Did you tell everyone to wear (her, his, their) hiking boots?

2. If someone really hunts for that book, (he, she, they) will find it.

3. Each of the women turned in (her, their) report on air pollution.

4. No one wants to give up (her, his, their) place by the front window.

5. Anyone who wants to cook (her, his, their) own breakfast is free to do so.

6. Everybody in the choir should sign (her, his, their) name in the guest book.

7. If anyone has information about the accident, (he, she, they) should report it immediately.

8. Everyone on the soccer team will buy (her, his, their) own bus ticket.

9. Somebody left (her, his, their) bicycle in the driveway.

Practice 3

In each sentence below, antecedents are joined by *and, or,* or *nor.* Underline the pronoun in parentheses that agrees in number with the antecedent.

1. Have you seen the paste and masking tape? I can't find (it, them).

2. Neither Mr. Stevens nor Mr. Feldman brought (his, their) tennis racket.

3. Karen and Edie will show slides of (her, their) hiking trip.

4. Mom and Aunt Lou don't want to give up (her, their) Saturday consumer-education classes.

5. I think Joe or Tim will lend us (his, their) bike.

6. If you see Anne or Betsy, ask (her, them) to call me.

7. My cousin and his wife took two Airedale puppies with (him, them) on vacation.

8. Neither Sonja nor her sister remembered (her, their) house key.

9. Water and grease have left (its, their) mark on this old wallpaper.

Practice 4

The pronoun in bold type in each sentence below does not agree in person with its antecedent. Replace each pronoun in bold type with one that agrees with its antecedent, and write that pronoun on the line after the sentence.

1. If somebody wants to sign up for the softball team, **you** had better do it today. _____

2. When people go to the movies, **you** should try not to disturb others. _____

3. If a person wants to use the tennis courts, **you** must wear sneakers. _____

4. When a student takes a test, **you** should try to be relaxed. _____

5. After a club member uses the kitchen, **you** should try to clean everything up. _____

6. People should be careful in using these tools, or **you** might get hurt. _____

7. No one should work so hard that **your** health suffers. _____

8. Often a bike rider forgets that **you** should use hand signals in traffic. _____

9. If someone wants to leave early, **you** may do so. _____

Name _____ Possible Score 15 My Score ☐

In some sentences, a pronoun seems to refer to either of two antecedents instead of just one.

Nan doesn't like to play tennis with her **sister** because **she** always wins. [double reference]

Who always wins? Does the pronoun *she* refer to *Nan* or to *sister?* To correct this kind of error, replace the pronoun with its specific antecedent.

Nan doesn't like to play tennis with her sister because **Nan** always wins.

Or, move the pronoun closer to its real antecedent.

Because **Nan** always wins, **she** doesn't like to play tennis with her sister.

Sometimes, in order to make the antecedent of a pronoun clear, you must rewrite a sentence to include a direct quotation.

Jim told **Don** that **he** might miss band practice. [double reference]

Jim told **Don**, "**You** might miss band practice."

Jim said, "Don, **I** might miss band practice."

Practice

Rewrite each sentence so that the pronoun in bold type refers specifically to the antecedent in bold type. Or, if necessary, rewrite the sentence, replacing the pronoun with its specific antecedent.

1. Ben doesn't cook for **Ray** because **he** likes spicy foods. _____

2. The **captain** called the judge to tell him that it was **his** responsibility. _____

3. "Anything Grows" is the **name** of our club, but I don't like **it**. _____

4. Carla studied **art** before she went mountain climbing. She said **it** was hard. _____

5. **Janie** doesn't see her friend Meg very often since **she** moved to Ohio. _____

6. Helen told **Beth** that **she** might be late if it rains.

_____

_____

7. **Carlos** often telephoned his brother while **he** was at camp.

_____

_____

8. Lynn asked her **sister** why **her** room was such a mess.

_____

_____

9. Our **car** hit the garage door, but **it** wasn't badly damaged.

_____

_____

10. **Mr. García** told Joe that **he** should check the oil level again.

_____

_____

11. **Julia** told Sandy that **she** should learn sign language.

_____

_____

12. Eric usually drives with **Sam,** but today **he** drove alone.

_____

_____

13. **Cindy** wrote to Nora when **she** became the swimming coach.

_____

_____

14. The mechanic told **Shelley** that **she** might need a new car.

_____

_____

15. Jim enjoys hiking with **Kent** because **he** knows all the trails.

_____

_____

Pronouns: Loose Reference

Name _____

A pronoun should have a specific antecedent. It should not be used to refer loosely to a general idea.

No one finished the **assignment, which** was too long. [specific reference]

No one finished the assignment, **which** was unfortunate. [loose reference]

In the first sentence, *which* refers specifically to the antecedent *assignment*. In the second sentence, *which* refers loosely to the fact that no one finished the assignment. To make the reference in the second sentence specific, you must rewrite the sentence.

That no one finished the assignment was unfortunate.

Unfortunately, no one finished the assignment.

Pronouns like *it, this, they, which,* and *that* are often used loosely. The problem of loose reference can often be solved by replacing the pronoun with specific words.

Last week I had three tests. **It** was much better this week. [loose reference]

Last week I had three tests. **My schedule** was much better this week. [specific words]

The doctor prescribed the wrong medication. **This** nearly cost the patient her life. [loose reference]

The doctor prescribed the wrong medication. **This mistake** nearly cost the patient her life. [specific words]

Practice

Rewrite each sentence below, replacing the pronoun in bold type with more specific words. Or, if necessary, revise the entire sentence.

1. Al twisted his ankle, **which** kept him from going biking with us.

_____

_____

2. **It** says that Spike Lee's new movie is excellent.

_____

_____

3. We decided to take the long trail to camp. **That** was a mistake.

_____

_____

4. **It** says in the paper that the mayor will run for reelection.

_____

_____

5. Ron and Daniella take turns doing chores. **This** seems to work.

_____

UNIT 2 Using the Right Words

6. Carmen found her watch by her locker, **which** was lucky.

_____

_____

7. Typing requires skill. **They** have to be accurate.

_____

_____

8. On rainy days, the boys play indoors. **It** was bad this morning.

_____

_____

9. Skiing looks like fun. **They** seem to glide downhill effortlessly.

_____

_____

10. Coaching is an interesting job. I'd like to be **one.**

_____

_____

11. Hank stubbed his toe and ripped his suit. **This** ruined his day.

_____

_____

12. Because jogging requires endurance, **they** must start out slowly.

_____

_____

13. **It** says in the article that politics can be a cutthroat game.

_____

_____

14. Tu's car broke down, **which** was unfortunate.

_____

_____

15. Jim succeeded in saving the puppy. **This** convinced him to become a veterinarian.

_____

_____

Pronouns: Wrong Reference

Name _____   Possible Score [7]   My Score [ ]

In some sentences, a pronoun refers to the wrong antecedent. This problem usually occurs because the wrong antecedent comes between the pronoun and its real antecedent. To correct this kind of pronoun error, place the pronoun as close as possible to the real antecedent.

> Ted took off his wet shoes, wiggled his bare **toes**, and put **them** in his knapsack. [wrong reference]

> Ted took off his wet **shoes**, put **them** in his knapsack, and wiggled his bare toes.

Sometimes, you have to switch the positions of the antecedent and pronoun and change the order of the sentence parts. This change is usually necessary in sentences that begin with words like *if, when, although, since,* and *while.*

> If the meat is too tough for the **kitten**, cut **it** into tiny pieces. [wrong reference]

> Cut the **meat** into tiny pieces if **it** is too tough for the kitten.

Practice

Rewrite each sentence below so that the pronoun in bold type refers to the antecedent in bold type.

1. If this **medicine** doesn't help the dog, throw **it** away. _____

   _____

2. Dan picked up his **notes,** turned to the pupils, and placed **them** on the desk. _____ _____

   _____

   _____

3. When the **reports** are ready for the lawyers, **they** should be stapled. _____

   _____

4. Beth got into the **car,** adjusted the mirror, and turned **it** on. _____

   _____

5. Since the **coats** are too small for the twins, **they** should be given away. _____

   _____

6. If the **collar** is too tight for the cat, punch another hole in **it**. _____

   _____

7. Pat picked up the **ball,** looked at the crowd, and tossed **it** through the hoop. _____

   _____

   _____

Application

A. Read the paragraphs below. Then underline the word or words in parentheses that correctly complete each sentence. In situations where more than one answer is correct, choose just one answer.

Not everyone is interested in auto mechanics or in doing minor maintenance and repairs on (her, his, their) own car. A person may feel that (her, his, their) car will perform better if a trained mechanic cares for (it, them). But even someone who has no interest in changing a flat tire or checking the oil and water still has an obligation to understand certain things about (her, his, their) car. (He, She, They) should know enough about the way (it operates, they operate) to be able to talk intelligently with the mechanic. The car owner should be able to describe what (he thinks, she thinks, you think) is wrong and to explain what (he wants, she wants, they want) done.

Of course, this situation applies both to teenagers and to adults since both will want (her, his, their) car to perform at (its, their) best. Today, many car owners are finding that a more thorough understanding of what is under the hood will help (them, you) avoid two things—being overcharged and having inferior work done on (their, your) car.

B. Each of the following items contains a pronoun in bold type with double reference, loose reference, or wrong reference. On a separate sheet of paper, rewrite each sentence, correcting the pronoun reference.

1. Ballet is a difficult profession because **they** have to practice so much.

2. Although I am studying accounting, I don't want to be **one**.

3. Julie dialed the same wrong number three times, **which** was embarrassing.

4. José usually walks with Bill to school, but today **he** took the bus.

5. Martha and Beth often study together, but yesterday **she** was sick.

6. Jessica told her sister that **she** was going to be late.

7. Phi took off his hat, combed his hair, and put **it** away.

8. Tanya knew how to fix the toaster, **which** was fortunate.

9. Dr. Voos made out two charts, examined the boys, and put **them** in the cabinet.

10. Ari picked up the shirts, thanked the salespeople, and put **them** under his arm.

11. Since the fruit drinks are too sweet for the guests, **they** should be thrown away.

12. Morty told Wes that **he** should buy a van.

13. Lisa ripped her backpack. **This** prevented her from meeting us on time.

14. Russ doesn't play basketball with Sal because **he** works on Saturdays.

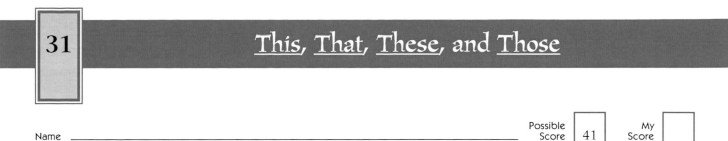

Name _____

Possible Score | 41 | My Score | ☐

The words *this, that, these,* and *those* are called *pointing words* or *demonstratives.* Notice that demonstratives can either stand alone as pronouns or be used as noun modifiers.

    This is Lee's book. [pronoun]   **These books** are Lee's. [modifier of noun <u>books</u>]

This and its plural *these* point to something near the speaker. *That* and its plural *those* point to something away from the speaker. Thus, adding the words *here* and *there* to *this, that, these,* and *those* is repetitious and incorrect.

    This here is mine. [nonstandard]   **That there box** is too heavy. [nonstandard]

    This is mine.   **That box** is too heavy.

However, you can use the word *here* or *there* correctly in other places in a sentence that contains a demonstrative.

    Let's put **these** boxes over **there** by the door.

Use the singular *this* and *that* with *kind, sort,* and *type.* Use the plural *these* and *those* with *kinds, sorts,* and *types.*

    Dad buys **this kind** of pear. [singular]   I like **that sort** of story. [singular]

    Dad buys **these kinds** of pears. [plural]   I like **those sorts** of stories. [plural]

Sometimes the singular words *kind, sort,* and *type* are followed by *of* and a plural noun. Be sure you use the singular words *this* and *that* to agree with *kind, sort,* and *type,* not with the plural noun that follows *of.*

    Have you tried **these kind of peaches?** [nonstandard]

    Have you tried **this kind of peaches?**

Practice 1

Write *I* next to each sentence in which *here* or *there* is used incorrectly. Write *C* next to each sentence in which *here* or *there* is used correctly.

_____ 1. That there student by the lunch counter is Rita's cousin.

_____ 2. Sally said that this here story is the best she's ever read.

_____ 3. These science reports should be kept right here where everyone can use them.

_____ 4. You'd better use Mrs. Collins's printer; that there one needs a new ink cartridge.

_____ 5. Why not move that plant over here near the window?

_____ 6. Just put those there crates against the garage wall.

_____ 7. That there swimmer is probably the best on the team.

_____ 8. Julian said he took two hours to do these here math problems.

_____ 9. Are there any more of those muffins left?

_____ 10. No one seems to have any idea where these here books belong.

_____ 11. The architect told us that the design of this here building was innovative in its time.

_____ 12. Did Ora program that there computer?

UNIT 2   Using the Right Words

_____ 13. Put those there chemicals in the test tube.

_____ 14. These here employees have organized a Memorial Day picnic.

_____ 15. Set that tray over there.

_____ 16. The chef made those there shrimp enchiladas.

_____ 17. These here teenages took a raft trip down the Colorado River last summer.

_____ 18. Tell me whether there are enough of these cheese puffs for everyone.

_____ 19. The lab assistant trained those there mice to run through a maze.

_____ 20. This here statue was carved by an islander thousands of years ago.

_____ 21. Leave the laundry bag over there.

Practice 2

Underline the word in parentheses that correctly completes each sentence below.

1. Betsy had never seen (that, those) kind of animals before.

2. It's always a pleasure to have (this, these) sort of campers in our national parks.

3. Dave weakened this argument by presenting (that, those) kinds of half-truths.

4. Do you like (this, these) type of coffee?

5. It's often a mistake to listen to (that, those) type of rumors.

6. Warm, moist weather seems to be good for (that, those) types of flowers.

7. It's very important to recognize (this, these) sort of mushroom as poisonous.

8. Sometimes, it's hard to be on the same team with (that, those) kinds of players.

9. Exact temperature control is important for (this, these) type of machines.

10. Jill doesn't like to write with (this, these) sorts of pens.

11. Janice seldom uses (that, those) kind of tool.

12. Film critics usually like (that, those) sorts of movies.

13. (This, These) types of advertisements often generate a great deal of business.

14. Homeowners generally avoid buying (this, these) sort of appliances.

15. My supervisor is often called upon to make (that, those) types of decisions.

16. Many serious students enroll in (this, these) kinds of courses.

17. No one in our class likes (this, those) type of paintings.

18. Amy reads (that, those) sort of novels.

19. Employment agencies often place teenagers in (this, these) kinds of jobs.

20. Builders often use (that, these) type of brick.

More about <u>This</u>, <u>That</u>, <u>These</u>, and <u>Those</u>

Name _____ Possible Score `22` My Score

The demonstratives *these* and *those* can stand alone as pronouns, or they can be used as noun modifiers.

These are Lee's books. [pronoun]   **These books** are Lee's. [modifier of noun <u>books</u>]

Them is a personal pronoun. Use *them* only in an object position.

Charlie saw **them**. [direct object]

Edie gave **them** the photographs. [indirect object]

Sue never heard of **them**. [object of preposition]

Do not use *them* in place of *these* or *those* as a subject or as a noun modifier.

Them are the ones I want. [nonstandard]   Paul chose **them shirts**. [nonstandard]

These are the ones I want. [subject]   Paul chose **those shirts**. [modifier]

Practice

Underline the word in parentheses that correctly completes each sentence.

1. Did you know that (them, those) commercials were written by a well-known songwriter?

2. (Them, These) are the three things you must have—a parka, strong boots, and warm gloves.

3. Two students are still writing; ask (them, those) to hand in their papers now.

4. Look! (Them, These) must be the magazines Carmen was looking for.

5. The twins were so excited about their birthday that we gave (them, these) one of their presents early.

6. (Them, These) beautiful old trees are being cut down because they have Dutch elm disease.

7. Watching (them, those) dolphins perform was the best part of the show at the aquarium.

8. The spareribs were delicious; everyone likes the way Uncle Mal cooks (them, these).

9. I think both (them, those) basset hounds should win a prize.

10. Now that the new bypass is complete, it's time to throw (them, those) old road maps away.

11. Corrine thinks (them, those) clouds look ominous.

12. (Them, These) are the race-car drivers who will take part in the competition on Sunday.

13. Tell (them, those) to meet me in the small conference room at one o'clock.

14. (Them, These) must be the engineers who attended the convention in Milwaukee last month.

15. Coach Landrum told (them, these) they would have to practice harder if they wanted to win.

16. (Them, Those) pilots have gathered at the north end of the airstrip for last-minute instructions.

17. Digging (them, these) ditches was hard work.

18. Lia adjusted her car's front seat for (them, those).

19. Stacey seldom watches (them, those) television shows.

20. On summer evenings, (them, these) girls play volleyball in Terminal Park.

21. Gordie bought (them, those) old campaign buttons in an antique store.

22. (Them, These) are the new roller blades we told you about.

Application

Name _____

Rewrite the following paragraphs. Remove the words *here* and *there* wherever they are not needed. Fix any incorrect demonstratives.

Arabian horses, which are noted for their beauty, stamina, and grace, have been used for hundreds of years to develop new breeds. But some admirers of these type of horses are interested in maintaining the pure breed in this here country.

A man named Homer Davenport, who first saw these kind of horses at the Chicago World's Fair in 1893, later succeeded in importing twenty-seven of them horses in 1906. One of the most famous of them Davenport imports was Buffalo Bill's horse, Muson.

Today, about 180 Arabian horses go back directly to the Davenport imports. Them highly prized horses are called Davenport Arabians and are found both in this here country and in Canada.

_____

_____

_____

_____

_____

_____

_____

_____

_____

_____

_____

_____

_____

_____

_____

_____

_____

_____

Name _____ Possible Score [59] My Score [ ]

The subject and the verb of a sentence must agree in number. That is, if the subject is singular, the verb must be singular. If the subject is plural, the verb must be plural. The verbs shown in the chart below are all present-tense verb forms because these are the forms most likely to cause agreement problems. Notice that the endings -s and -es are used both with nouns and with verbs. With nouns, -s and -es are signs of the plural. However, with verbs, these endings are signs of the singular. Notice, too, that the pronouns *I*, *we, they,* and *you* always occur with verbs that don't end in -s or -es.

Singular Subject + Singular Verb		Plural Subject + Plural Verb	
the cat	watch**es**	the cat**s**	watch
a box	break**s**	box**es**	break
he she it	work**s**	they	work
you alone I	remain	you three we	remain

Practice 1

Underline the verb or verbs in parentheses that correctly complete each sentence.

1. Chantha usually (ride, rides) her bike to school.

2. Jodie (watch, watches) the tryouts every chance she (get, gets).

3. My mother (take, takes) her vacation in August; she (hope, hopes) to visit her cousins in Missouri this year.

4. Ms. Rosas (urge, urges) us to practice speaking Spanish whenever we are with our Spanish-speaking friends.

5. Governor Stirling (drive, drives) a sports car on weekends.

6. Kathy Doyle (answer, answers) the telephone only when she is expecting a call.

7. My neighbors (swim, swims) at Juneway Beach when Farwell Beach is crowded.

8. Ask Brady if he (need, needs) help carrying that desk.

9. Every morning Ambassador Ibarra (drink, drinks) a glass of papaya juice and (eat, eats) an English muffin.

10. Whenever Lefty (borrow, borrows) my goggles, she (forget, forgets) to return them.

11. Although those snakes (look, looks) harmless, they are really quite dangerous.

12. Kelly (want, wants) to adopt every stray dog he (see, sees).

13. We (think, thinks) that the story (sound, sounds) too incredible to be true.

14. Pepe (expect, expects) us to meet him when he (arrive, arrives) at O'Hare Field.

15. The dresses (fit, fits) Marguerite perfectly.

16. The campus (look, looks) empty because many students have gone home for the weekend.

17. Whenever I (visit, visits) Mr. Kogutowicz, he (ask, asks) me to mow his lawn.

18. You always (guess, guesses) what I'm thinking.

19. They (seem, seems) to be interested in investment banking.

20. The pool (close, closes) at nine o'clock on Saturday.

21. We (plan, plans) to go skiing in Colorado next winter.

22. Elliot (say, says) that you (make, makes) the best avocado soup he has ever tasted.

23. That puppy (follow, follows) us wherever we (go, goes).

24. This boutique (sell, sells) imported silk shirts and scarves.

25. Molly (know, knows) that I (enjoy, enjoys) all types of sporting events.

Practice 2

Complete each sentence below correctly. Underline the verb form in parentheses that agrees in number with the subject.

1. These glasses (break, breaks) easily.

2. The rodeo (begin, begins) in forty-five minutes.

3. Her stockbroker usually (give, gives) her good advice.

4. Vines (cover, covers) the wall most of the year.

5. The winners (go, goes) first.

6. Stefan (order, orders) most of his shirts from that catalog.

7. Dr. Addison (sneeze, sneezes) whenever she is near cats.

8. You (draw, draws) very well.

9. That tennis player (wear, wears) a headband to keep the sweat out of his eyes.

10. This machine (start, starts) very fast.

11. Dorie Anton (coach, coaches) the twelfth-grade soccer team.

12. Maple leaves (turn, turns) golden in the fall.

13. Those singers (work, works) with Jeff and me.

14. These detectives (solve, solves) many crimes each year.

15. The ties (match, matches) your suit.

16. She (send, sends) her sister a check every month.

17. These cuts (sting, stings).

18. He (run, runs) two miles every day.

19. Mary (refuse, refuses) to wear a bathing cap when she is at the beach.

20. Darlene (remember, remembers) meeting us at the resort last year.

21. We (agree, agrees) with your assessment of the situation.

22. Earl (wait, waits) for me after school on Wednesdays.

23. I (teach, teaches) history and trigonometry.

Name _____ Possible Score [32] My Score [ ]

The verb *be* has three past-tense forms—*am, is,* and *are. Am* and *is* are used with singular subjects. *Are* is used with *you* and with plural subjects. The verb *be* also has two past-tense forms—*was* and *were. Was* is used with singular subjects. *Were* is used with *you* and with plural subjects.

    You may use a form of *be* as a main verb or as a helping verb.

      Those players **are** agile. [main verb]   I **am** leaving now. [helping verb]

    When you write a sentence with a form of *be* as the main verb, make sure the verb agrees with the subject, not with the noun or pronoun that follows the verb.

      The best present **were the books**. [nonstandard]

      The best **present was** the books. [standard]

    In informal writing, you may want to use a contraction of *be* or of a negative used with *be*. Notice that *'re* is a contraction of *are*, not *were*, and that *aren't* is used with negative questions with *I*.

      He's tired.   **We're** ready.   **I'm** listening.

      It's not broken.   **It isn't** broken.   **They're not** here.   **They aren't** here.

      I'm not hungry.   I'm on time, **aren't I**?

    Notice that adding *'nt* to a form of *be* doesn't affect the number agreement of subject and verb.

      She is my cousin.   **They were** the class clowns.

      She isn't my cousin.   **They weren't** the class clowns.

Practice 1

Complete each sentence below with an appropriate form of *be*. Use the tense form indicated in parentheses. Make sure the subject and verb agree in number.

1. Joe and Dee _____ watching that program on television. *(present)*

2. You _____ the first one to arrive. *(past)*

3. Jeff and Adam _____ upset about the extra rehearsal. *(present)*

4. The apples _____ in the refrigerator. *(past)*

5. Jake _____ working at the garage after school. *(past)*

6. Sharon's mother _____ a corporate lawyer. *(present)*

7. What _____ you planning to do on Saturday? *(past)*

8. _____ Linda at the movies this afternoon? *(present)*

9. I _____ painting the front porch. *(present)*

10. We _____ trying to telephone you. *(past)*

11. Tony _____ eating lunch when we got there. *(past)*

12. Diane _____ baby-sitting tonight. *(present)*

13. Our class _____ the first to use the new tool. *(past)*

14. My bicycle _____ that red-and-white one. *(present)*

15. _____ I supposed to let you know the address? *(present)*

Practice 2

Underline the verb form in parentheses that agrees in number with the subject.

1. The mystery (was, were) the footprints outside the window.

2. The frequent thunderstorms (was, were) a new experience for us.

3. The puppet shows (is, are) always a favorite entertainment for the children.

4. The two brothers (is, are) the backbone of the organization.

5. These plants (was, were) my responsibility last month.

6. The most disagreeable part (was, were) the traffic jams.

7. Phil's favorite fruit (is, are) blueberries.

8. The reason for the delay (is, are) those machines.

9. Piston rings (is, are) the seal between the piston and the cylinder wall.

10. The goal of dental hygiene (is, are) healthy gums and teeth.

Practice 3

Rewrite each sentence below. If the verb form in bold type is in the present tense, change it to the past tense; if it is in the past tense, change it to the present tense.

1. I **wasn't** the team captain.

   _____

2. **Weren't** you surprised by the news?

   _____

3. **I'm** not going to say anything.

   _____

4. We **aren't** the last to finish.

   _____

5. Why **isn't** the CD player working?

   _____

6. **Wasn't** I supposed to give my report?

   _____

7. **They're** not going camping.

   _____

Subject-Verb Agreement: Compound Subjects

Name _____ Possible Score [22] My Score [ ]

Sentences with compound subjects can cause agreement problems.

When you write a sentence with two subjects joined by *and*, use a plural verb.

Brad and Jim are reporting on the same book.

When you write a sentence with two singular subjects joined by *or* or *nor*, use a singular verb.

Kathy or Cecile is making the announcement tomorrow.

Neither **Kathy nor Cecile wants** to do it.

When you write a sentence with a singular subject and a plural subject joined by *or* or *nor*, make the verb agree in number with the subject closer to it.

Either Sam or the **girls are** going to wash the car.

Either the girls or **Sam is** going to wash the car.

Practice

Underline the verb form in parentheses that correctly completes each sentence.

1. Neither the sauce nor the pasta (is, are) ready yet.

2. Donna said that Helen and Judy (is, are) practicing hard.

3. Either Dad or my brothers (is, are) making pancakes.

4. Debbie and John (is, are) planning to bring their CDs.

5. Joe and Nick (is, are) building a tree house in the backyard.

6. Either the bus or the subway (is, are) convenient to get to the ball park.

7. Doug or Carole (is, are) going to meet us at the bus terminal.

8. I thought Jane or her brother (was, were) going to call us.

9. The saw and the hammer (was, were) in the tool chest.

10. Neither sun nor rain (damage, damages) this house paint.

11. Shawn and Rollo (enjoy, enjoys) traveling by boat.

12. Either the TV station manger or the program director (is, are) going to show us the control room.

13. Neither Ellie nor Jan (is, are) meeting us at Melvin's Café.

14. Either Roy or his sisters (work, works) at the Shelton Theater after school.

15. Gina and her friend (take, takes) turns driving on long trips.

16. Either the teachers or the administrator (is, are) demanding a new contract.

17. The cabbage soup and the pot roast (was, were) delicious.

18. I thought that Angelo and Michelle (was, were) working with the road crew.

19. Neither the clients nor the lawyer (plan, plans) to discuss the matter with the press.

20. The pilot and the flight attendants (try, tries) to make each flight as safe and comfortable as possible.

21. Either Dennis or Carmen (was, were) building a plastic cabinet for the living room.

22. Neither Greg nor Donna (play, plays) tennis at the Midtown Tennis Club anymore.

UNIT 2 Using the Right Words

Name _____   Possible Score **40**   My Score ☐

A phrase beginning with an expression like *as well as* or *in addition to*, which comes between the subject and the verb, is not part of the subject. Make the verb agree with the subject.

The **coach,** as well as the players, **is** going by bus.

The **players,** together with the coach, **are** going by bus.

If a prepositional phrase follows the subject, make the verb agree with the subject, not with the last word in the prepositional phrase.

The **ability** of the gymnasts **is** breathtaking.

Several **windows** in the building **were** broken.

If a negative expression beginning with *not* or *but not* follows the subject, make the verb agree with the subject, not with the last word in the expression.

Betsy and Joe, not their father, **are** weeding the garden.

Jeff, but not his sisters, **agrees** to baby-sit.

Practice

Cross out the interrupting phrase in each sentence below and underline the correct verb form.

1. Nancy, but not Sheryl, (is, are) working on the stage crew for the class play.

2. Ms. Scully, together with her students, (is, are) running around the track.

3. The announcement of the awards (is, are) scheduled for tomorrow night.

4. Chemistry, in addition to biology, (require, requires) several hours of lab work each week.

5. The bridge over the old railway tracks (was, were) being repaired last week.

6. The hot dogs, along with the potato salad, (was, were) kept in the refrigerator.

7. The points inside the distributor of a car (need, needs) changing every twelve thousand miles.

8. Corey, as well as his sister, (like, likes) bacon.

9. The washing machine, not the dishwasher, (is, are) making a strange noise.

10. The leftovers from dinner last night (was, were) used for lunch today.

11. The melted butter, as well as the lobster, (was, were) ready to be served.

12. Becky, but not Chuck, (is, are) entering the Lincoln Park Dance Marathon.

13. The members of that club (organize, organizes) a fund-raising dinner every spring.

14. Ken Hong, together with Dr. Kaplan, (jog, jogs) by the lake each evening.

15. Three names on this list (was, were) misspelled.

16. The marine biologist, in addition to the ecologists, (is, are) in favor of our latest proposal.

17. The handlebars on that bicycle (was, were) twisted out of shape.

18. Two girls in our physics class (is, are) building amateur radio sets.

19. Sharon, not my cousins, (believe, believes) that those stones mark ancient graves of prehistoric people.

20. The walls of this cavern (is, are) covered with prehistoric drawings.

Application

Name _____

Possible Score 59   My Score [ ]

A. On a separate sheet of paper, rewrite the following paragraph. Correct any errors in subject-verb agreement by changing the verb to make it agree in number with the subject.

> My brother Hank has a strange eating habit at breakfast. Each morning he wait until the last moment to get up. Then he has to rush to catch the bus, so he eat breakfast as he move around, picking up his books and coat. Mother keep trying to get him to sit down, but Dad say at least Hank is eating. It look to me as if Hank doesn't know what he is eating or what he is missing. He need to slow down enough to see what good things are on the table. Then he might get up early enough to enjoy them.

B. On a separate sheet of paper, rewrite the following paragraphs, adding the correct present- or past-tense form of *be* wherever you see the word *present* or *past* in parentheses. Make certain to choose singular verbs for singular subjects and plural verbs for plural subjects.

> Students (present) encouraged to develop the habit of reading at an early age. In elementary school, time (present) generally allocated daily for both regular reading instruction and for pleasure reading. In addition, many teachers (present) encouraging their students to develop reading logs, which (present) designed to chart reading experiences each year.
>
> Likewise, secondary-school teachers (present) equally committed to helping their students become "hooked" on reading. When novels, essays, biographies, and short stories (present) required reading for class, students (present) often given some in-class time to read these selections, rather than to do all of the reading outside of class. High-school graduates have testified that they (past) better prepared in reading for post-secondary education if they read regularly in and out of school, than if they (past) asked to read only out of school. Graduates have also said that frequent use of the library (present) an important part of maintaining the habit of reading.
>
> Finally, one of the best ways to be an active reader (present) to be surrounded by a variety of interesting reading materials. As one student said, "Keeping a book handy in my book bag (present) a simple way of having my reading materials no more than an arm's length away!"

C. On a separate sheet of paper, rewrite the following paragraphs, changing any verb that does not agree in number with its subject.

> Today the training of national park service rangers are much different than it was only a few years ago. And the rangers themselves have changed. Today's rangers includes women and members of minority groups. The new rangers comes mostly from urban areas. Most of them is college graduates.
>
> An important area of study are still ecology and the environment. Wilderness survival, in addition to fighting forest fires, are also part of the training program. And neither mountaineering nor rescue are ignored. However, administration and public relations is also studied, as are ways of handling overcrowding, traffic, and vandalism. Since teaching, not just lecturing, are now emphasized, the ability to listen courteously is an essential skill for rangers. An important qualification for today's park rangers are sensitivity to visitors with varying backgrounds and lifestyles.

D. For each sentence below, underline the verb form in parentheses that agrees in number with the subject.

1. Bret (camp, camps) at Raccoon Lake each summer.

2. The brakes on that car (squeak, squeaks).

3. This lawn mower (isn't, aren't) easy to maneuver.

4. A survey of the situation (reveal, reveals) several unique problems.

5. Neither Kathleen nor Don (want, wants) to work in the steel mills.

6. Kit's favorite vegetable (is, are) onions.

7. Fergie (wear, wears) the strangest shoes.

8. The traffic signals on the corner of Lake and Thatcher (is, are) broken.

9. María and her teammates (plan, plans) to win the tournament.

10. The library hours (wasn't, weren't) changed.

11. They (own, owns) five condominiums.

12. Chris, not his brothers, (expect, expects) to enter the five-hundred-yard freestyle event.

13. Senator Kirk (isn't, aren't) aware of the implications of her decision.

14. Tickets for the play (go, goes) on sale at noon.

15. Either Mason or the photographers (is, are) meeting us at Pine River Camp.

16. The drivers behind me (was, were) very impatient.

17. Those artists (share, shares) their ideas and goals.

18. The worst part (was, were) the crowds.

19. Tom, as well as his friends, (attend, attends) the baseball games each spring.

20. Karen or Marina (is, are) designing the program for the school play.

21. She (exercise, exercises) at the Lehman Health Club.

22. The problem (is, are) those two chimpanzees.

23. These swimmers (is, are) trying to grab the state championship.

24. Claudia (was, were) trimming the bushes.

25. The source of her irritation (was, were) the dirty dishes in the sink.

26. Those students (take, takes) a bus to school.

27. The television set (wasn't, weren't) working.

28. Either the manager or the cashiers (count, counts) the money at night.

29. The wheels on the chair (need, needs) oiling.

30. Glenna and Jodie (spend, spends) a great deal of time playing racquetball.

Subject-Verb Agreement: Verbs Preceding Subjects

Name _____ Possible Score [70] My Score [ ]

In questions, in sentences beginning with *here* or *there,* and in sentences beginning with prepositional phrases, the verb often comes before the subject. When you write these kinds of sentences, make sure the verb agrees in number with the subject.

Was Ella upset?

Here **comes** the **bus.**

On the shelf **were** a broken tennis **racket** and a **basketball.**

Practice

Circle the subject of each sentence below. Then underline the verb form in parentheses that agrees in number with the subject.

1. Just inside the front door (is, are) the old coat-rack and the umbrella stand that Grandfather made.

2. Here (is, are) the packages I told you about.

3. There (is, are) something important I want to tell you.

4. (Wasn't, Weren't) you at the dentist today?

5. Suddenly, around the corner (come, comes) Bob and Joan in a red truck.

6. By Friday afternoon there (wasn't, weren't) any tickets left.

7. Here (is, are) the strangest part of the whole story.

8. There (is, are) ten reporters in the courtroom.

9. (Was, Were) that quarterback in the TV commercial?

10. Near the lake (is, are) an outdoor theater.

11. (Is, Are) those divers on your team?

12. Across the street (is, are) some interesting Victorian homes.

13. Behind the desk (was, were) two boxes filled with toys.

14. Here (is, are) the medicine you wanted.

15. (Was, Were) the counselor helpful?

16. Along the road (is, are) many signs advertising that hair-care product.

17. There (is, are) three detectives on that case.

18. (Is, Are) Josh and Mindy expert tennis players?

19. There (was, were) a flaw in the material.

20. In the committee (is, are) several distinguished research scientists.

21. There (go, goes) the best athlete in the school.

22. On the counter (sit, sits) two jars of olives.

23. (Wasn't, Weren't) the vans parked in the garage?

24. Here (is, are) the telephones that Irene Torreno bought.

25. On top of the mountain (perch, perches) a ramshackle cabin.

26. (Wasn't, Weren't) that trail closed because of a mudslide?

27. Above the couch (hang, hangs) a lithograph and an oil painting.

28. There (wasn't, weren't) enough time to read the license number of the speeding car.

29. In the attic (is, are) a red couch and four orange chairs.

30. (Isn't, Aren't) these mangoes good?

31. Here (is, are) a good example of Gothic architecture.

32. (Was, Were) the Davidsons supposed to make the guacamole?

33. Around the corner from my house (is, are) a huge amusement park.

34. (Is, Are) tomatoes a fruit or a vegetable?

35. There (wasn't, weren't) any reason to check their story.

Subject-Verb Agreement: Determining Number

Name _____

Possible Score 15   My Score ☐

Some nouns look plural because they end in -s. Use a singular verb with a noun like *mumps*.

Civics is taught by Ms. Cohen.   The **news** about the wheat crop **is** good.

Some expressions referring to measurement or to amounts of time and money may be either singular or plural. When you want such expressions to mean items grouped together to form a single unit, use a singular verb. When you want such expressions to mean several separate items, use a plural verb.

Three eggs is a lot for one loaf of bread. [single unit]

Three eggs are on the table. [several items]

Two weeks seems like a long time to wait. [single unit]

Two weeks are set aside for reviewing and testing. [several items]

Use a singular verb if you want a fraction to tell *how much*. Use a plural verb if you want a fraction to tell *how many*.

Two thirds of the house **is** painted. [how much?]

Two thirds of the houses **are** painted. [how many?]

Use a singular verb with the title of a book, a play, a poem, a movie, or a television program.

***The Guns of August* is** a historical account of the months leading up to World War I.

Practice

Underline the verb form in parentheses that correctly completes each sentence. In sentences where either verb form might be correct, the words in brackets indicate which form you should use.

1. Do you think that measles (is, are) contagious?

2. Half the students in the sophomore class already (know, knows) how to swim.

3. *King Solomon's Mines* (remain, remains) one of my favorite old movies.

4. Three fourths of the money (was, were) set aside for paying the band.

5. Forty minutes (isn't, aren't) enough time to study for a test. [Consider the subject to be a single unit.]

6. Mathematics (is, are) Ron's favorite subject.

7. Fifteen pennies (was, were) lying on top of the newspapers. [Consider the subject to be several items.]

8. Billiards (require, requires) good hand-eye coordination.

9. Thirteen dollars (seem, seems) a lot to pay for a scarf. [Consider the subject to be a single unit.]

10. Two thirds of the orange juice (was, were) spilled when Jan knocked over the pitcher.

11. *Alice's Adventures in Wonderland* (is, are) Mary Beth's favorite book.

12. Optics (is, are) a science that deals with the properties of light.

13. Five eighths of the basketball players (want, wants) a new manager.

14. *Lilies of the Field* (was, were) a well-received film starring Sidney Poitier.

15. Pediatrics (is, are) the branch of medicine Bruce has chosen to study.

Name _____

Use a singular verb when you use one of the following indefinite pronouns as a subject: *everyone, everything, everybody, anyone, anybody, no one, nobody, someone, somebody, each, either, neither,* and *one.* A prepositional phrase following the subject does not affect the agreement of subject and verb.

Everyone is ready.   **Everything** in the serving bowls **is** hot.

Neither one of the owners **is** right.   **Each** of the shrubs **requires** water every day.

Use a plural verb when you use one of these indefinite pronouns as a subject: *many, few, several,* and *both.*

Many are homeless.   **Few** of us **were** able to escape.

Words like *none, some, any, most, part,* and *all* may be either singular or plural. Use a singular verb if you want the subject to tell *how much.* Use a plural verb if you want the subject to tell *how many.*

None of the floor **was** refinished. [how much?]

None of the floors **were** refinished. [how many?]

Practice 1

Underline the verb form in parentheses that agrees in number with the subject.

1. Everyone in the tour buses (is, are) eager to get started.

2. Everything (happen, happens) to me.

3. Somebody always (forget, forgets) to turn off the car lights.

4. Neither of the flashlights (work, works).

5. (Was, Were) anybody late for the game?

6. Many in the theater (was, were) upset by the movie.

7. Several of the new dishes (was, were) broken.

8. Both of my sisters (is, are) taking biology this year.

9. Few (was, were) hurt by the train's sudden stop.

10. (Is, Are) either of them taking that course in auto repair?

11. Nobody in the Outing Club (want, wants) to increase the dues this year.

12. Several of the community leaders (is, are) promoting the use of bicycle lanes in the main business area.

13. Both of the athletic directors (is, are) going to present their views.

14. Neither of the vending machines (was, were) working this morning.

15. Each of the gymnasts (come, comes) from a different country.

16. Everyone (was, were) at the beach all afternoon.

17. Few of the coaches (is, are) planning to attend the party.

18. Many of our clients (prefer, prefers) to do their own preliminary research.

19. No one (enjoy, enjoys) studying for exams.

20. Several of the batters (is, are) warming up.

Turn the page.   81

Practice 2

Decide whether the subject of each sentence is singular or plural by asking the questions *how much* and *how many*. Then underline the verb form in parentheses that agrees in number with the subject.

1. Fortunately, none of the ice (is, are) melting.

2. Most of the books on this reading list (is, are) paperbacks.

3. Part of the trouble (was, were) the broken handle.

4. All of the water (was, were) contaminated.

5. None of this explanation (make, makes) any sense to me.

6. (Is, Are) any of the iced tea left?

7. All of the papers left near the open window (was, were) damaged by the rain.

8. Some of the oil (was, were) spilled.

9. Most of the spectators (was, were) quiet as the performance began.

10. None of the apartments (was, were) for rent.

11. (Is, Are) any of these photographs for sale?

12. Part of the school (was, were) built in 1980.

13. All of the partners (is, are) flying to Iowa tomorrow.

14. Most of the highway (is, are) being repaired this summer.

15. Some of the committee members (want, wants) to appoint Senator Gutierrez.

16. None of the detectives (know, knows) who committed the crime.

17. All of the dental students (is, are) learning that technique.

18. Most of the figures in the wax museum (look, looks) quite real.

19. Part of the shore (was, were) eroded by high winds and torrential rains.

20. Some of the lettuce (is, are) left.

21. (Is, Are) any of the workers striking for higher pay?

22. All of the milk (is, are) gone.

23. Some of this pizza (is, are) still in the refrigerator.

24. None of the citizens (plan, plans) to sign this petition.

25. Part of his face (was, were) sunburned.

Application

Name _____   Possible Score [60]   My Score [ ]

A. Underline the verb form in parentheses that correctly completes each sentence.

1. Cryogenics (is, are) the study of the behavior of matter at extremely cold temperatures.

2. Inside her locker (is, are) a sandwich and some old gym shoes.

3. Somebody in the apartment upstairs (play, plays) the piano at six o'clock each morning.

4. (Wasn't, Weren't) they at the rodeo on Sunday?

5. Part of the steak (was, were) undercooked.

6. *Chicanos: A History of Mexican Americans* (was, were) written by Matt S. Meier and Feliciano Rivera.

7. (Is, Are) Jeanette in the chemistry lab now?

8. Half of the flowers in the garden (is, are) azaleas.

9. Here (is, are) a ticket to the jazz concert.

10. Many of the builders (read, reads) that magazine.

11. Marbles (was, were) the game they played most often.

12. Everyone (is, are) at the window.

13. Two cups of cream (seem, seems) to be all we need. [Consider the subject to be a single unit.]

14. *Lights of New York* (was, were) the first full-length, all-talking film ever made.

15. There (is, are) the Oriental rug Mr. Jacoby bought.

16. Most of the facts (support, supports) our conclusion.

17. Seven hundred dollars (is, are) too much money for that camping gear. [Consider the subject to be a single unit.]

18. Across the fields (is, are) an abandoned shack.

19. (Is, Are) any of your friends at the stables?

20. Two months (isn't, aren't) enough time to explore the ruins in South America. [Consider the subject to be a single unit.]

21. Part of the dinner (was, were) made by Dennis.

22. Among those in attendance (was, were) Ophelia and Lynn.

23. Everything (is, are) all right now.

24. (Was, Were) Dave sick?

25. Four fifths of the watermelon (was, were) eaten yesterday.

26. Three cartons of juice (is, are) in the refrigerator. [Consider the subject to be several items.]

27. Few (was, were) as sad as Brian and Lisa.

28. *12 Monkeys* (was, were) the name of a movie starring Madeleine Stowe, Bruce Willis, and Brad Pitt.

29. Either of them (is, are) sure to be a good lead singer.

30. Three fourths of her movies (deal, deals) with social problems.

B. Underline the verb form in parentheses that correctly completes the sentence.

1. (Is, Are) Lisa learning to sky dive?

2. Linguistics (was, were) the course Dan took in night school.

3. No one (like, likes) this recording of the song as much as the original version.

4. Thirty dollars (seem, seems) quite inexpensive for a watch like that. [Consider the subject to be a single unit.]

5. On top of the washing machine (is, are) all of your towels.

6. Several of them (is, are) waiting at the bottom of the ski slope.

7. Three fourths of the Scouts (attend, attends) weekly meetings.

8. The news (seem, seems) ominous.

9. There (go, goes) Brandon and Fay.

10. Neither of the layouts (look, looks) good.

11. In front of the window (is, are) all of her racquetball trophies.

12. *Braveheart* (was, were) directed by Mel Gibson.

13. (Was, Were) the fight on TV last night?

14. Ten minutes (is, are) too much time to waste. [Consider the subject to be a single unit.]

15. Everything in the basement (was, were) damaged by the flood.

16. Thousands of dollars (is, are) spent by the Bureau of Streets and Sanitation each year. [Consider the subject to be several items.]

17. All of the scenes in the play (is, are) well written.

18. "Distant Galaxies" (was, were) the name of the poem she wrote.

19. (Isn't, Aren't) Bill the editor of the school magazine?

20. Two thirds of the trees in this forest (is, are) elm trees.

21. (Is, Are) anyone sure that those two committed the crime?

22. Under the bed (is, are) a dirty shirt and a scarf.

23. Checkers (is, are) more fun than chess.

24. Everyone (suspect, suspects) Roy Meade.

25. Nobody (want, wants) to explore the attic of that old house.

26. Both of these words (is, are) misspelled.

27. *The Hundred Secret Senses* (was, were) published in 1995.

28. Here (is, are) a reprint of that advertisement.

29. Four quarters (is, are) on top of the dashboard. [Consider the subject to be several items.]

30. Some of these families (is, are) homeless as a result of the fire.

40

Verbs: Irregular Verbs

Name _____

Every English verb has three basic forms: simple, past, and past participle. These forms are called the principal parts of a verb. A fourth form—the *-ing* form—is made by adding *-ing* to the simple form.

Simple	Past	Past Participle	-ing Form
walk	walked	(have) walked	walking

Most verbs are regular. That is, their past and past-participle forms are made by adding *-ed* or *-d* to their simple forms.

Simple	Past	Past Participle
look	look**ed**	(have) look**ed**
race	race**d**	(have) race**d**

Some verbs are irregular. Such verbs have no regular way to make their past and past-participle forms. You must learn the parts of these verbs. Below are several examples of irregular verbs:

Simple	Past	Past Participle	Simple	Past	Past Participle
beg**in**	beg**an**	(have) beg**un**	find	found	(have) found
f**all**	f**ell**	(have) fall**en**	take	took	(have) tak**en**
go	went	(have) gone	am, is, are	was, were	(have) been
burst	burst	(have) burst	cost	cost	(have) cost

Be careful not to use the past form of an irregular verb when you need the past participle. Note that the past form is never used with a helping verb; the past participle always requires one.

Dave **broke** the record for the 100-yard dash [past form]

Dave **had broken** another track record six months before. [have + past participle]

The record for the 100-yard dash **was broken** by Dave. [be + past participle]

Another track record **has been broken** by Dave. [have + be + past participle]

Practice 1

Each of the following sentences is written correctly. Identify each irregular verb form in bold type by writing *simple, past,* or *past participle.*

1. Somsak **wrote** home once a week when she was at camp. _____

2. We sometimes **choose** apple juice just for a change. _____

3. Jeanne **tore** her coat on the door handle yesterday. _____

4. Haven't you ever **seen** the giraffes at the zoo? _____

5. When you're ready, **begin** to write. _____

6. Ted **caught** the last bus leaving for the city. _____

7. Jeff and Willis often **buy** lunch at the cafeteria. _____

8. Had the bell **rung** by the time you arrived? _____

9. I **took** this photograph two years ago. _____

10. Uncle Hank has **driven** to Iowa for his vacation. _____

11. These plants were **grown** under artificial lights. _____

12. Kay and Phil **became** upset about working overtime. _____

Practice 2

Complete each of the following sentences correctly. Use either the past or the past-participle form of the irregular verb in parentheses.

1. Mr. and Mrs. Reilly _____ vegetables in the community lot. (grow)

2. I _____ about your plans for a surprise party. (know)

3. Eva has _____ to Puerto Rico to visit her sister. (fly)

4. Two bikes were _____ last week outside the gym. (steal)

5. The gears _____ in very cold weather. (stick)

6. We usually _____ milk with supper. (drink)

7. Each summer, my cousins from New Jersey _____ to visit. (come)

8. The class has _____ a contribution to the new library. (give)

9. The national anthem is _____ before the game. (sing)

10. Carmen and Patty _____ the bus instead of the train. (ride)

11. Gretchen had _____ the newspaper away. (throw)

12. I _____ my math problems home for Aunt Julie to read. (bring)

13. The seats near the front have already been _____ . (take)

14. Was anyone _____ in the accident? (hurt)

15. The union leaders have _____ to the reporters. (speak)

16. The instructors _____ diving as well as swimming. (teach)

17. Carol and Dick _____ blue jeans as often as possible. (wear)

18. During the hot weather, the campers _____ twice a day. (swim)

19. The battle against the common cold is still being _____ . (fight)

20. This horse is always _____ by the new students. (ride)

21. The surface of the pond had _____ suddenly. (freeze)

22. I don't know how my jeans were _____ . (tear)

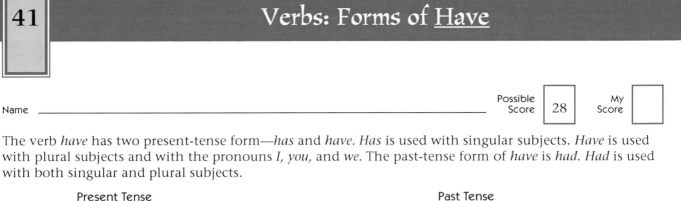

41

Verbs: Forms of <u>Have</u>

Name _____   Possible Score | 28 | My Score | ☐

The verb *have* has two present-tense form—*has* and *have. Has* is used with singular subjects. *Have* is used with plural subjects and with the pronouns *I, you,* and *we.* The past-tense form of *have* is *had. Had* is used with both singular and plural subjects.

Present Tense	Past Tense
She **has** a new car.	Mae **had** the right answer.
My cousins **have** no money.	We **had** your wallet.

You may use a form of *have* as a main verb or as a helping verb.

Janelle **has** the keys. [main verb]   Mike **had passed** that shop. [helping verb]

When you express a wish about the past, *had* is the right form to use, not *would have.*

I wish you **had** asked me first.

I wish you **would have** asked me first. [nonstandard]

Had is also the correct form to use as a helping verb when you express the earlier of two past actions. Avoid using *would have* after *if* in sentences like this one:

If I **had** guessed right [earlier past action], I could have won.

If I **would have** guessed right, I could have won. [nonstandard]

The contracted forms of *have* are *'s* and *'ve.*

She **has** been very patient.	Tyler should **have** warned us.
She**'s** been very patient.	Tyler should**'ve** warned us

In speech, the contraction *'ve* often sounds like the word *of.* Don't let this similarity of sounds fool you into writing *of* when you mean *'ve* or *have.*

Tyler should **of** warned us. [nonstandard]

Practice 1

Complete the following statements by adding *have* or *has* in the spaces provided.

1. I _____ never understood that problem.

2. Anatoliy _____ something to say to you.

3. Professional soccer _____ been played there since 1885.

4. Who _____ the time to explain this to me?

5. You _____ to swim the length of the pool and back.

6. _____ anyone seen my social studies book?

7. Perhaps we _____ misunderstood Mrs. Sellers.

8. Those plants _____ flourished in the warm, wet weather.

9. Did you know that sweet potatoes _____ high energy value?

10. Kevin _____ to go to the dentist tomorrow.

Practice 2

The following sentences are correct with *had*. In the spaces provided, change *had* to *has* or *have*.

1. Carmen **had** a lot to tell us about her vacation. _____

2. The factory workers **had** a new contract. _____

3. The guard **had** checked all the windows and doors. _____

4. Ben **had** already seen that movie twice. _____

5. We **had** to redo all the posters. _____

6. At camp, we **had** to set tables and sweep the floor. _____

7. Ashley **had** forgotten to leave the key for us. _____

8. Mary Jo **had** a new job at the supermarket on weekends. _____

Practice 3

The following sentences express the earlier of two past actions after *if* or state a wish about the past. In the spaces provided, write the helping verb *had* and the appropriate form of the main verb in parentheses.

1. Graduates sometimes wish that they _____ other courses in high school. (take)

2. If Samantha _____ about the traffic jam earlier, she could have avoided the expressway. (hear)

3. Jody wishes that she _____ out for track last year. (try)

4. If Mario _____ less nervous, he might have done better on the exam. (be)

5. I would have telephoned you if I _____ your number. (know)

Practice 4

Rewrite sentences 1–3, replacing *have* or *has* with the contracted forms. Rewrite sentences 4 and 5, replacing the nonstandard *of* with the correct form of *have*.

1. We have been waiting for the bus for twenty minutes. _____

   _____

2. Jack has been trying to talk to you all afternoon. _____

   _____

3. You have got plenty of time to eat lunch. _____

   _____

4. You could of walked home with us. _____

   _____

5. Somebody must of been using the VCR. _____

   _____

Name _____ Possible Score **35** My Score [ ]

Because the verb *do* has many uses, choosing the correct form of *do* is sometimes a problem. *Do* may be used as a main verb. It may also be used to form a question or a negative, to show emphasis, to substitute for another verb already mentioned, and to form a short question at the end of a statement.

   Ben **does** his chores. [main verb]   They **do** understand. [emphasis]

   When **do** they play? [question]   I played as often as you **did.** [substitute]

   She **doesn't** sing. [negative]   We didn't look angry, **did** we? [short question]

Do has two present-tense forms—*does* and *do*. *Does* is used with singular subjects. *Do* is used with plural subjects and with the pronouns *I, we,* and *you*.

   Beth **does** her homework.   The boys **do** the dishes each night.

The negative form of *does* is *doesn't;* the negative form of *do* is *don't*. *Doesn't* is used like *does*—with singular subjects. *Don't* is used like *do*—with plural subjects and with the pronouns *I, you,* and *we*.

   She **does** like volleyball.   **Do** I know them?

   She **doesn't** like volleyball.   **Don't** I know them?

The past-tense form of *do* is *did*. *Did* is used with both singular and plural subjects. Be careful not to confuse the past form *did* with the past-participle form *done*. *Did* is used alone, however, *done* is always used with a helping verb like *have, has,* or *had*.

   We **did** it all by ourselves

   We **had done** it all by ourselves.

   We **done** it all by ourselves. [nonstandard]

Practice 1

Complete each of the following sentences correctly with *does* or *do*.

1. Carol certainly enjoys speaking Spanish more than her brother _____ .

2. The twins _____ the dishes each night after dinner.

3. Ignacio likes listening to that group as much as we _____ .

4. When _____ the bus leave for the knowledge bowl?

5. Diane and Jose often _____ their math assignment together.

6. She _____ try hard in social studies!

7. _____ Pete want to go to the movie with us?

8. Jon practices the guitar more often than I _____ .

9. Where _____ this iron belong?

10. _____ you think you can be ready by six?

11. Our coach always _____ her best to help us improve.

UNIT 2 Using the Right Words

12. No one else makes pizza the way Joe _____ .

13. _____ you mind if I borrow your bike?

14. Why _____ this car start in drive instead of in park?

15. I _____ get lots of exercise!

Practice 2

Complete each of the following sentences correctly with *doesn't* or *don't*.

1. Jan skates very well, _____ she?

2. _____ Mr. Malina always lock the doors at five?

3. Why _____ Gus and Al look at the secondhand motorcycle?

4. _____ he want to try out for the team?

5. Mom _____ get home until six o'clock on Thursdays.

6. Bev says she _____ like broccoli.

7. _____ she usually do her homework in the library?

8. He _____ like interruptions when he's talking.

9. _____ this phone need to be recharged?

10. These articles _____ have the information I'm looking for.

Practice 3

Complete each of the following sentences correctly with *did* or *done*.

1. What have you _____ with my old Rolling Stones records?

2. Sally said she _____ ten push-ups in gym this morning.

3. I think Dad has already _____ the dishes.

4. Whoever _____ this had better speak up soon.

5. The Feldmans _____ everything possible to make us happy.

6. Heidi _____ all the driving on the trip home.

7. We _____ our best to persuade Jack to stay for the movie.

8. The entertainment committee has already _____ the planning for the variety night.

9. Last night Eric and Isabel _____ the rest of the posters for the track meet.

10. I'm sure you _____ what you thought was right.

Verbs: Subjunctive Forms

Name _____

Possible Score | 40 | My Score |

English verbs have three moods—indicative, imperative, and subjunctive. Those verb forms that state facts or ask questions are in the indicative mood.

Jody **likes** to read detective thrillers.   **Does** she really?

The verbs in requests and commands are in the imperative mood.

Please **let** him stay.   **Close** that door.

The verbs in certain other kinds of requests, in contrary-to-fact statements, and in wishes are in the subjunctive mood. Verb forms in the subjunctive mood differ form those used for ordinary statements. For example, forms normally ending in -s appear without the -s, and *were* is used instead of *was*.

In *that* clauses after verbs like *suggest, ask, insist, recommend,* and *demand,* use the simple form (the subjunctive form) of the verb, not the -s form.

We suggest that a graduating senior **speak** at the sports banquet. [not speaks]

They asked that the library **remain** open until half past ten. [not remains]

The words *if, as if,* and *as though* are often used to express something that is unreal or contrary to fact. When the verb in a contrary-to-fact statement is *be*, use the form *were* with all subjects, singular and plural.

If my brother were here, we would have a family reunion. [My brother isn't here.]

They treated me **as if I were** a porcelain doll. [I'm not a porcelain doll.]

When the verb after the word *wish* is a form of *be*, use *were* with all subjects, singular and plural.

Jake **wishes it were** warm today.   We **wish we were** free to go.

Practice 1

Underline the verb form in parentheses that correctly completes each sentence.

1. The citizens' group asked that the bus company (add, adds) two stops to its Main Street route.

2. Uncle Joe still talks to Ellie as if she (was, were) a child.

3. If Terri's hair (was, were) a little darker, she would look just like her sister.

4. Alex's counselor suggested that he (go, goes) on several job interviews during summer vacation.

5. Don't you wish Dan (was, were) able to go with us tomorrow?

6. Marty always behaves as though everything (was, were) all right.

7. If Dad (was, were) a regular passenger, he would get to know the other commuters on the morning train.

8. The tenants demanded that the owner (repair, repairs) the stairway immediately.

9. I feel as if I (was, were) walking on a cloud.

10. Gene recommended that Nan (play, plays) forward.

11. Dave acted as though he (was, were) not disappointed by the news.

12. I wish that I (was, were) a senior and graduating this June.

13. The police officer recommended that every bicycle (have, has) reflecting lights.

14. Diane tried to look as if she (was, were) having a good time.

15. The judge insisted that the witness (answer, answers) the question.

Practice 2

Underline the verb form in parentheses that correctly completes each of the following sentences.

1. If Manuel (was, were) here now, we could go fishing together.

2. Mom suggested that Mark (learn, learns) to cook.

3. Luís wishes the game (was, were) being played on Saturday instead of on Friday.

4. If Alexander (was, were) my dog, I'd enter him in a show this year.

5. Connie suggested that each member (contribute, contributes) a dollar.

6. I wish I (was, were) as good a tennis player as Rosie is.

7. We recommended that the ticket price (remain, remains) unchanged.

8. I wonder what she would do if she (was, were) in my position.

9. My sister isn't living near us anymore, but I wish she (was, were).

10. The speaker continued as though he (was, were) unaware of the hecklers.

11. All of the family would be together if Kate (was, were) here.

12. Do you ever wish he (was, were) a better skier?

13. Why does Mr. Zavaleta act as if I (was, were) responsible for his problems?

14. Her adviser recommended that Rita (take, takes) trigonometry.

15. What would you do if she (was, were) too sick to go?

16. Dr. Russo insisted that Dad (remain, remains) hospitalized.

17. My brother treats me as though I (was, were) an expert photographer.

18. We all wish that Jean (was, were) the team captain.

19. Sometimes I feel as if I (was, were) a robot.

20. Curtis suggested that they (search, searches) for the lost ship.

21. If Letitia (was, were) here, she could fix the car.

22. The trainer wishes she (was, were) able to teach that elephant some tricks.

23. They demanded that the mechanics (repair, repairs) the plane.

24. The Greenewalts wish they (was, were) going sailing tomorrow.

25. I insist that you (join, joins) us for dinner.

Application

Name _____   Possible Score `48`   My Score `☐`

A. Complete the sentences in the following paragraphs correctly. Use either the past or the past-participle form of each verb in parentheses.

Early in the 1940s, zoos (become) _____ increasingly concerned about the preservation

of rare and endangered species, and they (begin) _____ to develop breeding programs for

their animals in captivity. They (hope) _____ in this way to preserve some species that were

(know) _____ to be facing extinction in their natural habitat.

In the past, zoos might have (keep) _____ one animal of a rare species. They may now buy

several, with the aim of developing breeding herds. Animals may also be (give) _____ or

(trade) _____ from zoo to zoo, often to form breeding pairs.

Medical facilities at many zoos have (grow) _____ to include nurseries, providing special care

for newborn animals. The success of these nurseries can be (see) _____ in the recent births in

captivity of pandas, gorillas, a sea otter, and a rare American bald eagle.

B. Complete sentences 1–10 with *have* or *has*. Complete sentences 11–16 with *had* plus the correct form of the verb in parentheses.

1. Jolanda _____ to leave at ten o'clock tomorrow morning.

2. We _____ been watching you from the sidelines.

3. You _____ to listen carefully.

4. They _____ got to finish the float in time for the parade.

5. It _____ always worked for us.

6. Leo _____ a part-time job mowing lawns.

7. They must _____ been late for the performance.

8. Roberta says that she _____ lots of patience.

9. The motor _____ been on for five minutes.

10. We _____ enough space for our furniture.

11. If she _____, she wouldn't have been angry. (know)

12. I wish I _____ what you meant. (understand)

13. If someone _____ it to me, I would have got the right answer. (explain)

14. Carl wishes he _____ to the concert. (go)

15. If Leroy _____ harder, he would have succeeded. (try)

16. They wish they _____ more often. (practice)

C. Underline the form of *do* in parentheses that correctly completes each sentence in the dialogue below.

"Pete saw you running with your dog, Lady, yesterday. (Do, Does) she run with you every day?"

"Yes, she usually (do, does). I think it's (did, done) us both a lot of good."

"Did she run with you last winter, too?"

"Yes, but not as often. If it's cold or wet out, she (doesn't, don't) like to run any more than I (do, does). Has Pete (did, done) much running?"

"He (did, done) a lot a few years ago, but he hasn't (did, done) any recently."

"Then why (doesn't, don't) he join us some morning? It (doesn't, don't) take long, and Lady really (do, does) like it."

D. Underline the verb form in parentheses that correctly completes each sentence.

1. We demand that you (refund, refunds) our money immediately.

2. If Nick (was, were) the cook, he would have made a spicy meal.

3. Karen wishes her car (was, were) smaller so that she could save money on gasoline.

4. I recommend that you (see, sees) your doctor at once.

5. If Josh (was, were) meeting us, he would have been here by now.

6. Barb acts as though she (was, were) too sick to go hiking.

7. I wonder how I would feel if I (was, were) playing in the semifinals tomorrow.

8. Shana wishes we (was, were) going to that Japanese restaurant instead of to this one.

9. Professor Schultz suggests that you (take, takes) this poetry course first.

10. The customers asked that the grocer (clean, cleans) the alley behind the store more thoroughly.

11. The detective looked as though she (was, were) about to solve the case.

12. Murphy insists that everyone (go, goes) horseback riding after the picnic.

Indirect Quotations

Name _____

There are important differences in writing direct and indirect quotations besides the use of quotation marks. Notice the differences between a statement written as a direct and as an indirect quotation.

Jo said, **"I can't go."** [direct]

Jo said **that she couldn't go.** [indirect]

Jo said **she couldn't go.** [indirect]

Pronoun *I* shifts to *she*; verb *can't* shifts to its past form *couldn't* to agree with tense of *said*; *that* may be added.

A question that can be answered by *yes* or *no* is a *yes/no* question. Notice the differences between a *yes/no* question written as a direct and as an indirect quotation.

Roy asked us, **"Do you like pizza?"** [direct]

Roy asked us **if we liked pizza.** [indirect]

Roy asked us **whether we liked pizza.** [indirect]

Roy asked us **whether or not we liked pizza.** [indirect]

Period replaces question mark; pronoun *you* shifts to *we*; verb *like* shifts to its past form *liked* to agree with tense of *asked*; words *if*, *whether*, or *whether or not* are added to replace *do*.

A *wh*-question is one that begins with a question word like *why*, *when*, *where*, *what*, *which*, or *how*. Notice the differences between a *wh*- question written as a direct and as an indirect quotation.

I asked them, **"When will you be ready?"** [direct]

I asked them **when they would be ready.** [indirect]

Period replaces question mark; pronoun *you* shifts to *they* and moves to position directly after *when*; verb *will* shifts to its past form *would* to agree with tense of *asked*.

Practice

Rewrite each sentence below, changing the direct quotation to an indirect quotation. Sentences 1 and 2 are statements. Sentences 3 and 4 contain *yes/no* questions. Sentences 5–7 contain *wh*-questions.

1. Joe promised, "I won't do it again." _____

_____

2. Spiros said, "The song is sure to be a hit." _____

_____

3. Ellie asked me, "Do you know Paul's number?" _____

_____

4. Jill asked him, "is your watch broken?" _____

_____

5. Mom asked us, "When will you be home?" _____

_____

6. Hugo asked us, "Where are you going?" _____

_____

7. The coach asked us, "Why are you late?" _____

_____

Application

Rewrite each of the following sentences, changing the direct quotation to an indirect quotation.

1. Tamara asked me, "Have you seen the new dolphins at the aquarium?"

   _____

   _____

2. I told her, "I haven't, but I've read about them."

   _____

   _____

3. She explained, "I'm taking my brother on Saturday."

   _____

   _____

4. Then she asked me, "Do you want to go with us?"

   _____

   _____

5. I asked her, "What time are you going?"

   _____

   _____

6. Then I asked her, "How long will you be gone?"

   _____

   _____

7. She told me, "We can go right after lunch."

   _____

   _____

8. Then she added, "We'll be back before five."

   _____

   _____

9. I told her, "That sounds fine."

   _____

   _____

Raise/Rise, Set/Sit, Lay/Lie

Name _____

Possible Score **30** My Score ☐

Raise means "to cause something to go up." It is always followed by an object and can be used in the passive. *Rise* means "to get up" or "to go up." It is never followed by an object, nor can it be used in the passive.

> Two scouts **raised** the flag carefully. [object—flag]
>
> The flag **was raised** carefully by two scouts. [passive]
>
> Please **rise** when the guest speaker enters. [no object, not passive]

Here are the forms *raise* and *rise* take:

raise	raising	raised	(have) raised
rise	rising	rose	(have) risen

Set means "to put or place something." It is always followed by an object and can be used in the passive. *Sit* means "to take a sitting position" or "to occupy a place." It does not take an object, nor can it be used in the passive.

> Beth **set** the plants in the sun. [object—plants]
>
> The plants **were set** in the sun. [passive]
>
> The house **sits** on a small hill. [no object, not passive]

Certain expressions are exceptions to these general rules—for example, *cement sets, the sun sets, a table sits ten, a hen sets,* and *a person sits a horse.*

Here are the forms *set* and *sit* take:

set	setting	set	(have) set
sit	sitting	sat	(have) sat

Lay means "to put or place something." It is always followed by an object and can be used in the passive. *Lie* means "to recline" or " to be in a position or location." it does not take an object, nor can it by used in the passive.

> We always **lay** the mail on that table. [object—mail]
>
> The mail **is** always **laid** on that table. [passive]
>
> I always **lie** down after lunch for a nap. [no object, not passive]
>
> The mail **lay** on the table for two days. [past tense of lie]

Here are the forms *lay* and *lie* take:

lay	laying	laid	(have) laid
lie	lying	lay	(have) lain

Practice 1

Underline the work in parentheses that correctly completes each of the following sentences.

1. My aunt (raises, rises) turkeys as well as chickens.

2. The water level is (raising, rising) rapidly because of the heavy rains.

3. The band has (raised, risen) nearly all the money it needs for new uniforms.

4. In 1775, the colonists (raised, rose) in rebellion.

5. Attendance has (raised, risen) since we started serving refreshments at club meetings.

6. Our morale (raised, rose) after we heard the good news.

7. Several hands were (raised, risen) when the speaker agreed to answer questions.

8. Two zoologists are (raising, rising) a baby chimpanzee in their home.

9. The sun (raises, rises) at 6:45 A.M. tomorrow.

10. Julian (raised, rose) the question of student parking facilities.

Practice 2

Underline the word in parentheses that correctly completes each of the following sentences.

1. Someone has (set, sat) a wet glass on the tabletop.

2. Mr. Anderson invited us to (set, sit) down and rest.

3. The cabin (sets, sits) on a bluff overlooking the lake.

4. This plant should be (set, sat) in strong light.

5. Last night María and I just (set, sat) and watched television.

6. We were (setting, sitting) the chairs outdoors when it started to rain.

7. Just (set, sit) the packages over there, please.

8. Everyone was (setting, sitting) in the wrong room and wondering where the teacher was.

9. Where should this trunk be (set, sat)?

10. After Jim had (set, sat) for three hours on the bus, he was tired and stiff.

Practice 3

Underline the word in parentheses that correctly completes each of the following sentences.

1. If you have a headache, why don't you (lay, lie) down for a while?

2. Ms. Cardenas is (laying, lying) the carpeting in the hall today.

3. The cornerstone of the new library will be (laid, lain) next week.

4. Millie was (laying, lying) in a hammock, reading *Sports Illustrated*.

5. (Lay, Lie) the parcels on the counter in the kitchen.

6. Steve (laid, lay) under a huge oak tree.

7. The negotiator (laid, lay) his cards on the table.

8. The kitten has (laid, lain) asleep all afternoon.

9. New railroad track is being (laid, lain) along the old roadbed.

10. The bike path (lays, lies) along the course of the river.

Let/Leave

Name _____

Possible Score 40   My Score [ ]

The verbs *leave* and *let* are frequently confused. Use *leave* when you mean "depart" or "cause to remain." Use *let* when you mean "allow" or "permit."

They usually **leave** by eight. [depart]

We are **leaving** the rest for you. [cause to remain]

Why don't you **let** them go to the movies? [allow]

You can use either verb correctly with the word *alone*, as in the sentence "**Leave** her alone" and "**Let** her alone." Both of these sentences mean "Don't bother her."

Notice the different forms *leave* and *let* take:

| leave | leaving | left | (have) left |
| let | letting | let | (have) let |

Practice

Underline the form of *leave* or *let* that correctly completes each of the following sentences.

1. Will you (leave, let) me out at the next intersection, please?

2. Just (leave, let) the books on the table.

3. Why don't you (leave, let) them try to fix it themselves?

4. We have only two days (left, let) before vacation.

5. Don't (leave, let) the cat through the gate!

6. What time are you (leaving, letting)?

7. Why are you (leaving, letting) them stay up late?

8. Please don't (leave, let) you bike in the driveway.

9. They've (left, let) that problem get out of hand.

10. Just (leave, let) a message if I'm not home.

11. Will you (leave, let) me help?

12. Don't (leave, let) it bother you.

13. He (left, let) his watch to be repaired.

14. I wish you'd (leave, let) me explain.

15. Just (leave, let) her tell the story herself.

16. We (left, let) him decorate the table.

17. We (left, let) the table for him to decorate.

18. Just (leave, let) it to me.

19. You shouldn't (leave, let) her get away with that!

20. Don't tease your brother; (leave, let) him alone!

21. Dad is (leaving, letting) on the 6:00 bus.

22. She is (leaving, letting) me use her new mountain bike.

23. Alfonso (left, let) a note for his sister.

24. Elisa (left, let) them know about the parade.

25. Just (leave, let) the back door unlocked.

26. The police aren't (leaving, letting) anyone enter.

27. I think you should (leave, let) Ernestine finish the course.

28. He hopes the doctor will (leave, let) him go home.

29. They had to (leave, let) their plants behind.

30. Don't (leave, let) the dishes in the sink.

31. Tessie (leave, let) us read the newsletter.

32. Did you (leave, let) them win?

33. Robert is (leaving, letting) for the Bahamas at noon.

34. We applauded as she (left, let) the podium.

35. The treasurer (left, let) the money on the desk.

36. Please (leave, let) me know if you can meet us.

37. Don't (leave, let) the gorilla frighten you.

38. The police commissioner (left, let) the file in her office.

39. Ms. Dietz is (leaving, letting) the company.

40. I am (leaving, letting) them use the sailboat.

Application

Name _____

Possible Score | 14 | My Score | ☐

A. Underline the word that correctly completes each sentence in the paragraphs below.

   (Raising, Rising) a puppy is not easy. My brother and I have found that we have to protect anything chewable, like a shoe (laying, lying) on the floor. Also, we cannot (set, sit) plates of food in a spot the puppy might reach.

   Mom and Dad discovered another hazard when they were trying to (lay, lie) new tiles on the kitchen floor. (Laying, Lying) tiles is usually not difficult, but it is almost impossible with an inquisitive puppy underfoot.

   (Raising, Rising) costs of veterinary fees and dog food make it expensive to keep a puppy. But the effort will seem justified when we can all (set, sit) back and enjoy a healthy, well-trained dog as a member of the family.

B. Write sentences of your own, using the verbs below. Be careful not to confuse *let* and *leave*.

1. have left _____

_____

2. leave _____

_____

3. are letting _____

_____

4. left _____

_____

5. had let _____

_____

6. is leaving _____

_____

7. let _____

_____

Possessives with Gerunds

Name _____

A gerund is an *-ing* verb form that is used as a noun. When a pronoun or a noun comes directly before a gerund, that noun or pronoun is usually in the possessive form.

Her jogging keeps Mari trim.   We enjoyed **Paul's cooking.**

You would *not* normally use a possessive noun or pronoun before a gerund in these situations.

1. The word before the gerund is a plural noun.

   In those days, many people didn't approve of **women** voting. [not women's]

2. The noun before the gerund does not refer to something living.

   Everyone talked about the **river** rising to flood level. [not river's]

3. A phrase comes between the noun and the gerund.

   We were surprised at the **owner** of a new car parking there. [not owner's]

4. The noun or pronoun before the gerund needs to be strongly emphasized.

   Can you imagine **me** getting the highest score? [not my]

Practice

Underline the word or words that correctly complete each of the following sentences.

1. (Pat, Pat's) threatening to make us do the cooking stopped our complaints about the food.

2. Fortunately, no one asked for my opinion of (him, his) acting.

3. (Him, His) running the two-hundred-meter dash won Michael Johnson a gold medal in the 1996 Olympics.

4. We didn't understand the (builder, builder's) of the mall objecting to the zoning regulations.

5. A sure sign of the beginning of the ragweed season is (Sarah, Sarah's) sneezing.

6. The mayor feared that the (hurricane, hurricane's) striking at night would add to the danger.

7. (Sharon, Sharon's) calling the vet so promptly saved the collie's life.

8. The (baby, baby's) crying brought worried members of the family from all rooms of the house.

9. Everyone was distressed by the (building, building's) burning to the ground.

10. We appreciate (you, your) defending our viewpoint.

11. In most American homes, the idea of (men, men's) helping with the housekeeping is no longer a strange one.

12. (Me, My) pretending to understand is not going to help either of us.

13. We really didn't mind (you, your) interrupting.

14. Most people today accept the idea of (women, women's) participating in competitive sports.

15. The accident was caused by the (driver, driver's) of the station wagon failing to see the red light.

16. (Jill, Jill's) practicing the drums doesn't seem to bother the neighbors.

17. Mom was upset at (me, my) missing the bus again.

18. The (cat, cat's) keeping her kittens in the coat closet considerably changed our family habits.

19. (Tom, Tom's) forgetting his lunch meant that he had to borrow money from me.

20. We had to go to a laundromat because of the (washing machine, washing machine's) breaking down.

Application

Name _____

Possible Score | 12 | My Score | ☐

Use a possessive noun or pronoun plus a gerund to correctly complete each of the following sentences. Write each sentence you make.

1. No one talked about _____

   _____ .

2. She didn't mind _____

   _____ .

3. I don't understand _____

   _____ .

4. He didn't explain _____

   _____ .

5. We were upset by _____

   _____ .

6. _____

   _____ pleased us.

7. _____

   _____ surprised everyone.

8. _____

   _____ was disappointing.

9. _____

   _____ offended us.

10. _____

    _____ didn't bother anyone.

11. _____

    _____ interrupted the meeting.

12. _____

    _____ seemed unimportant at the time.

Negative Words

Name _____ Possible Score [20] My Score [ ]

There are many negative words in English—for example, *not* and its contraction *n't*, *no*, *none*, *never*, *nothing*, *no one*, and *nowhere*. As a rule, avoid using double negatives—more than one negative—in a clause. Notice that the double negatives in the following clauses can be corrected in different ways:

I **didn't** see **no one**. [nonstandard]   We **don't** have **nothing** to do. [nonstandard]

I **didn't** see **anyone**.   We **don't** have **anything** to do.

I saw **no one**.   We have **nothing** to do.

The words *hardly, scarcely*, and *barely* are considered negatives because they mean "almost none" or "almost not." Don't use another negative in a clause with one of these words.

I **can't hardly** do that. [nonstandard]   He **couldn't barely** see them. [nonstandard]

I **can hardly** do that.   He **could barely** see them.

Avoid using *ain't* in place of *am not, is not, are not, has not, have not*, and their contractions.

Julie **ain't** my cousin [nonstandard]   They **ain't** here. [nonstandard]

Julie **isn't** my cousin.   They **aren't** here.

Julie**'s not** my cousin.   They**'re not** here.

Practice

Underline the word or words that correctly complete each of the following sentences.

1. There isn't (any, no) easy way to explain what happened in the last quarter of the game.

2. There (is, isn't) hardly any milk left.

3. Angela worked all afternoon but couldn't find (anything, nothing) wrong with the motor.

4. (Ain't, Hasn't) Mr. Kucera explained the homework yet?

5. Once Noberto starts talking about his motorcycle, there isn't (anyone, no one) that can stop him.

6. You (ain't, aren't) surprised at Jeff's attitude, are you?

7. We talked for an hour but (didn't get, got) nowhere.

8. Marcy (could, couldn't) barely get to her seat before the kickoff.

9. Unless you get there by six o'clock, you won't find (anywhere, nowhere) to park.

10. Sally said she didn't want (any, no) special favors from us.

11. Wayne hasn't (ever, never) been to a track meet before.

12. I (can, can't) scarcely hear you when the stereo's on.

13. I'm going with Ms. Alvarado, (ain't, aren't) I?

14. The security guard (didn't see, saw) no one.

15. There (was, wasn't) hardly anyone there when María got to the clubhouse.

16. Why (ain't, isn't) Charlene planning to compete in the sixty-yard dash tomorrow?

17. By eight o'clock there (was, wasn't) nothing left to eat.

18. I haven't made (any, no) progress with my guitar lessons.

19. Al (could, couldn't) hardly understand Inez when she spoke Spanish.

20. (I ain't, I'm not) going to lunch right now.

Application

Name _____

Possible Score | 30 | My Score | [ ]

A. Underline the word or words that correctly complete each sentence in the following paragraph.

Some days I can't seem to do (anything, nothing) right. This morning I got up late and didn't have (any, no) time for breakfast. On the way to school, it started to rain, and I didn't have (a, no) raincoat. There (was, wasn't) barely time for me to wipe off my wet boots and to run to class. When I got there, I couldn't find (any, no) paper. Then I realized I didn't have (any, no) lunch. I couldn't find it (anywhere, nowhere). I had to buy my lunch, and I didn't see (any, none) of my friends to eat with. I'm glad there (ain't, aren't) too many days like today. And tomorrow I (ain't, am not) going to get up late.

B. Underline the word or words that correctly complete each of the following sentences.

1. Callie looked for directions but didn't find (any, none).

2. Can't you give me (any, no) reason for their strange behavior?

3. There (is, isn't) barely room for six of us in your car.

4. (Ain't, Haven't) you seen that movie yet?

5. The committee members don't want (anyone, no one) to know about the awards before the presentation.

6. We looked in the freezer for meat but (didn't find, found) none.

7. She (was, wasn't) barely polite to me after I apologized.

8. Pat (ain't, hasn't) found the instructions for making the kite yet.

9. That cactus can live in a desert; it won't need (any, no) water for weeks.

10. I (don't want, want) no advice from them.

11. Juan couldn't find (anyone, no one) to explain the road map.

12. Isn't there (anyplace, no place) to hide the presents for Dad?

13. I (can, can't) hardly believe that I climbed that cliff.

14. Those are the headphones we're supposed to use, (ain't, aren't) they?

15. Only tourists come to Alcatraz Island now. There haven't been (any, no) prisoners there since 1963.

16. Gina (didn't seen, saw) nothing she wanted to buy at the garage sale.

17. There (was, wasn't) scarcely enough kindling to start a fire.

18. Those sportswriters (ain't, haven't) written enough about professional soccer.

19. The children (can, can't) hardly wait for the puppet show to begin.

20. (Ain't, Isn't) the straight steal used more often than the delayed steal in softball?

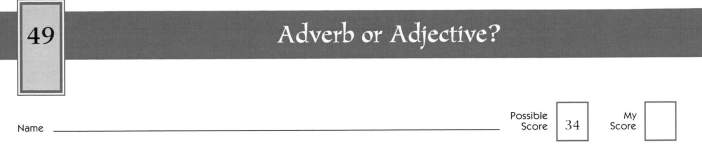

Name _____   Possible Score | 34 | My Score | |

Most often, an adverb is formed by adding the ending *-ly* to an adjective. For example, the adjective *rapid* becomes the adverb *rapidly*, and the adjective *clear* becomes the adverb *clearly*. When you write, be careful that you don't use an adjective where an adverb is required. Use an adverb if the modifier following the verb describes the action of the verb; use an adjective if the modifier describes the subject.

Dave works **efficient**. [nonstandard]

Dave seems **efficient**. [adjective modifies the subject <u>Dave</u>]

Dave works **efficiently**. [adverb modifies the verb <u>works</u>]

A few adverbs like *loud* and *slow* may be used with or without the *-ly* ending, though the *-ly* ending is usually preferred. Other adverbs, like *hard* and *fast*, have no *-ly* form.

Beth sang **loud**.   Beth sang **loudly**.   They moved **fast**.

Go **slow**!   Go **slowly**!   You play **hard**.

Use an adjective to modify the subject when you want verbs such as *look, taste, sound, smell, feel, remain,* and *appear* to describe what something is like. Use an adverb to modify the verb when you want these same verbs to name an action.

The hikers looked **eager.** [adjective modifying noun <u>hikers</u>]

The hikers looked **eagerly** up the trail. [adverb modifying verb <u>looked</u>]

To be sure you have used the right form after a verb like *look*, try substituting *is, are, was,* or *were* for the verb in the sentence. If the sentence still makes sense, an adjective is the right form. If the sentence doesn't make sense, an adverb is the right form. For example, since *The hikers were eager* makes sense, you know you need the adjective form *eager* in the first sentence. And since *The hikers were eagerly up the trail* doesn't make sense, you know the adverb *eagerly* is the right form for the second sentence.

Practice 1

Underline the word in parentheses that correctly completes each of the following sentences.

1. Holly listened (patient, patiently) to her sister.

2. Holly was (patient, patiently) whenever she listened to her sister.

3. Be sure to answer (polite, politely) if anyone asks you about the score.

4. Sometimes Mr. Gerhart seems (sarcastic, sarcastically) to strangers.

5. The stage crew worked (steady, steadily) from eight to half past ten.

6. Don't be (reckless, recklessly) when you take your driver's test.

7. If you drive (reckless, recklessly), you won't get your license.

8. The spectators cheered (loud, loudly) when the home team scored a touchdown.

9. Watch (careful, carefully) while I turn on the motor.

UNIT 2 Using the Right Words

10. Our dog always waits (quiet, **quietly**) for us to take him for a walk.

11. Your idea sounds (**sensible**, sensibly).

12. We looked (hasty, **hastily**) for the car keys.

13. The fire alarm sounded (sudden, **suddenly**) and startled everyone.

14. They looked (**angry**, angrily) about the news.

15. Jake tasted the apple juice (cautious, **cautiously**).

16. The apple juice tasted (**sweet**, sweetly).

17. The wood felt (**rough**, roughly) before we sanded it.

18. Drive (slow, **slowly**). The streets are icy.

19. Jacob felt (**hopeful**, hopefully) when he saw us.

20. The hot rolls smell (**delicious**, deliciously).

21. The neighbors objected (strong, **strongly**).

22. That wrestler appears (**strong**, strongly).

Practice 2

Underline the word in parentheses that correctly completes each of the following sentences.

1. Ginny looked (**sad**, sadly) at the broken roller blades.

2. The German-shepherd puppy looked (**sad**, sadly).

3. Owen and I stayed (**calm**, calmly) as the floodwaters began to rise.

4. The detective stayed (**calm**, calmly) at the scene of the crime.

5. The nurse remained (patient, **patiently**) at Sharon's bedside.

6. We remained (**patient**, patiently) as we waited for the show to begin.

7. The tennis players appeared (**eager**, eagerly) to start the match.

8. They waited (eager, **eagerly**) for the parade to begin.

9. The court reporter looked (**sleepy**, sleepily).

10. Angelina looked (sleepy, **sleepily**) at the report on her desk.

11. Alex was (**cautious**, cautiously) because he didn't know how to ski.

12. She felt (cautious, **cautiously**) for broken bones.

Adjective and Adverb Comparison

Name _____   Possible Score 28   My Score ☐

Most adjectives and adverbs have three different forms—positive, comparative, and superlative—to show increasing degrees of the quality they name. Use these rules to make the comparative and superlative forms of most adjectives and adverbs.

1. Add the endings -er and -est to most one-syllable adjectives and adverbs.

	Positive	Comparative	Superlative
Adjective	tall	taller	tallest
Adverb	soon	sooner	soonest

2. Add the words *more* and *most* before most adjectives and adverbs of more than two syllables as well as before all adverbs ending in -*ly*.

	Positive	Comparative	Superlative
Adjective	unusual	more unusual	most unusual
Adverb	unusually	more unusually	most unusually

3. Use the words *more* and *most* with most two-syllable words. With some, especially those ending in -*y*, you may use either form of comparison. If you are not sure which form to use, check your dictionary.

	Positive	Comparative	Superlative
Adjective	angry	angrier, more angry	angriest, most angry
Adverb	angrily	more angrily	most angrily

A few frequently used adjectives and adverbs have irregular forms. That is, they do not form the comparative and superlative by adding either -*er* and -*est* or *more* and *most*.

Positive	Comparative	Superlative	Positive	Comparative	Superlative
good/well	better	best	much/many	more	most
bad/badly	worse	worst	little	less	least

Be careful not to use double comparisons like *more faster* and *most fastest*.
Use the comparative form for comparing two items; use the superlative for more than two.

Of the two problems, the second is the **more** difficult. [comparative]

Of the three problems, the second is the **most** difficult. [superlative]

When you compare a person or a thing to the rest of the group it belongs to, use the words *any other*.

Sally is taller than **any** girl in her class. [nonstandard]

Sally is taller than **any other** girl in her class.

Practice 1

Complete each of the following sentences correctly. Add either the comparative or the superlative form of the word in parentheses.

1. Although Lee is _____ than his brother, they are both the same height. (young)

2. A giant sequoia tree in California is the world's _____ living thing. (large)

3. Of the four candidates, Stan spoke the _____ . (convincingly)

4. Which of those four CDs did you like _____ ? (well)

5. The photographer arrived _____ than Ken did. (late)

6. "But the second part of the story is even _____ than the first," said Naomi. (peculiar)

7. Touro Synagogue in Rhode Island, built in 1763, is the _____ existing synagogue in the United States. (old)

8. In 1970, high tides and a tropical cyclone hit Bangladesh, creating the _____ natural disaster since the turn of the century. (bad)

9. Edie's behavior is _____ than Jan's. (predictable)

10. "That is the _____ sunset I've ever seen," said Sam. (spectacular)

11. Brenda learned the game _____ than Linda did. (easily)

12. Of the three sisters, Sandi seems the _____ . (ambitious)

13. You play tennis _____ than Hal does. (skillfully)

14. Which of the seven stars in the Big Dipper is the _____ to Earth? (close)

15. The brain of a horse is _____ than the brain of a human. (light)

16. A brittle star can move _____ than a starfish. (quickly)

Practice 2

Underline the word or words in parentheses that correctly complete each of the following sentences.

1. This chili is (hotter, more hotter) than the chili we had last week.

2. Do you think that test was harder than (any, any other) we've taken?

3. The (most quickest, quickest) way to get there is by the tollway.

4. Sid seemed (more nervous, nervouser) than I had ever seen him before.

5. I liked all the food, but the fruit salad was the (best, bestest).

6. We think our dog, Rex, is smarter than (any, any other) dog on the block.

7. That was the (more awkward, most awkward) moment I've ever spent.

8. Which river is (longer, longest), the Amazon or the Mississippi?

9. Danny said his cold was (worse, worser) yesterday.

10. "I'd rather go to Colorado than to (any, any other) state," said Van.

11. Dena said she had the (least, leastest) trouble with the final chapter of the book.

12. The last day of classes always seems the (most slowest, slowest).

Good/Well, Bad/Badly

Name _____

Good is always an adjective (noun modifier). Use *good* after such verbs as *be, seem, feel, taste, smell, look,* and *sound* when you want to describe a person or a thing.

Those soccer players are very **good**.   Your work seems **good**.

Use *well* as an adverb (verb modifier) when you want to describe an action. Use *well* as an adjective when you are referring to someone's health.

They played soccer **well**. [adverb]   She feels **well** now. [adjective]

Use *bad* in the same way you use *good*—as an adjective after such verbs as *be, seem, feel, taste, smell, look,* and *sound.* Use *badly* in the same way you use the adverb *well*—as an adverb that describes an action.

Juan's first driver's test was **bad**. [adjective]   Juan drove **badly**. [adverb]

Practice

Underline the word in parentheses that correctly completes each sentence below.

1. Draginja certainly looks (good, well) now that she has recovered from her cold.

2. Don't you agree that the team played (bad, badly) yesterday?

3. If you think this recording sounds (good, well), you can order one for yourself.

4. Andy feels (good, well) now that he is home from the hospital.

5. This pen writes just as (bad, badly) as the other one.

6. If you speak French (good, well), you will certainly enjoy your trip to Quebec.

7. Jeff can't see (good, well) without his glasses.

8. Wendi's bike is as (good, well) now as it was when it was new.

9. The movie wasn't as (bad, badly) as I thought it would be.

10. Did you feel (bad, badly) when you heard the news?

11. When Uncle Ed bakes bread, the whole house smells (good, well).

12. The director scheduled another rehearsal today after the band performed so (bad, badly) last night.

13. The patient responded (good, well) to the treatment of complete rest.

14. The weather was so (bad, badly) that Mrs. Neumann canceled the hike.

15. Unfortunately, the motor doesn't run (good, well) when it rains.

Application

Name _____

Underline the word or words in parentheses that correctly complete each sentence.

1. The line that was painted down the middle of the bike path yesterday looks (crooked, crookedly).

2. Pat looked (suspicious, suspiciously) at the strange box on the shelf.

3. The dark-haired mechanic works (more quickly, quicklier) than the blond mechanic.

4. Belinda feels (good, well) now that her fever has dropped.

5. The vegetable soup that Tom made tastes (spicy, spicily).

6. The baby tasted the cooked cereal (wary, warily).

7. You are the (more dependable, most dependable) person on the staff.

8. These hiking boots are (comfortabler, more comfortable) than the ones I tried on earlier.

9. Which car runs (more smoothly, most smoothly), this sports car or that station wagon?

10. My cousins were ill yesterday, but now they are (good, well).

11. The music coming from that outdoor café sounds (strange, strangely).

12. Lawanda arrived the (sooner, soonest) of the two.

13. The taco and the enchiladas taste (bad, badly).

14. These are the (worst, worstest) hamburgers I have ever eaten.

15. This air conditioner runs better than (any, any other) air conditioner.

16. Jane and Nancy smelled the newly baked bread (eager, eagerly).

17. The stories Steve Shapiro has written for the school paper are quite (good, well).

18. Moving the furniture was (more difficulter, more difficult) than we had thought it would be.

19. Michael feels (bad, badly) about the trouble he caused you.

20. We jumped as the foghorn sounded (sudden, suddenly).

21. Our hockey team played (bad, badly) today even though we were favored to win.

22. Chris felt the hot iron (cautious, cautiously) to avoid burning his hand.

23. Of the three senators on the committee, Ms. Fayer did the (best, better) job.

24. Your brother has felt (good, well) ever since he's begun jogging on a regular basis.

25. Jan said the pizza baking in the oven smelled (good, well).

26. The material we bought at the discount store felt (rough, roughly).

27. The story she told us was the (stranger, strangest) story of all.

28. Who is (older, oldest), you or your sister Denise?

29. The inexperienced driver drove (bad, badly).

30. Of the two baby elephants, this one is (heavier, heaviest).

Name _____   Number Correct × 2 = [ ]

Underline the word or phrase in parentheses that correctly completes each of the following sentences.

1. Paul and (her, she) saw a four-car accident early this morning.

2. Do you suppose it was (he, him) who called?

3. Just before he left, Mike gave Sally and (I, me) directions to the ball park.

4. After practicing with her uncle, Mary Beth spoke Italian as well as (he, him).

5. Since you've lost weight, that coat fits you better than (her, she).

6. (Who, Whom) did Yolanda visit when she and Myra Hollister went to St. Louis last summer?

7. I remember now (who, whom) the man in the red shirt is.

8. Tina is the foreign-exchange student (which, who) has just joined the volleyball team.

9. Nobody in Ms. Helm's physics class wanted to be the first to give (his, their) oral report.

10. A hiker must have the right equipment, or (her, their) safety may be endangered.

11. Neither Ailene nor her sister expected to see (her, their) name on the list of finalists.

12. Levi says he doesn't write Paul very often since (he, Paul) moved to Rochester.

13. Many people want to grow their own vegetables. (This, This interest) has caused an increased enrollment in gardening classes.

14. (It says, The article says) that the president's speech on energy contained several dramatic proposals.

15. The senator greeted the reporters, (faced the TV lights, and then hoped they wouldn't ask about the fuel shortage, hoped they wouldn't ask about the fuel shortage, and then faced the TV lights).

16. In spite of your explanation, I still don't understand (these, this) kind of story.

17. Actors often enjoy playing (that, those) types of parts.

18. Betsy said that she liked (them, those) wooden candlesticks best of all the presents.

19. (Them, These) are the people we met at the Antique Boat and Auto Show.

20. I (teach, teaches) mathematics at Oak Park Junior College.

21. The Superdome (cover, covers) fifty-two acres near the business district in New Orleans.

22. The players (want, wants) to practice indoors today.

23. He (wasn't, weren't) at the amusement park last night.

24. I thought you (was, were) going to work at the supermarket again this weekend.

25. Clare or her brother always (take, takes) care of the animals in the morning.

26. The flowers in the window box (need, needs) watering.

27. Across the street (are, is) a hot-dog stand and a delicatessen.

28. Three fourths of the table (was, were) varnished.

29. Each of the boxes (are, is) marked with a code number and a shipping date.

30. We have already (taken, took) the new soccer equipment over to the field house.

31. That movie has (ran, run) for two months.

32. Last summer Aunt Lou (grew, growed) tomatoes in wooden tubs on her apartment balcony.

33. If Mr. Taglia (had, would have) asked, the salesperson would have demonstrated the new model.

34. Mrs. Stathos must (have, of) sprained her ankle when she slipped on the rug yesterday.

35. In some states, a motorcyclist (doesn't, don't) have to wear a helmet for protection.

36. The stage crew (did, done) everything they could before the props were unpacked.

37. If Hank (was, were) here to explain this problem, I would understand it better.

38. Before Ann began her trip, her parents suggested that she (learn, learns) to change a flat tire.

39. Leon asked me (if I was going to take the bus today, was I going to take the bus today).

40. Judy asked us (did we want to go to the football game, if we wanted to go to the football game).

41. Dad has (laid, lain) down for a nap before starting his six-hour drive to Door County.

42. After my brother talked about the camping trip for a week, Mom decided to (leave, let) him go.

43. Everyone enjoyed (John, John's) acting in *Death of a Salesman*.

44. Juan sent in his application a week ago, but he hasn't heard (anything, nothing) about it yet.

45. After twenty-five years of promoting fire safety, Smokey the Bear retired (peaceful, peacefully) to the zoo.

46. Arriving home hungry and cold, Dee thought the hot soup tasted (delicious, deliciously).

47. Don't you think that our band's uniforms look (better, more better) than that band's uniforms?

48. Debbie finished that problem faster than (any, any other) student in her study group.

49. Unfortunately, Andy's old pickup truck doesn't run (good, well) in cold weather.

50. Bev wants to take flute lessons this fall because she thinks she plays (bad, badly).

Name _____   Number Correct × 5 = ☐

Each numbered sentence is partly or wholly underlined. Three of the four choices that follow each sentence represent different ways of rewriting the underlined material. If you feel that the underlined part of the sentence does not need to be rewritten, circle *A, no change*. If you feel the underlined part needs to be rewritten, circle the letter of the choice (*B* or *C* or *D*) that represents the best rewriting.

1. John prepared an italian meatloaf from his mother's recipe.

   A. no change   C. italian Meatloaf

   B. Italian meatloaf   D. Italian Meatloaf

2. "Drive North," said Mom, "Until you reach the county line, which is marked with a sign."

   A. no change   C. North," said Mom, "until

   B. north," said Mom, "until   D. north," said Mom, "Until

3. Neal asked the waitress for ham, and eggs, potatoes, toast, and milk.

   A. no change   C. ham and eggs potatoes and toast and milk.

   B. ham and eggs; potatoes; toast and milk.   D. ham and eggs, potatoes, toast, and milk.

4. I wanted to color my hair yet I was afraid of getting split ends if I did.

   A. no change   C. hair, yet I was afraid of getting split ends if

   B. hair yet I was afraid of getting split ends, if   D. hair; yet I was afraid of getting split ends if

5. When the Holly mansion was torn down the village had to look elsewhere for tax revenue.

   A. no change   C. was torn down, the village

   B. was torn down. The village   D. was torn down; the village

6. Our income, according to the accountants, should be up by thirty percent over last year's.

   A. no change   C. income, according to the accountants should

   B. income according to the accountants should   D. income according to the accountants, should

7. The Valiants who finished last in 1996 actually came in second in their league this year.

   A. no change   C. Valiants who finished last in 1996, actually

   B. Valiants, who finished last in 1996, actually   D. Valiants, who finished last in 1996 actually

8. A company that has a long record of paying dividends to stockholders is a good bet for an investment.

   A. no change

   B. company, that has a long record of paying dividends to stockholders is

   C. company that has a long record of paying dividends to stockholders, is

   D. company, that has a long record of paying dividends to stockholders, is

9. Detroit predicted a bad year the blame was put on union troubles and increased competition from foreign compacts.

   A. no change   C. a bad year, however, the

   B. a bad year, the   D. a bad year; the

10. Cory knows how to speak Basque, which is related to no other language, Spanish, and Portuguese.

    A. no change

    B. Basque which is related to no other language, Spanish, and Portuguese

    C. Basque, which is related to no other language; Spanish; and Portuguese.

    D. Basque, which is related to no other language, Spanish and Portuguese.

11. At the prom on Saturday night—have you ever had so much fun—we danced until midnight.

    A. no change   C. night: have you ever had so much fun, we

    B. night, have you ever had so much fun—we   D. night—have you ever had so much fun?—we

12. The camp for overweight teenagers advertised its reasons for success balanced diets, a variety of strenuous outdoor activities, and counseling.

    A. no change   C. for success, balanced

    B. for success; balanced   D. for success: balanced

13. Tim wondered if the dentist would find any new cavities during the routine six months' examination

    A. no change   C. examination!

    B. examination?   D. examination.

14. Donna said that she'd never be able to finish the dress without help from Melanie.

    A. no change

    B. Donna said, "That she'd never be able to finish the dress without help from Melanie."

    C. Donna said, "She'd never be able to finish the dress without help from Melanie."

    D. Donna said, I'll never be able to finish the dress without help from Melanie.

15. The woman shouted, You'll never get any of my money; then she laughed hysterically.

    A. no change

    B. shouted you'll never get any of my money; then

    C. shouted, "You'll never get any of my money"; then

    D. shouted, "You'll never get any of my money;" then

16. The three carpenters toolboxes were stolen during their lunch break.

    A. no change   C. three carpenters' toolboxes

    B. three carpenter's toolboxes   D. three carpenters toolbox's

17. He told them to call the police if he wasn't back in an hours time.

    A. no change   C. an hours' time.

    B. an hour's time.   D. an hour time.

18. Were expected for dinner at six, you know.

    A. no change   C. We're expected

    B. Were you expected   D. Wer'e expected

19. The nursing home is planning a special celebration for Ms. Yu, a one hundred five year old resident.

    A. no change   C. a 105-year-old resident.

    B. a one-hundred-five-year-old resident.   D. a one-hundred-5-year-old resident.

20. Approximately three fourths of the people who take out home loans pay off their mortgages early.

    A. no change   C. three-fourths of the people

    B. ¾ of the people   D. .75 of the people

Capitalization

Name _____

Capitalize the first word of every sentence.

We walked home from the movie.

Capitalize proper nouns and proper adjectives.

Boston **B**ruins   125 **T**welfth **S**treet   **G**erman recipe   **V**ictorian furniture   the **W**ar of 1812

Capitalize titles with names, and also capitalize the titles when they stand in place of names.

General **P**atton   **S**enator **B**yrd   "Come here, **M**om."   "Welcome home, **S**enator."

Capitalize the days of the week, the months of the year, and holidays but not the seasons.

Thursday   **O**ctober   **M**emorial **D**ay   **a**utumn   **L**abor **D**ay   **s**pring   **M**onday

Capitalize the regions of a country but not directions or the points on a compass.

Sheila has lived in the **S**outh all her life.   He flew **s**outh for the winter.

Capitalize the first word and all important words in the titles of books, paintings, and the like.

David Copperfield   **M**ona **L**isa   *West Side Story*   "**O**de on a **G**recian **U**rn"

Practice 1

Underline the words that need capital letters in the following phrases. If a phrase does not require any capital letters, write *C* after it.

1. fine french wines
2. speaks chinese
3. brazilian coffee
4. the north
5. drive north
6. san francisco team
7. english bone china

8. governor ella grasso
9. the new governor
10. the ailing king
11. democrats
12. uncle joel
13. my youngest uncle
14. vogue pattern

15. east on first avenue
16. the revolutionary war
17. old war hero
18. doctor nan fowler
19. king richard III
20. aunt alice
21. her daughter-in-law

Practice 2

Underline the words that need capital letters in the following sentences.

1. when you get to watson road, turn northwest.

2. david and maureen took the twelfth street bus to dee's house.

3. mrs. poe sent both of her children to camp iroquois for the entire summer.

4. the ringling brothers and barnum & bailey circus is in louisville during the second week of may.

5. the film *a river runs through it* was made in montana.

6. two english families fought the war of the roses to determine who would be the next king.

7. senator jackson fought long and hard to retain control of the committee.

8. the civil war destroyed the south but left the north relatively unscarred.

9. colonel richards left the white house, pleased with her new duties.

10. cadet wildon arrived at west point confident and eager to begin her studies.

Application

A. Rewrite the following paragraphs on a separate sheet of paper, changing lowercase letters to capital letters wherever necessary.

when dick found out westinghouse wanted him to go to a convention in cleveland, he asked me to go along. we left toledo on a thursday afternoon, driving on the ohio turnpike. near the lorain exit, we had a flat; but we inflated the tire with a can of pump-it-up and made it to a gas station. dick wasn't satisfied with his spare, so he bought a used goodyear tire to replace the one that blew.

as we rolled into cleveland on interstate 71, we passed a mayflower moving van that had flipped over. furniture was scattered all over the highway and part of the west 150th street exit ramp. city police and the cuyahoga county sheriff's patrol were already at the scene, waving the traffic on. but that wasn't the last accident of the day. while dick went to his meeting, i watched an excellent production of *othello* at the lakewood shakespeare festival. as othello was killing desdemona, the wall of their bedroom slowly fell down on top of them.

B. Rewrite the following paragraphs on a separate sheet of paper, changing lowercase letters to capital letters wherever necessary.

philadelphia, the fourth largest city in the united states, lies on the delaware river in southeastern pennsylvania. the city was founded in 1682 by william penn, an englishman who had been persecuted for his quaker beliefs. penn envisioned philadelphia as a center of religious freedom, and the city attracted thousands of colonists who had suffered religious persecution in england. appropriately, *philadelphia* is a greek word meaning "brotherly love"; and, in fact, philadelphia has been nicknamed the city of brotherly love. in 1683, philadelphia became the capital of pennsylvania. by the early 1700s, it had become the largest and wealthiest city in the colonies.

philadelphia is a city rich in the early history of the united states. it was here, in carpenter's hall, that the first continental congress met in 1774. in independence hall, the declaration of independence and the constitution were adopted. nearby stands the liberty bell, which was rung to announce the declaration of independence in 1776. congress hall was the seat of congress until 1800. betsy ross may have produced the first american flag in her house on arch street. and in christ church, built in the early 1700s, one can see the pews of washington and franklin. during the revolutionary war, philadelphia served as the capital of the colonies. and until 1800, it served as the capital of the united states.

C. Underline the words that require capital letters in the following phrases. If the phrase is correct as it stands, write *C* after it.

1. turkish coffee
2. the midwest
3. canadian bacon
4. colonel richardson
5. "good morning, governor"
6. president clinton
7. new york jets
8. armistice day
9. north by northeast
10. iranian oil
11. winter
12. *independence day*

Name _____

Use commas to separate words, phrases, and short clauses in a series.

> Alice ordered folders, stationery, and stamps. [words]
>
> I hiked to the beach, past the boathouse, and through a grove of trees. [phrases]
>
> He studied, he practiced, and he worried. [clauses]

Use commas to separate the items in dates and addresses.

> The bombing of Pearl Harbor, December 7, 1941, forced the United States to fight Japan.
>
> The Hollys moved to 772 Wicker Street, Seattle, Washington, last year.

Some words are usually thought of as pairs, like *ham and eggs* and *bread and butter*. When such a pair occurs with other items in a series, set it off with commas as a single item. However, if you want the words to be considered separately, put a comma between them.

> Joe fixed soup, **bread and butter**, pudding, and milk. [as a pair]
>
> Reva bought soda, pickles, **bread**, and **butter**. [separately]

Two or more words that modify the same noun should be separated by commas.

> The mayor's sister is a **tall, frail** woman.

Look at the word *dark* in the following sentence; what word does it modify?

> Ellie crocheted a **dark** green sweater for her mother.

Dark tells what kind of *green*, doesn't it? Since *dark* modifies *green*, these two words should not be separated by a comma. However, in the following sentence, a comma follows the word *dark* since the words *dark* and *gloomy* both modify *night*:

> It was a **dark, gloomy** night.

Practice 1

Add commas to the following sentences wherever necessary. If a sentence is correct as given, circle the number of the sentence.

1. The Dawsons the Gattis the Podjarskis and the Janssens play bridge every Thursday.

2. That laundry will sew on missing buttons repair zippers and do reweaving.

3. Lou left his money to his sons his house to Mrs. Kane and his stocks to Marie's trust fund.

4. Molly served ham and eggs rolls and tea at her brunch.

5. Ms. Tolliver's portfolio included common stocks municipal bonds and sinking-fund debentures.

6. The decorator matched the wallpaper with the sofa the carpet and the dining-room chairs.

7. Doru Lisa and Carl share the ride to school

8. The October 1 1996 issue of *Time* was sold out.

9. Many movie stars live in Palm Springs California between their film assignments.

10. She modeled a soft dove-gray silk skirt.

11. Mike and Larissa Nick and Donna and Jack and Lee are the other couples I invited to the party.

12. The medical secretary makes appointments prepares bills and orders supplies.

13. Who is the dark handsome man over by the fireplace?

14. The light brown horse is being ridden by a nervous inexperienced jockey.

15. The high scorers in last Wednesday's basketball game were Ann Rita and Inna.

16. Jeff bought a light blue jacket for his trip to Sacramento.

17. We loaded the boat hoisted the sails and set off on our journey along the Pacific coast.

18. Tony's mother thought the medium-gray suit looked the best on him.

19. The townspeople fought floods fire and famine in their battle for survival.

20. A police officer stopped the car questioned the driver and issued a ticket for speeding.

Practice 2

Add commas wherever necessary to the following sentences.

1. My brother was born on May 11 1985 in the little town of Wyanet.

2. The movers loaded the truck locked the doors securely and headed across town to our new house.

3. Our newest classmate used to live in London England.

4. Off in the distance we could see horses cows and a tall red silo.

5. My sister and I toured the White House when we were in Washington D.C.

6. Ms. Johnson wants us to buy a hoe two pitchforks and a rake.

7. We walked to the waterfront then along the beach and finally out onto the pier.

8. The fourth observation post in this section of the park was completed on July 17 1996.

9. The boys found a wooden trunk a box of photographs and a rusty sword in the attic.

10. Our insurance company has moved to 1011 W. Ohio Street Chicago Illinois.

11. The bus turned the corner swerved to avoid a pothole and lurched to a stop.

12. On our last vacation we visited San Diego San Francisco and Los Angeles.

13. The biology department ordered test tubes slides and pipettes.

14. Arturo and his family arrived in the United States on April 24 1997.

15. The new supervisor promised her employees better working conditions a later starting time and new coffee and sandwich machines.

16. Tony and Nancy Pablo and Rita and David and Drew all hiked to the bottom of the canyon.

17. The signing of the new trade agreement January 18 1997 meant an end to unfair trade practices that had been damaging to the economy.

18. Pete prepared the salad set the table and waited for his guests to arrive.

19. The bank has moved its headquarters to 65 E. Washington Street Peoria.

20. The clouds gathered the sky darkened and a torrential rain lashed the valley.

21. Sue ordered a cheeseburger a soda and fries.

22. Ms. Raymond Mr. O'Malley and Dr. Sánchez left for the convention this morning.

23. Our dentist recently visited Cairo Egypt.

24. Doretha's latest book of poems was published on December 10 1996.

25. Our club collected newspapers old books and aluminum cans for recycling.

Name _____   Possible Score | 10 | My Score | |

You can express two ideas in two separate sentences.

    Margarita ran for office.   She won easily.

  Or you can show that two ideas are closely related by joining them to form one compound sentence.

    Margarita ran for office, **and** she won easily.

  Notice that two things are necessary to join ideas in a compound sentence. The first is a comma. The second is a connecting word, or conjunction, like one of these: *and, but, for, nor, or, yet,* or *so.*

Practice 1

Add commas wherever necessary to the following sentences.

1. Either you honor the contract or the company will be forced to take legal action.

2. We couldn't make much of a contribution nor did they expect a big one from us.

3. Capelletti won the Heisman Trophy and he later joined a professional football team.

4. Jessie saw the mouse run in and out she went for traps.

5. The dentist found only one cavity but he made another appointment for me to get it filled.

Practice 2

Rewrite each pair of sentences as a compound sentence. Use commas and conjunctions correctly.

1. You could use compost. You might choose chemical fertilizers to enrich this plot. _____

_____

_____

2. Food stamps help millions of Americans. Without this program many would go hungry. _____

_____

_____

3. Allen wants to become an architect. He is weak in math. _____

_____

_____

4. Dee couldn't run in the marathon. She was still weak from the flu. _____

_____

_____

5. The team fought hard. They won the game. _____

_____

Name _____

Possible Score | 13 | My Score | [ ]

Use a comma to set off introductory elements from the rest of the sentence.

> **When the tide went out,** the men dug clams. [clause]
>
> **Running easily,** the fox outdistanced the hounds. [phrase]
>
> **Luckily,** Terry found the kitten before darkness set in. [word]

Use commas to set off material that interrupts the general flow of the sentence.

> You know**, of course,** that her flight was delayed.
>
> Cory will be admitted**, I think,** after he gets a pass.

Practice 1

Add commas to the following sentences to set off introductory and interrupting elements.

1. When the map was finally located it led us to an empty underground cavern.

2. The company found so I'm told that their new product was not selling well in the Midwest.

3. Unhappily I had to settle for curtains instead of shutters.

4. Leaving early Melissa and John reached the lake before noon.

5. The best course to follow in my opinion is to give Ms. Holt a raise and some new duties.

Practice 2

Use each of the following introducers and interrupters in a sentence. Add commas wherever necessary.

Introducers:	When the music starts	Strolling along the pier	Suddenly
Interrupters:	so I've heard	as we see it	in the meantime

1. _____

_____

2. _____

_____

3. _____

_____

4. _____

_____

5. _____

_____

6. _____

Commas: Nonessential Elements

Name _____ Possible Score [36]   My Score [ ]

Commas are used to set off nonessential words, phrases, or clauses from the main structure of a sentence. Essential words, phrases, or clauses are not separated from the sentences in which they appear.

How can you tell whether a sentence part is essential or not? If the word, phrase, or clause answers the question *which particular one* about the person or thing it refers to, it is essential to the meaning of the sentence and should not be set off with commas.

> We need a flower **that blooms well in the shade**.

The *that* clause is essential to identify *which particular kind of flower* is needed. In other words, the *that* clause restricts *flower* to one particular kind. Such essential elements are often called *restrictive*.

If the word, phrase, or clause does not identify the word it refers to as one specific person or thing, it is nonessential and should be set off from the rest of the sentence with commas.

> The impatiens, **which blooms well in the shade,** is available in all colors of the red-to-white range.

In this sentence, the *which* clause provides additional information about the impatiens but does not restrict or limit the meaning of the word in any way. Such nonessential elements are often called *nonrestrictive*.

Here are some examples of essential and nonessential phrases. Pay special attention to where and why commas are used:

> The gift **wrapped in expensive red paper** is yours. [essential]

> The gift, **wrapped in expensive red paper,** took her last penny. [nonessential]

> Any team **in the tournament for the first time** is at a disadvantage. [essential]

> Our team, **in the tournament for the first time,** is at a disadvantage. [nonessential]

Practice 1

Decide which of the following sentences includes nonessential elements and then add commas where necessary. If the sentence is correct as given, circle its number.

1. Mr. Bixby our neighbor left his lawn mower outside.

2. My sister and her best friend Ellen Dukes bought their tickets together for the concert.

3. The cat in the third cage may have feline distemper.

4. Hodgkin's disease which is a form of cancer often strikes the lymph nodes first.

5. A person with two jobs is entitled to relax at the end of the day.

6. Willy my best friend is from Texas.

7. A dentist who tells his or her patients to use dental floss regularly is doing them a favor.

8. *Moby Dick* which some critics call the great American novel has been filmed more than once.

9. Churchill's mother who was born in the United States married into the British aristocracy.

10. The pin heavily adorned with rubies was complemented by the black velvet box it rested in.

11. My new car which has a wiper on the hatchback window is well equipped.

12. The Republican Party with far fewer registered voters still beat the Democrats on that occasion.

13. Jackie Dawson playing chess for the first time outscored all the other contestants.

14. The cottage next to ours at Pine Lake is up for sale.

15. Assessor Reinke who has control over our property-tax bills has just recommended a rate increase.

Practice 2

Use word groups 1–5 as nonessential elements in sentences of your own. Use word groups 6–10 as essential elements in sentences. Use commas wherever necessary.

1. finished by hand   2. who ran as a Democrat   3. whose mother is Jewish
4. which doesn't need much space   5. recently named the starter at first base

6. on the left   7. laughing his head off   8. with a smile   9. known for her honesty
10. that comes in blue

1. _____

_____

2. _____

_____

3. _____

_____

4. _____

_____

5. _____

_____

6. _____

_____

7. _____

_____

8. _____

_____

9. _____

_____

10. _____

_____

Application

Name _____

A. Rewrite the following sentences, adding commas wherever necessary.

1. Nearly half the people in that country work on farms plantations and ranches. _____

_____

_____

2. Using reverse thrusters the pilot brought the plane to a halt. _____

_____

_____

3. The planet Mars in my opinion is the most interesting in our solar system. _____

_____

_____

4. Sue hoped to sing the lead but she realized that Gail had a better voice. _____

_____

_____

5. Coughing sputtering and billowing smoke the old roadster wheezed into town. _____

_____

_____

6. Bev needed some history books so she went to the library to look for them. _____

_____

_____

7. Officer Foley who was cited for heroism lives next door to us. _____

_____

_____

8. Determined to win Carolyn trained daily for the marathon. _____

_____

_____

B. Read the following paragraphs carefully. Then rewrite them, adding commas wherever necessary.

The Navaho Indians who settled in the southwestern United States in the late 1600s are known for their colorful handwoven blankets. Initially most Navaho blankets were woven from naturally colored wool—black white and a mixture of the two that produced gray. Occasionally the wool was dyed with roots herbs and minerals to produce dark colors.

As in most Indian nations weaving is done by the women. Navaho women in addition to weaving also create abstract geometrical designs. The Navaho men on the other hand create designs showing people animals birds and fish.

Semicolons

Name _____

A semicolon is a stronger separator than a comma but not as strong as a period. Use a semicolon to join two closely related sentences. Do not use a connective word like *and, or, but, for, nor, yet,* and *so* between the sentences.

> Lea studied the maps for an hour; she passed the geography test easily.

If either of the sentences you wish to join already contains a comma, use a semicolon to join them, even though a connective word is also used.

> Lieutenant Vasco, a Stockton native, scored 570 points; **but** one of the recruits did just as well.

Use a semicolon between items in a series if any of the items already contains a comma.

> Joy knows Hindi, the official language of the North; Tamil, a Ceylonese tongue; and Sanskrit.

When two sentences are joined by a conjunctive adverb like *however, therefore, in fact, for example,* or *on the other hand*, you must use a semicolon before the conjunctive adverb. A comma usually follows the adverb.

> She invested shrewdly; **however,** she lost everything when gold stocks collapsed.

Practice

Circle the incorrect commas that should be changed to semicolons in the following sentences. If the sentence is correct, circle its number.

1. They moved often, living in La Porte, Indiana, Rye, New York, and Memphis, Tennessee.

2. She fell out of the swing, but I didn't push her.

3. Atlanta is growing rapidly, it offers a good business climate and a stable working population.

4. Billy, who is just three, ate his brother's apple, and this action caused a terrible fight when Henry got home.

5. Pencils don't contain lead anymore, they're made of graphite, which isn't poisonous.

6. Supply and demand govern prices, so when goods are in short supply and demand is great, prices rise.

7. Neil's victory was no surprise, he'd been practicing that dive for six months.

8. Jenny has a collection of antique bottles, let her explain the differences between pressed and cut glass.

9. The price-earnings ratio is good, therefore, I recommend that you buy the stock as soon as possible.

10. A new store would bring in more business, however, we just don't have enough capital to expand now.

11. Clean your work area, and then lock the door.

12. Dad replaced the screens just in time, the seventeen-year locusts invaded the next night.

13. Karen scored well in the school figures, she lost only because Nancy's free-skating routine was so good.

14. Grandpa bought a new tiller, some blood meal, and special enzyme tablets, which will break down the composed vegetable matter faster.

15. Nick keeps jumper cables in his car, so we don't really have anything to worry about.

Name _____   Possible Score | 15 | My Score | |

A colon in a sentence is a signal to the reader that something important follows. Use a colon after a statement that is followed by an explanatory clause or expression.

> Henry James was never really a popular novelist: none of his novels ever attained the sales of a modern best-seller.

Use a colon to introduce a list when you don't use the words *for example* or *such as*.

> The cake called for unusual ingredients: mace, citron, and coffee.

However, do **not** use a colon when the list immediately follows a verb or a preposition.

> Beth's favorite foods **are** peanuts, salami, cheese, and grapes.
> Amy sent invitations **to** band members, players, coaches, and cheerleaders.

Colons also have some purely conventional uses:

1. to introduce a long or formal quotation,

> In her review of the film, Rona Barrett said: "*One Flew Over the Cuckoo's Nest* is about mental institutions. By the end of the movie you will be thinking about the cuckoos in your own nest."

2. to separate hours from minutes,

> 8:15 A.M.   2:12 E.S.T.   the 6:25 bus

3. to follow the greeting in a business letter.

> Dear Sir or Madam: Ladies and Gentlemen: Dear Ms. Adams:

Practice

Add colons wherever necessary to the following sentences.

1. We caught the bus at 330.

2. Harry missed the 504 to New York, so he waited until the next one came at 635.

3. We ignored the confusion a new restaurant on opening day is always in chaos.

4. Emory gave several reasons for staying in Dallas the winter climate, his high salary, and his low mortgage rate.

5. Dad added three items to the list checkbook, lug wrench, and picnic tablecloth.

6. It takes a long time to become a doctor four years of college, four years of medical school, and one or two more years of internship.

7. You may quote from these books only *Compton's, World Book,* and the *Farmer's Almanac.*

8. Ruth invented a foolproof method for weeding she mulches the garden so weeds can't grow at all.

9. Our hotel bill included the following telephone charges, telegrams, and room service.

10. The automaker predicted a record-breaking year one company's sales rose thirty percent.

11. That model has been discontinued it needed frequent repairs and was too expensive.

12. All participants need the following hiking boots, heavy jeans, and a wide-brimmed hat.

13. When the 745 bus failed to depart as scheduled, Charles knew he was going to be late.

14. Ellen's proposal won acclaim it was both simple and cost effective.

Name _____ Possible Score | 40 | My Score | |

Occasionally, you may want to insert words into a sentence that sharply interrupt its normal word order. In such cases, you will need stronger separators than commas.

Parentheses indicate the greatest degree of separation between the enclosed word group and the rest of the sentence.

> The cyclamen (called the poor person's orchid) makes a good houseplant for cool rooms.

If the word group in parentheses occurs within the sentence, don't start the word group with a capital letter or end it with a period, even if it is a complete sentence.

> Jim's wool jacket (we bought it last week) keeps him warm in subzero weather.

If the word group is a question or an exclamation, place a question mark or an exclamation point inside the parentheses, but don't start the word group with a capital letter.

> That play (it was a comedy, wasn't it?) left me cold.

If the material in parentheses is a complete sentence standing by itself, begin it with a capital letter and end it with a period inside the closing parentheses.

> We left L.A. early. (It was just in time, too.) The earthquake hit soon after ten o'clock.

Use dashes to indicate greater separation than commas but less separation than parentheses.

> Dennis Rodman—forward for the Chicago Bulls—has written his autobiography.

Use a single dash to emphasize an added comment.

> Ken could win a gold medal—provided he stays in excellent physical shape.

If the interrupting word group is a statement, neither a capital letter nor a period is needed inside the dashes. If it is a question or an exclamation, you must add a question mark or an exclamation point before the second dash, but don't begin the word group with a capital letter.

> Paul Newman—can you believe he's over seventy?—shuns publicity and leads a quiet life.

Brackets are used to show that a clarification or explanation has been added to a sentence, especially to a quotation. The bracketed words in this example provide a clear reference for the pronoun:

> Speaking of the vice-president's foreign policy, Senator Clare Boothe Luce said: "Much of what he [Henry Wallace] calls his global thinking is, no matter how you slice it, still Globaloney."

Practice 1

Add parentheses wherever necessary to the following sentences.

1. Humus decayed plant matter improves garden soil.

2. Stan "the Man" Musial owns a restaurant in St. Louis.

3. Maxwell House "good to the last drop" and Folgers "it's mountain grown" are brands of coffee.

4. Aunt Lil's present it was custom-made came from the best store in Dallas.

5. The carolers appreciated their host's wassail a hot, spicy punch and eggnog.

6. Hot-rod accessories glass-pack mufflers, headers, etc. took Hal's entire allowance.

7. Agatha Christie's detective wasn't Albert Finney great in the role? always solves the case creatively.

8. Rita and Leann opened a law office together. They're Colgate grads. Their practice is real estate.

9. Berg polled seventeen percent of the vote. He ran as an independent. Such a showing is rare for a splinter candidate.

10. Two restaurant critics bought a dinner in Paris it cost four thousand dollars that included nine different wines.

11. The red Ferrari it was the Ferrari team's only entry blew an engine on the first lap.

12. As the sun set we spent many such evenings watching the sun set the air turned chilly.

13. She asked Rob did you ask him, too? if he wanted to join us on Saturday.

14. Meteors called shooting stars regularly strike the earth's atmosphere.

15. The crowd rather small for a holiday grew restless as the game wore on.

16. A warning Danger! No Diving! was clearly posted on the pier.

17. An old ship it was dry-docked early in this century has been made into a restaurant.

18. Beth opened the door slowly. It creaked, as in some old horror movie. Inside, was nothing.

19. The chief some of the Indians called him Black Cloud began the ceremony with a chant.

20. Fish emulsion what an odor! is often used to fertilize houseplants.

Practice 2

Add dashes and brackets wherever necessary to the following sentences.

1. Chuck made the most elusive golf shot a hole in one on the back nine at Firestone.

2. Bordeaux mixture and Paris green these are not exotic French compounds but common garden preparations.

3. All these make Ms. Dodge a fine boss to work for good humor, patience, and tolerance.

4. Wines are rated on bouquet how they smell as well as on flavor.

5. The details on that blouse pin tucks and bound buttonholes make it a bargain at thirty dollars.

6. Melissa Smith she lettered in tennis all four years of high school will attend the University of Utah next year on an athletic scholarship.

7. The Jordans adopted a sixth child isn't that great? in addition to their five other children.

8. P. T. Barnum said, "There's one a sucker born every minute."

9. Lena has the talent to win the piano competition assuming she continues to practice daily.

10. The author notes that "she Mrs. Johnson was reluctant to join the committee."

11. Washington slammed the next pitch another curve! into the upper deck in left field.

12. The water in the pool was warm too warm.

13. Our choir seventy-five voices strong will travel to Quebec at the end of the month.

14. We left or I should say *fled* the hotel the very next morning.

15. An invitation was sent to Dr. Bowler surgeon, director of health, philanthropist and her husband.

16. The memo stated that "he the chairman has already vetoed the idea."

17. The alleged bicycle thieves decided to plead guilty all except one.

18. Optional equipment air conditioning, power windows, and leather upholstery have driven up the price of that car.

19. Jerry will almost certainly win the speech prize if he doesn't catch another cold!

20. Our new house what a headache! won't be ready for another two months.

Application

Name _____

A. Rewrite the following paragraphs on a separate sheet of paper, adding semicolons wherever necessary.

The cosmetic industry is a powerhouse in our economy it accounts for billions in sales every year. The cosmetic giants—Revlon, L'Oreál, Clinique, Estée Lauder—give one another stiff competition. They need new products all the time they must keep an exclusive image they must finance expensive research.

For example, to bring out a new moisturizer, the chemists must formulate emollients, which are skin softeners humectants, which hold moisture to the skin surface and binders, to keep the cream smooth. The product must smell and look good it must have a shelf life of eighteen months before spoilage it must be attractively packaged by the advertising agents. If any one of these qualities is missing, the new moisturizer will fail in the marketplace. Ball-point lipsticks makeup-setting mists, one of which was nothing but water and glitter mascaras are just three famous marketing flops in the industry.

B. Rewrite the following paragraph on a separate sheet of paper, adding colons wherever necessary.

The actors arrived on flight seven at 615. At 620, troubles started for the troupe no cabs were available, baggage disappeared, and the hotel lost their reservations. Later, the prop master and the stage manager argued about who was responsible for some missing properties. Finally, a list was posted. It read, "Please find the following before tonight one pair of blue tights, one tiara, one velvet cape, one shovel." When the tights finally showed up, they were much too small for the star. He had to give Hamlet's famous speech, "To be or not to be that is the question," while standing behind a table to keep his legs hidden from the audience.

C. Write twelve sentences of your own, using the following expressions to illustrate the correct use of parentheses, dashes, and brackets.

1. —I admit that I love them— _____

_____

_____

2. (Boy, was that a relief!) _____

_____

_____

3. He [the president] _____

_____

_____

4. (one of the all-time greats) _____

_____

_____

5. (who could forget those eyes?) _____

_____

_____

6. —at an incredible $7.95— _____

_____

_____

7. (six of the fourteen survivors) _____

_____

_____

8. —all these make a good teacher. _____

_____

_____

9. (never one of my favorites) _____

_____

_____

10. —she actually went there!— _____

_____

_____

11. (a real disappointment) _____

_____

_____

12. —those were the days— _____

_____

_____

Name _____   Possible Score | 16 | My Score | |

Periods, question marks, and exclamation points usually signal the ends of sentences. Such end punctuation also tells the reader what kind of sentence he or she has just finished reading—a statement, a question, or an emphatic expression.

If you want to indicate a statement of fact or opinion, end your sentence with a period.

The school paper should come out twice a month so we can stay within our budget**.**

If you want to indicate a direct question, use a question mark as end punctuation.

Do you think we should publish the paper every week or only twice a month**?**

But an indirect question or a polite request phrased as a question should end with a period.

The principal asked if we would change our class schedule**.** [indirect question]

May we expect payment by the fifteenth**.** [polite request]

Reserve the exclamation point for use in sentences that express very strong feelings.

Wow**!** That trade was a lucky break for the Phillies**!**

A command could end either with a period or an exclamation point, depending on the force you want to convey.

Don't slam the door, Molly**.** [mild]   Don't tell my parents on me**!** [more forceful]

As a general rule, end punctuation goes inside any quotation marks that may be present. But question marks or exclamation points that refer to the whole sentence, not just to the quotation, go outside the quotation marks.

Maria wondered, "Can I finish this and still make it to woodshop on time**?**"

Did you finish reading "The Raven"**?**

Practice

Rewrite these sentences, supplying the appropriate end punctuation.

1. Inez won by the slimmest of margins _____

_____

2. Do you believe that Inez finally won _____

_____

3. How fantastic that Inez finally won _____

_____

4. Get the plumb line out of the toolbox, Luis _____

_____

UNIT 3   Mastering the Mechanics

5. May I have New Year's Eve off if I work on Christmas _____

   _____

6. May we expect to hear from you by return mail _____

   _____

7. Your credit rating may be damaged if you let this bill go until next month _____

   _____

8. If you wait right there, I'll join you in a few minutes _____

   _____

9. Will you wait for me if I'm late _____

   _____

10. Get out of the doorway, for heaven's sake _____

    _____

11. Tim called angrily, "That'll be the day" _____

    _____

12. Kate asked, "Don't you want me to be your friend" _____

    _____

13. Did you see Grandma Moses's painting *Out for the Christmas Trees* _____

    _____

14. They wondered whether the picnic was Friday or Saturday _____

    _____

15. How incredible that he just said, "OK wih me" _____

    _____

16. Jack was wondering if we could help him with dinner tonight _____

    _____

Application

Name _____   Possible Score 25   My Score [ ]

Read the following paragraphs. Then rewrite them, supplying the appropriate end punctuation.

When Mr. Denton came home from work, he was tired as usual and hungry He wearily sat down at the kitchen table and reached for the evening paper as his wife set the spaghetti dinner before them As she sat down, she said, "Ben, I've been thinking" Her voice caught his attention immediately

He look up, smiled, as he picked up his fork, and asked, "About what, Sara"

"Ben," she began and paused She had his full attention now "I think I'm going to get a job" Ben looked up from his plate and passed her the garlic bread

Sara continued as she began to eat, "We could use the extra money, Ben, now that Tim will be going to college next year"

"Sounds good to me," Ben responded "In fact, great, if your heart's in it We could use the money What kind of job are you thinking about"

"There are several possibilities," Sara replied "When I talked with Juanita yesterday, she told me that Boutelles's has several openings now The pay's good there, and the hours would be a good fit with us What do you think, Ben"

"Sara, it's your call I want you to do what you want to do I'm willing to pull my added share of the load here at home" He paused and then said seriously, "But the seasoning is going to change when I make the spaghetti sauce" Then he grinned

"We'll work on that together," Sara smiled "I may even ask to help with the yard work"

_____

_____

_____

_____

_____

_____

_____

_____

_____

_____

_____

_____

_____

_____

Name _____ Possible Score 22 My Score ☐

Use quotation marks when you record someone's exact words.

> Paul said, **"My bike has a flat tire."** [direct quotation]

Don't use quotation marks if you are reporting in your own words what someone has said.

> Paul said that his bike had a flat tire. [indirect quotation]

Often, in an indirect quotation, the word *that* is omitted.

> Paul said his bike had a flat tire. [indirect quotation]

Use quotation marks to record dialogue—conversation between two or more speakers. Each time the speaker changes, you should begin a new paragraph.

> "Does it end happily ever after?" asked Sue, sitting up suddenly. Her eyes were wide open now.
> "You know," said her father.
> "No, I don't," she protested.
> "She was a princess, wasn't she?" he asked.
> "Of course."
> "Well then," he replied, "it has to end happily ever after, doesn't it?"

Besides enclosing direct quotations and dialogue, quotation marks are also used to enclose the titles of short works—magazine articles, short poems, essays, stories, and songs.

> Brenda just finished reading Faulkner's short story **"A Rose for Emily."**

The titles of longer works—books, long poems, plays, magazines, movies—and the names of ships and artwork are italicized. In handwritten or typed manuscripts, this is done by underlining.

> Tonight we are going to see Tennessee Williams's play **A Streetcar Named Desire**.
> Edward Hopper's **Nighthawks** hangs in the Art Institute of Chicago.

Words used as words in a sentence are also italicized or underlined.

> In my English composition, I used **irony,** but the right word was really **satire**.

Practice 1

The following sentences have been written without punctuation. If a sentence needs quotation marks, write *direct quotation* in the space provided. If the sentence does not need quotation marks, write *indirect quotation*.

1. _____ Jamie said that he would take the train

2. _____ Jamie said I'll take the train

3. _____ Linda shouted that she was leaving

4. _____ The dentist said it wouldn't hurt a bit

5. _____ Carol said I know you can do it

6. _____ The driver told us we were on the wrong bus

7. _____ The driver told us you are on the wrong bus

8. _____ Bill promised I won't do it again

9. _____ Bill promised he wouldn't do it again

10. _____ Sally replied I practice every afternoon

Practice 2

Rewrite the following sentences, adding quotation marks or italics (underlining) wherever necessary.

1. The Queen Mary is anchored in Long Beach, California. _____

_____

2. Shaw's story The Eighty-Yard Run appeared in Esquire magazine. _____

_____

3. The film Phenomenon starred John Travolta. _____

_____

4. John used the word amount when he should have used number. _____

_____

5. The Joy Luck Club is a novel by Amy Tan. _____

_____

6. Grant Wood's American Gothic is a very famous painting. _____

_____

7. Stopping by Woods on a Snowy Evening is one of Robert Frost's best-known poems. _____

_____

8. We reprinted her article Losing Weight and Keeping Fit. _____

_____

9. Ms. Albert wrote woody when I think she meant wordy. _____

_____

Name _____ Possible Score | 17 | My Score | |

Direct quotations and dialogue are always enclosed in quotation marks. But where do commas, periods, semicolons, and other marks of punctuation belong in relation to quotation marks?

Commas and periods always go *inside* the closing quotation marks.

"Nobody," Linda announced, "should miss that movie."

"That movie is great," Linda announced. "Nobody should miss it."

Semicolons and colons go *outside* the quotation marks because they are not considered part of the quoted material.

She said, "My daughter is too good for Mr. Carson"; then she swept out of the room.

The critic said, "An understanding of Shakespeare is not enough": we have to love the bard as well.

If the material quoted is a question or an exclamation, the question mark or exclamation point goes *inside* the closing quotation mark.

She responded by saying, "What if it happens to you?"

But if the whole sentence is a question or an exclamation, put the question mark or the exclamation point outside the closing quotation mark.

Did Mr. Chaffee say, "Read chapter 2"?

I could scream when she starts with "If I were you"!

If the quoted material and the whole statement both end with question marks or exclamation points, use just one question mark or exclamation point *inside* the closing quotation mark.

Do you remember her asking, "Can someone give me a lift to the train station?"

When one quotation occurs inside another, use single quotation marks around the *inside* quotation.

"Why do I get yelled at," he asked, "when Dad can say 'Shut up!' all he wants?"

Practice

Add quotation marks where necessary, deciding whether punctuation marks go inside or outside of them.

1. Yalini said, You did better than Ivy on the history test.

2. They caught the vandals who spray painted the steps last Saturday, Lorraine announced.

3. Milton's *Paradise Lost* is really long, but he also wrote shorter poems, like On His Blindness.

4. I'll drop off that overdue book on the way to the grocery, said Mom, if it will save you a trip.

5. Lawrence's short story The Rocking-Horse Winner is about a boy who has the gift of prophecy.

6. If you don't get out of here, I'll call the police! shouted Granny to the burglar.

7. The dentist said, After the shot, you won't feel a thing; he was right, too.

8. How I hate it when he says I told you so!

9. When Bobby ran over to the stereo, Julia said, Don't touch it!

10. Day Tripper is my dad's favorite Beatles song, Norm said.

11. Tomorrow, Ms. Johnson said, we'll hear a recording of Robert Frost's poem Mending Wall.

12. Mr. Albert said, William can explain what's wrong with the expression between you and I.

Application

Name _____

Possible
Score | 26

My
Score | [ ]

A. Rewrite the following dialogue on a separate sheet of paper, adding quotation marks where they are needed. Be sure it is clear whether the punctuation marks are inside or outside of the quotation marks.

Don't worry, said Mom calmly. There's no point in getting married unless you're really sure. Granny used to say that if you marry in haste, you'll repent at leisure.

I smiled up at her. I thought to myself how Granny used these folksy sayings all the time. Meanwhile, Mother went on ironing.

How long did you actually know Bruce before he proposed? she asked.

Oh, about seven months, I said.

Did you like his parents? Mom asked.

That's just it, I said. I felt like *they* didn't approve of *me*. His father didn't say two words all through dinner. And his mother kept giving me these funny looks. I don't think I've ever felt so uncomfortable in my life. And frankly, Bruce wasn't much help. I could have used a little more support.

What kind of people are they? Mom asked.

They're pretty well off, I guess. And they sure wanted me to know it. When I went up to one of their paintings, his mother asked me if I knew it was an original. I told her I knew.

Mother winced. That's my daughter, she said, a monster of tact.

Anyhow, I went on, it was strictly downhill after that. In fact, when I told Bruce we should call things off, he actually looked a little relieved.

There was a short pause as Mother folded the tablecloth she had been ironing.

Well, you know that Granny used to say that you just don't marry a man. You marry a family.

Yeah, Mom, I said, and I sure didn't want to marry his mother.

B. On a separate sheet of paper, write ten original sentences, supplying the information called for and the punctuation required for each sentence.

1. a sentence with the titles of two short poems

2. a sentence with a word used as a word

3. a sentence referring to the title of an article and the magazine that it comes from

4. a question containing the title of a movie

5. a question ending with a quotation

6. a quotation inside another quotation

7. a sentence with the title of a musical play or movie and the title of one of its songs

8. a sentence ending with an exclamation point, including a quotation anywhere in the sentence

9. a sentence ending with a quotation that includes a question mark

10. a sentence with a quotation followed immediately by a semicolon

Name _____ Possible Score | 35 | My Score | |

Until about three hundred years ago, the apostrophe was not used to show ownership. Possessives were simply written with the letter *s*, the same as most plurals. Today, though, you must use an apostrophe to indicate ownership.

To make a singular noun or an indefinite pronoun show ownership, add *'s*.

the boss**'s** office	Kathleen**'s** ring
Ms. Travis**'s** coat	the team**'s** mascot
everyone**'s** duty	somebody**'s** purse
Marx**'s** theories	the index**'s** entries

Remember that the possessive pronouns never have apostrophes, even though some end in *s*.

my/mine	your/yours	her/hers	his
our/ours	their/theirs	whose	its

Most plural nouns already end with the letters *s* or *es*. So to make them show ownership, add just an apostrophe.

the boys' bikes	five carpenters' toolboxes
the Burches' house	soldiers' rations

If a plural noun ends with a letter other than *s*, make it possessive by adding *'s*.

the men**'s** room	children**'s** toys

Certain expressions of time and money are always written with apostrophes, although these apostrophes do not indicate ownership in the usual sense.

a dollar**'s** worth	two month**s**' work
a week**'s** vacation	three hour**s**' relief

Practice 1

Rewrite the following phrases, making the nouns in bold type possessive by adding *'s* or just an apostrophe.

1. **doctor** recommendations _____

2. **fox** tail _____

3. **women** room _____

4. **ladies** dresses _____

5. **Joann** lap top _____

6. **plumbers** wrenches _____

7. **leaders** demands _____

8. **teacher** pen _____

9. **cat** food _____

UNIT 3 Mastering the Mechanics

10. **winner** number _____

11. **driver** techniques _____

12. **car** accessories _____

13. **oxen** yokes _____

14. **nobody** business _____

15. **anybody** guess _____

16. **Louise** scarf _____

17. **Democrats** strategy _____

18. **a month** rent _____

19. **bird** nest _____

20. **Tess** predicament _____

Practice 2

Fill in the blanks in the following sentences by adding possessive nouns that end with an apostrophe or 's.

1. I left _____ notebook at home this morning.

2. My dad donated half _____ income to the fund drive!

3. How can she get the job done on five _____ notice?

4. The _____ barn burned to the ground in thirty minutes.

5. _____ sewing machine breaks the thread too often.

6. The _____ room is a mess; they should clean it up today.

7. Reluctantly, I left my _____ son at the nursery-school door; Sherry couldn't drop him off that day.

8. I put the _____ appointment book beside the switchboard.

9. That _____ clothes are always at the height of fashion.

10. Dad makes good soup, but my _____ soup is much better.

11. The _____ victory was unexpected, considering their record.

12. The cat clawed up _____ social-studies homework.

13. The _____ limousine was an old hearse.

14. Though the _____ race is expected to be close, Morris will probably win.

15. I found _____ silk tie in the laundry hamper.

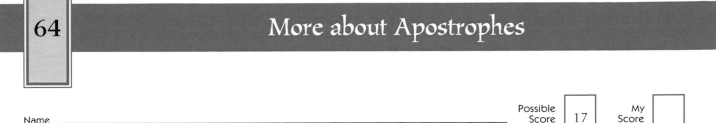

Name _____   Possible Score [17]   My Score [ ]

Apostrophes indicate possession. But they also have other common uses. Apostrophes take the place of missing letters in contractions—shortened forms of common expressions.

we're (we are)	he'll (he will)	they're (they are)
she's (she is)	she's (she has)	I've (I have)
you're (you are)	won't (will not)	it's (it is)

Another use for the apostrophe is in forming special plurals. To form the plural of figures, letters, symbols, and words referred to as words, you should add *'s*.

The picture order included some 5 × 7**'s**.

María got B**'s** and C**'s** on all of her math homework.

The +**'s** on the forecast map indicate areas of rain.

You have too many *because***'s** in that sentence.

When you choose to write out numbers and symbols, no apostrophe is needed.

Willie can count by **fives** to one hundred; he's only six years old.

Lee got two **minuses** in reading.

Practice 1

Make contractions of the phrases in parentheses and write the contractions in the spaces provided.

1. _____ (She had) arrived in Abilene before the storm.

2. _____ Are you sure (he will) come to the study session?

3. _____ Rehearsal starts at eight, but (they are) often late.

4. _____ (Let us) try the new bypass north of St. Louis.

5. _____ (We have) been planning the party since October.

6. _____ (She has) never been elected to office before.

7. _____ That geranium (does not) need pinching to bloom well.

8. _____ (He is) the new tenor in the senior choir.

9. _____ John is checking the cafeteria to see if (she is) there.

10. _____ (I will) design the entranceway as you have specified.

Practice 2

Add an apostrophe or an *'s* wherever necessary in the following sentences.

1. Lilly's third-grade report card has seven +s and no −s.

2. The cards I need are 3 × 5s not 5 × 7s.

3. How many ss are there in *Mississippi?*

4. The type slug is broken, so all of the 8s are blurry.

5. To find substitutes for those extra *think*s in paragraph one, look up some synonyms in the thesaurus.

Application

Name _____

Possible Score | 17

My Score

A. Write eight sentences of your own, using the possessive forms of the words listed below.

women   Bess   brother   Smith   fish   students   someone   coaches

1. _____

_____

2. _____

_____

3. _____

_____

4. _____

_____

5. _____

_____

6. _____

_____

7. _____

_____

8. _____

_____

B. Rewrite the following paragraph on a separate sheet of paper, adding apostrophes wherever necessary.

Ive found that spoken language, with its regional differences in pronunciation and local expressions, is often more fresh and interesting than standard written English. New Yorkers, for example, "graduate high school," while the rest of us "graduate *from* high school." Chicagoans make their *couldnts* into one-syllable words. Montana natives use a contraction youll almost never hear elsewhere: *maynt* for *may not.* Many Americans drop final *rs*, but Bostonians are the only ones to drop *rs* in the middle of words. They "pahk" their "cahs." People from Brooklyn, on the other hand, add *rs* where they dont exist. They "berl" water; the rest of us "boil" it. Regionalisms like these cause trouble only if theyre transferred to a printed page where only standard written English is acceptable.

Name _____ Possible Score | 13 | My Score | |

Spell out any number that can be written in one or two words. (Compound numbers from twenty-one to ninety-nine are hyphenated.) Use figures for numbers requiring more than two written words.

eight thousand immigrants   **twenty-six** years   **174** acres   **13.9** percent

Use figures for dates, hours (with A.M. or P.M.), addresses, page numbers, exact sums of money, and measurements expressed with common abbreviations.

June **4, 1812** [but *The **fourth** of June was overcast.*]   **733** E. **38th** Street

8:00 A.M. or **8** A.M. [but *eight* o'clock]   Interstate **80**   page **54**

a **$29.95** blouse [but *Can you change a **ten** for me?*]   a **50'** drop   **−7**°F

Spell out round numbers, indefinite numbers, and ordinal numbers.

a **hundred** shares of stock   **millions** of chances to win   **thirty-first** president

Do not begin a sentence with a figure.

1995 saw a long steelworkers' strike. [nonstandard]

The year 1995 saw a long steelworkers' strike. [standard]

Spelled-out fractions are hyphenated if they are used as adjectives but not hyphenated if they are used as nouns.

Melaine won by a **three-fourths** majority. [adjective]

Three fourths of the class voted in the election. [noun]

If one number in a series of numbers should be written as a figure, then write all the numbers in the series as figures.

The troop ordered **50** blue ribbons, **73** red, and **124** white.

Practice

Rewrite the following sentences on a separate sheet of paper, changing any numbers that are expressed incorrectly. If a sentence is correct as given, write *correct.*

1. We adopted 6 stray cats over the the years.

2. Neil ordered 24 crocus bulbs, 36 narcissus bulbs, and 150 Red Emperor tulip bulbs from the nursery.

3. The Martinellis moved to 3544 Drexel Avenue last year.

4. Viv canceled her 5 o'clock appointment and asked if she could come in around 10:30 A.M. on Saturday.

5. You could go through Atlanta on I-75 or take the I-475 bypass around the city, which is faster.

6. On the Celsius scale, zero degrees is +32°F.

7. She probably gets 1,000 autograph requests a year.

8. Our 1st trip to Iowa was uneventful, but on our second one there we won $650,000 in the lottery.

9. You can elect to take your full social-security benefit at age 65 or a reduced benefit at age 62.

10. The skirt pattern called for a 3" hem.

11. One of the most attractive features of the house is its three-quarter-acre lot.

12. My birthday falls on the 23rd of December, and nobody pays much attention to it because of Christmas.

Application

Name _____

Possible Score | 10 | My Score | ☐

Write ten sentences of your own, using each of the following number phrases. Be sure to change to spelled-out numbers if figures are not correct.

1. 80 days
2. a forged $50 bill
3. a 3-toed sloth
4. 27 new tomato hybrids
5. at 6:15 A.M.
6. June thirteenth, 1993
7. 1,000's of insects
8. our 25th anniversary
9. ⅗ of the men over 50
10. a 16' 8" pole vault

1. _____

   _____

2. _____

   _____

3. _____

   _____

4. _____

   _____

5. _____

   _____

6. _____

   _____

7. _____

   _____

8. _____

   _____

9. _____

   _____

10. _____

   _____

Name _____   Number Correct × 5 = [ ]

Each numbered sentence is partly or wholly underlined. Three of the four choices that follow each sentence represent different ways of rewriting the underlined material. If you feel that the underlined part of the sentence does not need to be rewritten, circle *A, no change*. If you feel the underlined part needs to be rewritten, circle the letter of the choice (*B* or *C* or *D*) that represents the best rewriting.

1. The british soldiers advanced to the river's edge, where they camped for the night.
   A. no change
   B. British soldiers
   C. british Soldiers
   D. British Soldiers

2. "Birds fly South," he said, "as a result of instinct and environmental factors."
   A. no change
   B. south," he said, "as
   C. South," he said, "As
   D. south," he said, "As

3. The rich old man called from his sickbed for paper, pen, and ink, and a clipboard to write on.
   A. no change
   B. paper; pen and ink; and a clipboard to write on.
   C. paper, pen and ink, and a clipboard to write on.
   D. paper pen and ink and a clipboard to write on.

4. Pedro needed extra money so he took a job when school let out for the summer.
   A. no change
   B. money so he took a job, when
   C. money; so he took a job when
   D. money, so he took a job when

5. After the neighbors moved into the house next door we were less worried about vandalism on our block.
   A. no change
   B. house next door, we were
   C. house next door. We were
   D. house next door; we were

6. A critic to my way of thinking should tell us why a piece of literature is good.
   A. no change
   B. critic to my way thinking, should tell
   C. critic, to my way of thinking should tell
   D. critic, to my way of thinking, should tell

7. Logan who was elected by a coalition of urban residents introduced legislation to help the poor.
   A. no change
   B. Logan, who was elected by a coalition of urban residents, introduced
   C. Logan, who was elected by a coalition of urban residents introduced
   D. Logan who was elected by a coalition of urban residents, introduced

8. Flowers that bloom readily in any soil are a must for our garden.
   A. no change
   B. Flowers, that bloom readily in any soil, are
   C. Flowers that bloom readily in any soil, are
   D. Flowers, that bloom readily in any soil are

9. Ferns need constant moisture they do very well in plastic pots because water can't evaporate through such containers.
   A. no change
   B. constant moisture, therefore they
   C. constant moisture, they
   D. constant moisture; they

10. Joe bought a pair of <u>running shoes, which are the only shoes he wears, some sweat socks, and a new bandanna.</u>

    A. no change

    B. running shoes which are the only shoes he wears, some sweat socks, and a new bandanna.

    C. running shoes, which are the only shoes he wears, some sweat socks and a new bandanna.

    D. running shoes, which are the only shoes he wears; some sweat socks; and a new bandanna.

11. Mr. Timothy <u>Schultz—have you read about him—drove</u> the corporation into bankruptcy.

    A. no change

    B. Schultz, have you read about him, drove

    C. Schultz: have you read about him, drove

    D. Schultz—have you read about him?—drove

12. Buying your own home offers many <u>advantages tax deductions,</u> a hedge against inflation, and the right to design your own personal environment.

    A. no change

    B. advantages: tax deductions,

    C. advantages, tax deductions,

    D. advantages; tax deductions,

13. I asked if the county-fair board would let us set up a booth with an antipollution <u>theme</u>

    A. no change

    B. theme?

    C. theme.

    D. theme!

14. <u>The teacher said that we had better review our class notes before Monday's quiz.</u>

    A. no change

    B. The teacher said, "That we had better review our class notes before Monday's quiz."

    C. The teacher said, you had better review your class notes before Monday's quiz.

    D. The teacher said, "We had better review our class notes before Monday' quiz."

15. The lawyer <u>said, You shouldn't ever sign a contract without letting me check it; then</u> he reread the document.

    A. no change

    B. said, "You shouldn't ever sign a contract without letting me check it"; then

    C. said you shouldn't ever sign a contract without letting me check it; then

    D. said, "You shouldn't ever sign a contract without letting me check it," then

16. The <u>mens rations</u> ran out after a week.

    A. no change

    B. mens' rations

    C. men's rations

    D. mens ration's

17. Mrs. Cárdenas had <u>a months vacation</u> due her when she quit her job at the agency.

    A. no change

    B. a months' vacation

    C. a month vacation

    D. a month's vacation

18. <u>Bunnys coming</u> with us for the weekend picnic.

    A. no change

    B. Bunnies coming

    C. Bunnys' coming

    D. Bunny's coming

19. The Harrisons bought <u>a two hundred twelve-acre farm</u> in southern New Jersey.

    A. no change

    B. a 212-acre farm

    C. a two hundred-12-acre farm

    D. a two-hundred-twelve-acre farm

20. A glass of skim milk provides about <u>one fifth of an adult's daily requirement</u> of protein.

    A. no change

    B. one-fifth of an adult's daily requirement

    C. .20 of an adult's daily requirement

    D. ⅕ of an adult's daily requirement

IMPROVING SPELLING SKILLS

Pretest

Name _____   Number Correct × 2 = ☐

Underline the word or phrase in parentheses that correctly completes each of the following sentences.

1. Next fall the (athaletics, athletics) program at Springfield High will include three team sports.

2. Jonah and I were (hungery, hungry) an hour after breakfast.

3. Because environmentalists feared the (dangerous, dangrous) effects of aerosol sprays on the earth's ozone layer, pump sprays were developed.

4. (Several, Sevral) of these photographs are out of focus.

5. "I (beleive, believe)," said the mayor, "that a mass-transit program is essential for our city."

6. The plaster on the living room (ceiling, cieling) has started to peel.

7. Although no one had intended to (deceive, decieve) Mr. Greco, he was upset by the incident.

8. This (freight, frieght) train is heading toward Chico, Texas.

9. We were surprised by the (begining, beginning) of the story, but not the ending.

10. The sudden (occurence, occurrence) of the hailstorm took even the weather bureau by surprise.

11. Pete (benefited, benefitted) greatly by studying an extra hour.

12. The day was warm and (sunny, suny).

13. They felt (compeled, compelled) to attend the award dinner.

14. Marc and Nona refused to take (danceing, dancing) lessons.

15. The patient's condition had seemed (hopeless, hopless).

16. Fortunately, the scar on Tina's arm was hardly (noticable, noticeable) after a few weeks.

17. At first, Ed found the schedule of housework and office work barely (managable, manageable).

18. This is (probablely, probably) the worst movie I've ever seen.

19. We were, of course, (worried, worryed) at the thought of their driving in such a bad storm.

20. They (tried, tryed) unsuccessfully to clear the snow from the driveway.

21. By noon, the tables had been (gaily, gayly) decorated for the fund-raising dinner.

22. The (babie's, baby's) toys are already packed.

23. He had a great deal of difficulty overcoming his (shiness, shyness).

24. Although the theater had to be searched because of a bomb threat, no one (paniced, panicked).

25. The cocker-spaniel puppies are (frolicing, frolicking) in the backyard.

26. The price of this camping gear has been (drastically, drastickally) reduced.

27. Francine is studying (economicks, economics) this semester.

28. That statement is completely (illogical, ilogical).

29. To his surprise, Tom found that he had (mispelled, misspelled) more words than his younger sister.

30. Have you seen my raincoat? It seems to have (disappeared, dissappeared).

31. The plane was in the (midAtlantic, mid-Atlantic) when the passengers heard the election results.

32. It is important to exercise (selfdiscipline, self-discipline).

33. Those (toothbrushes, toothbrushs) are on sale for one dollar.

34. As a result of his frequent (journeys, journies) to France, Greg now speaks fluent French.

35. Three of the (factories, factorys) on this street will be demolished next spring.

36. Alex bought two clock (radioes, radios) for gifts.

37. The Irish setters that had barked at the smell of smoke were the (heroes, heros) of the day.

38. The (roofs, rooves) of those buildings are covered with red tile.

39. Keeping (knifes, knives) out of the reach of young children is a good safety precaution.

40. The (womans, women) in our office plan to go bowling tonight.

41. Ms. Chen says (its, it's) not too late to sign up for the senior lifesaving course.

42. (Their, There, They're) planning to jog after school every day.

43. Do you know (whose, who's) going on the camping trip?

44. (All together, Altogether), only twenty of the thirty-five members completed the questionnaire.

45. My (principal, principle) reason for taking this auto-repair course is to save money.

46. We've been traveling through Europe for the (passed, past) two months.

47. Everyone (accept, except) Beth is going to Lake Geneva.

48. I decided I needed a (thorough, through) review of the driver's manual before renewing my license.

49. Do you think María was (conscience, conscious) when the dentist pulled her wisdom tooth?

50. She will call for you (later, latter) this afternoon.

Spelling by Syllables

Name _____ Possible Score | 61 | My Score | |

Dividing a word into syllables often makes the work easier to spell. Suppose you want to spell a long word like *environment*. Say the word and count the vowel sounds. Usually, there is one vowel sound for each syllable. Then write the word, repeating the syllables aloud as you spell one syllable at a time—**en vi ron ment**. Spelling by syllables helps you avoid two frequent errors: (1) adding a syllable that isn't part of a word and (2) omitting a syllable that is part of a word.

Here are three common patterns that are helpful for dividing words into syllables:

Consonant/Consonant	Vowel/Vowel	Vowel/Consonant
wo**n** / **d**er	n**e** / **o**n	h**o** / **t**el
stru**c** / **t**ure	r**i** / **o**t	t**i** / **g**er

Practice 1

Say each word in the following list. Decide how many syllables the word has. Then draw a line or lines dividing the word into syllables. Use a dictionary to check your answers.

1. basis	5. final	9. license	13. rodeo	17. awkward	21. ultimate
2. domestic	6. fluid	10. pliers	14. society	18. impulsive	22. fantastic
3. entertain	7. forty	11. pursue	15. stadium	19. giant	23. compliment
4. except	8. identity	12. quiet	16. vitamin	20. multiply	24. courteous

Practice 2

The following words are sometimes pronounced with an extra syllable. Next to each word, write *1,2,3,* or *4* to show how many syllables each word has. Use a dictionary to check your answers.

_____ 1. athletics	_____ 5. disastrous	_____ 9. evidently	_____ 13. lightning
_____ 2. barbarous	_____ 6. drowned	_____ 10. hindrance	_____ 14. remembrance
_____ 3. burglar	_____ 7. entrance	_____ 11. hungry	_____ 15. umbrella
_____ 4. wondrous	_____ 8. necklace	_____ 12. monstrous	_____ 16. mischievous

Practice 3

One word in each of the following pairs is misspelled because a syllable has been left out. Say each pair aloud. Then underline the word whose spelling accounts for all the syllables.

1. experiment/experment	8. incidently/incidentally	15. ultraviolet/ultravilet
2. elementry/elementary	9. mathmatics/mathematics	16. crulty/cruelty
3. dangerous/dangrous	10. memory/memry	17. history/histry
4. defnite/definite	11. miniture/miniature	18. similar/simlar
5. diffrent/different	12. probly/probably	19. salary/salry
6. favorite/favrite	13. separate/seprate	20. accompny/accompany
7. genral/general	14. sevral/several	21. factory/factry

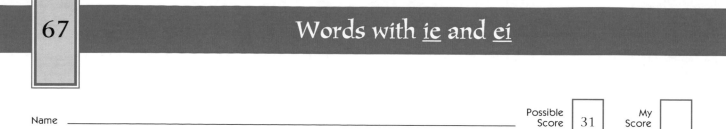

Name _____   Possible Score 31   My Score ☐

When the letters *e* and *i* occur together in a word, it's hard to know what order to put them in. Do you write *ie* or *ei*? The following rule expressed as a rhyme can help you decide which combination to use for a particular word. The symbol /ā/ stands for the "long a" sound in *able, pane, neighbor,* and *say*.

> **Use *i* before *e*, except after *c*,**
> **Or when sounded like /ā/,**
> **As in *neighbor* and *weigh*.**

Here are some examples of words that follow the rule, as well as three exceptions.

i before **e**	**ei** after **c**	**ei** for /ā/	exceptions
believe	ceiling	beige	efficient
chief	conceit	freight	height
friend	receive	vein	their

Practice 1

The following words are spelled correctly. Match each word with the description that fits the word.

a. *i* before *e*   c. *ei* for /ā/
b. *ei* after *c*   d. exception

_____ 1. cashier   _____ 6. mischief   _____ 11. seize

_____ 2. brief   _____ 7. neighborhood   12. series

_____ 3. deceive   _____ 8. receipt   _____ 13. species

_____ 4. foreign   _____ 9. reign   _____ 14. weight

_____ 5. leisure   _____ 10. relief   _____ 15. yield

Practice 2

Rewrite the following words, completing each by adding *ie* or *ei* according to the rule. There are no exceptions in this list.

1. ach—ve _____
2. conc—ve _____
3. dec—t _____
4. d—sel _____
5. f—rce _____
6. front—r _____
7. gr—ve _____
8. hyg—ne _____

9. perc—ve _____
10. p—ce _____
11. r—ns _____
12. rel—ve _____
13. rev—w _____
14. unv—l _____
15. windsh—ld _____
16. bel—f _____

Doubled Consonants before Suffixes

Name _____ Possible Score [26] My Score [ ]

Double the final consonant of a word before adding a suffix when *all three* of the following conditions are present:

1. The suffix you are adding begins with a vowel—for example: *-ing, -ed, -able, -er, -est,* and *-y.*
   forget + **ing** = forge**tt**ing

2. The word you are adding a suffix to ends in a single consonant preceded by a single vowel.
   begi**n** + ing =begi**nn**ing

3. The word has only one syllable, or the final syllable is stressed. This mark (´) indicates stress.
   pin + ed =pi**nn**ed   pre/**fér** + ed = prefe**rr**ed

Practice 1

Combine each word with the suffix indicated. Write each new word, using the three-part rule to decide whether you should double the final consonant before adding the suffix.

1. plan + ed   _____
2. remít + ance   _____
3. occúr + ed   _____
4. rob + cry   _____
5. compél + ing   _____
6. regrét + able   _____
7. sun + y   _____

8. refér + al   _____
9. propél + ing   _____
10. big + er   _____
11 jog + ing   _____
12. bag + age   _____
13. red + est   _____
14. drag + ed   _____

Practice 2

Combine each word with the suffix indicated. First, decide if all three conditions necessary for doubling consonants are present. Then, write the new words correctly.

1. meet + ing   _____
2. repel + ed   _____
3. exist + ence   _____
4. omit + ing   _____
5. commit + ment   _____
6. refer + ed   _____

7. drug + ist   _____
8. benefit + ed   _____
9. expel + ed   _____
10. regret + ful   _____
11. fun + y   _____
12. differ + ent   _____

Application

Name _____

Possible Score 23 My Score ☐

UNIT 4 Improving Spelling Skills

A. Rewrite each of the following words, adding a letter or letters wherever necessary.

1. sev—ral _____
2. ent—rance _____
3. disast—rous _____
4. drown—ed _____
5. fav—rite _____

6. math—matics _____
7. incident—ly _____
8. mini—ture _____
9. hung—ry _____
10. umb—rella _____

B. Write the word from the list that has a meaning similar to the word or words in bold type in each sentence below.

> brief   freight   deceive   yield   leisure

1. The railroad cars were at the dock to receive the **goods for transportation**. _____

2. An agreement was reached after each side agreed to **give up possession** of some of its demands. _____

3. Fortunately, we had only a **short** wait outside the theater in the bitter cold. _____

4. With a shorter workweek, many people will have some **free time** for hobbies. _____

5. The company's lawyer claimed that its advertising was not intended to **mislead** the public. _____

C. Read the paragraphs below. Then underline the correct spelling of each word in parentheses.

> Flag football as an alternative to touch football has become increasingly popular with both men and women. In this variety of football, the equivalent of tackling has (occured, occurred) when a player has removed the plastic streamers from the ballcarrier's belt.
>
> Flag football is often (prefered, preferred) for intramural programs. It is frequently played by those who like to participate in sports but who are not totally (commited, committed) to (wining, winning). In fact, players with enthusiasm but with (differing, differring) degrees of ability are welcomed.
>
> Players of flag football have (suffered, sufferred) fewer injuries from this variety of the game. Players are also (begining, beginning) to enjoy a (biger, bigger) part in an active sports program.

Name _____ Possible Score | 74 | My Score | |

Follow these rules when adding suffixes to most words that end in *e*:

1. If the suffix you are adding begins with a vowel, drop the final *e*.

   danc**e** + ing = dancing   sens**e** + ible = sensible   guid**e** + ance = guidance

2. If the suffix you are adding begins with a consonant, keep the final *e*.

   hop**e** + less = hop**e**less   extrem**e** + ly = extrem**e**ly   us**e** + ful = us**e**ful

3. If the word ends in *ce* or *ge*, keep the final *e* before *-able* or *-ous*.

   notic**e** + able = notic**e**able   courag**e** + ous = courag**e**ous

Here are some exceptions to the rules given above:

1. In spelling the following words, *keep* the final *e* before a suffix beginning with a vowel.

   dy**e** + ing = dy**e**ing   mil**e** + age = mil**e**age   ho**e** + ing = ho**e**ing

2. In spelling the following words, *drop* the final *e* before a suffix beginning with a consonant.

   argu**e** + ment = argument   aw**e** + ful = awful   whol**e** + ly = wholly

   judg**e** + ment = judgment   tru**e** + ly = truly   nin**e** + th = ninth

3. In spelling most words that end in *le*, drop the *le* before adding *-ly*.

   possibl**e** + ly = possibly   probabl**e** + ly = probably   doubl**e** + ly = doubly

4. In a few words that end in *ie*, drop the *e* and change the *i* to *y* befor adding *-ing*.

   l**ie** + ing = l**y**ing   d**ie** + ing = d**y**ing   t**ie** + ing = t**y**ing

Practice 1

Combine each word with the suffix indicated. There are no exceptions in this list.

1. advise + ed _____
2. difinite + ly _____
3. continue + ous _____
4. retire + ment _____
5. desire + able _____
6. chose + en _____
7. nine + ty _____
8. service + able _____
9. prepare + ation _____

10. separate + ly _____
11. value + able _____
12. change + able _____
13. nerve + ous _____
14. write + ing _____
15. expense + ive _____
16. like + ly _____
17. decide + ing _____
18. scene + ic _____

Practice 2

Combine each word with the suffix indicated. Indicate the seventeen exceptions in this list by drawing a circle around the number.

1. behave + ing _____
2. argue + ment _____

3. tune + ing _____
4. umpire + ing _____

UNIT 4   Improving Spelling Skills

5. charge + able   _____

6. pursue + ing   _____

7. tie + ing   _____

8. immediate + ly   _____

9. awe + ful   _____

10. probable + ly   _____

11. make + ing   _____

12. nine + th   _____

13. persuade + ed   _____

14. criticize + ed   _____

15. explore + er   _____

16. safe + ty   _____

17. manage + able   _____

18. enforce + able   _____

19. whole + ly   _____

20. peace + able   _____

21. judge + ment   _____

22. use + ing   _____

23. mile + age   _____

24. lose + er   _____

25. acquire + ed   _____

26. lie + ing   _____

27. possible + ly   _____

28. true + ly   _____

29. appropriate + ly   _____

30. outrage + ous   _____

31. unique + ly   _____

32. amaze + ment   _____

33. double + ly   _____

34. utilize + ation   _____

35. ache + ing   _____

36. universe + al   _____

37. erode + ed   _____

38. hostile + ity   _____

39. wise + ly   _____

40. achieve + ment   _____

41. die + ing   _____

42. live + ly   _____

43. endure + ance   _____

44. waste + ing   _____

45. advise + able   _____

46. please + ure   _____

47. dose + age   _____

48. effective + ly   _____

49. gesture + ed   _____

50. dye + ing   _____

51. contrive + ed   _____

52. hoe + ing   _____

53. fame + ous   _____

54. humble + ly   _____

55. baffle + ing   _____

56. use + ful   _____

Name _____ Possible Score [70] My Score [ ]

Follow these rules when adding suffixes to most words that end in *y*:

1. When the final *y* is preceded by a consonant, change the *y* to *i* before adding the suffix.

   wor**y** + ed = worr**i**ed   funn**y** + er = funn**i**er   read**y** + ness = read**i**ness

2. However, when the final *y* is preceded by a consonant and the suffix begins with *i*, leave the *y* unchanged.

   worr**y** + ing = worr**y**ing   fort**y** + ish = fort**y**ish

3. When the final *y* is preceded by a vowel, leave the *y* unchanged.

   rela**y** + ed = rela**y**ed   pla**y** + er = pla**y**er   enjo**y** + able = enjo**y**able

The rules above do not apply to the plurals of proper nouns or to nouns that add the possessive ending 's.

    the **Kellys**   the **baby's** blanket

In the following words, even though a vowel precedes the *y*, change the *y* to *i*.

    da**y** + ly = da**i**ly   ga**y** + ly = ga**i**ly

And in these words, the final *y* remains, even though a consonant precedes it.

    sh**y** + ly = sh**y**ly   sh**y** + ness = sh**y**ness

    sl**y** + ly = sl**y**ly   sl**y** + ness = sl**y**ness

Depending on its use in a sentence, the word *dry* has two different spellings when the suffix *-er* is added:

    We've had **drier** weather lately. [adjective]   This clothes **dryer** doesn't work. [noun]

Practice 1

Combine each word with the suffix indicated. There are no exceptions in this list.

1. early + est _____
2. hurry + ing _____
3. library + an _____
4. ready + ness _____
5. sorry + er _____
6. employ + able _____
7. study + ing _____
8. destroy + ed _____
9. empty + ness _____
10. company + es _____

11. annoy + ance _____
12. lucky + er _____
13. alley + s _____
14. ally + s _____
15. study + ed _____
16. convey + ance _____
17. rely + ance _____
18. busy + ness _____
19. try + ed _____
20. apology + es _____

UNIT 4 Improving Spelling Skills

Practice 2

Combine each word with the suffix indicated. Indicate the eleven exceptions in this list by drawing a circle around the number.

1. easy + ly _____
2. Toby + 's _____
3. cry + ed _____
4. mystery + ous _____
5. satisfy + ed _____
6. family + 's _____
7. lazy + est _____
8. anybody + 's _____
9. employ + er _____
10. country + es _____
11. justify + ed _____
12. Murphy + s _____
13. gloomy + ly _____
14. qualify + ed _____
15. baby + es _____
16. employ + ment _____
17. convey + s _____
18. try + es _____
19. decoy + s _____
20. dry + ness _____
21. Brady + s _____
22. lovely + ness _____
23. hurry + ed _____
24. monkey + s _____
25. pay + able _____

26. qualify + ing _____
27. necessary + ly _____
28. satisfy + ing _____
29. Kennedy + s _____
30. acccuracy + es _____
31. day + ly _____
32. lonely + ness _____
33. shy + ness _____
34. apply + ance _____
35. lady + 's _____
36. weary + ly _____
37. comply + ance _____
38. busy + ly _____
39. identify + es _____
40. journey + ed _____
41. Ronny + 's _____
42. terrify + ing _____
43. dismay + ed _____
44. happy + er _____
45. sly + ly _____
46. carry + ing _____
47. delay + ed _____
48. lady + es _____
49. deny + al _____
50. survey + s _____

Suffixes after Final <u>c</u>

Name _____

Possible Score | 32 | My Score |

UNIT 4 Improving Spelling Skills

The letter *c* usually represents an /s/ sound when it comes before the letters *i* and *e*, as in exer**ci**se and **ce**llar. When the letter *c* represents a /k/ sound before a suffix beginning with *i* or *e*, you must add the letter *k* after the *c* to indicate the /k/ pronunciation.

> picni**c** + **k** + **i**ng = picni**cki**ng /k/   shella**c** + **k** + **e**d = shella**cke**d /k/

Of course, when the letter *c* represents the /s/ sound before a suffix beginning with *i* or *e*, you do not add a *k*.

> criti**c** + **i**ze =criti**ci**ze /s/   fanati**c** + **i**sm = fanati**ci**sm /s/

If a letter other than *i* or *e* begins the suffix, no spelling change is needed to indicate that the letter *c* represents the /k/ sound.

> histori**c** + **a**l = histori**cal** /k/   economi**c** + **s** = economi**cs** /k/

Practice

Combine each word with the suffix indicated, saying each new word to yourself. Then write each new word, adding a *k* if it is needed.

1. mimic + ing _____
2. domestic + ate _____
3. critic + al _____
4. frolic + ed _____
5. tactic + s _____
6. basic + ally _____
7. panic + ing _____
8. electric + al _____
9. critic + ism _____
10. classic + al _____
11. traffic + ing _____
12. analytic + al _____
13. panic + ed _____
14. frolic + some _____
15. topic + al _____
16. elastic + ity _____

17. traffic + ed _____
18. politic + al _____
19. shellac + ing _____
20. politic + ize _____
21. picnic + ed _____
22. frolic + ing _____
23. symmetric + al _____
24. mimic + ed _____
25. critic + ize _____
26. fanatic + ism _____
27. drastic + ally _____
28. mechanic + al _____
29. civic + s _____
30. cynic + ism _____
31. frantic + ally _____
32. comic + al _____

Words with Prefixes

UNIT 4   Improving Spelling Skills

Name _____   Possible Score | 20 | My Score | ☐

When you add a prefix to a word, you usually make no change in the spelling of the prefix or in the spelling of the word.

anti + freeze = antifreeze   un + aware = unaware   dis + regard = disregard

Even when the last letter of a prefix and the first letter of a word are the same, the resulting double letters are used in the new word.

su**b** + **b**asement = su**bb**asement   i**l** + **l**ogical = i**ll**ogical   mi**s** + **s**pell = mi**ss**pell

i**m** + **m**oral = i**mm**oral   tran**s** + **s**hip = tran**ss**hip   i**r** + **r**egular = i**rr**egular

Sometimes, the double letter is a vowel, as in *re* + *elect*. In such a case, you may find the new word spelled *reelect* or *re-elect*. Because there may be alternative spellings for a word like *reelect*, you should check your dictionary and use the spelling recommended by your teacher.

Occasionally, you will need to use a hyphen after a prefix to distinguish a word you want to use from another word with an identical spelling but with an entirely different meaning.

recollect [to remember]

re-collect [to collect again]

Always use a hyphen to join a prefix to a proper noun or to a proper adjective.

mid-Atlantic   pre-Islamic   inter-American

Finally, use a hyphen to join the prefix *self-* to a word.

self-disciplined   self-esteem   self-supporting

Practice

Combine each prefix with the word indicated. Write each new word, making any change necessary to spell it correctly.

1. dis + appear   _____

2. mid + point   _____

3. un + natural   _____

4. in + capable   _____

5. pre + Incan   _____

6. sub + zero   _____

7. inter + act   _____

8. in + exact   _____

9. non + toxic   _____

10. ir + regular   _____

11. in + justice   _____

12. self + rule   _____

13. anti + smog   _____

14. re + commend   _____

15. in + secure   _____

16. un + usual   _____

17. self + made   _____

18. im + balance   _____

19. re + cover (cover again) _____

20. in + active   _____

Application

UNIT 4 Improving Spelling Skills

Name _____   Possible Score | 42 | My Score | |

A. Each of the words in the following list is spelled correctly. Choose one that has a meaning similar to the word or words in bold type in each of the numbered sentences.

antiwar	disagree	illegal	nervous	re-signed
basically	dying	illiterate	panicked	ridiculous
bicentennial	expensive	immature	picnicking	self-respect
chosen	extremely	improvement	political	semiannually
continuous	fanaticism	irrelevant	pre-Columbian	semicircle
courageous	frolicked	mimicking	prepackaged	shellacked
criticism	hopeless	misstated	resigned	trafficked

1. Jeff and Don look **absurd** in those costumes. _____

2. Lynn and Dave were **selected** by the committee members. _____

3. Three **brave** teenagers rescued the child from the burning building. _____

4. The African violets and the English ivy are **barely alive**. _____

5. Rich has shown **increased skill** in his typing. _____

6. People who are **easily excited or upset** usually dislike speaking in public. _____

7. That radio station plays **uninterrupted** music. _____

8. This pair of boots was quite **costly**. _____

9. The weather the past three winters has been **very** bad. _____

10. The situation in which they found themselves was **without hope**. _____

11. Ms. Sapolski encouraged us to use constructive **evaluation and analysis** when we discussed our reports.

_____

12. After the table had been sanded, it was **coated with shellac.** _____

13. Mr. LeFevre was pleased at our **precisely imitating** his pronunciation in French class. _____

14. Heavily **traveled** roads must be cleared of parked cars during rush hours. _____

15. At recess, the children **played and ran happily**. _____

16. Although the pilot had to make an emergency landing, no one **became suddenly and**

overpoweringly frightened. _____

17. The students agreed that Svetlana's plan was **fundamentally** sound. _____

18. Sue has always been interested in anything **relating to the conduct of government**. _____

19. Mary was disturbed by the speaker's **excessive, uncritical enthusiasm**. _____

20. Our family enjoys **eating outdoors** during the hot summer months. _____

21. People who are **unable to read or write** will not be considered for the job. _____

22. Paul asked, "Is it **unlawful** to change lanes without signaling?" _____

23. One should have **respect for oneself as a human being**. _____

24. Because commuting took three hours a day, Jody finally **quit her job**. _____

25. Your presentation of the lawyer's viewpoint was **not accurately expressed**. _____

26. The United States observed its **two-hundredth anniversary** in 1976. _____

27. Since no witnesses were present the first time, the will had to be **signed again**. _____

28. Do you object to buying fruit that is **packaged before being offered for sale?** _____

29. Mark suggested that club elections be held **twice a year**. _____

30. The judge ruled that the lawyer's interruption was **not relating to the matter at hand**. _____

31. Claire and Andy remain friends even though they **differ in opinion** about politics. _____

32. As the music began, the square dancers joined hands and formed a **half circle**. _____

33. The guide didn't know when the jewelry was made, but she thought it was **before the time of**

    Christopher Columbus. _____

34. "In foreign policy," said the candidate, "I am firmly **against armed conflict**." _____

35. Shrubs that are **not fully grown or developed** must be protected against the cold. _____

B. There are seven misspellings of words with suffixes in the paragraphs below. Underline the misspelled words. Then write the words correctly on the lines beneath the paragraphs.

> The koala, which looks like a toy teddy bear, was first identifyed by explorers as a bear. However, it is a marsupial, that is, a mammal with a pouch for carrying its young.
>
> Koala babys are not developed enough at birth to live outside the mother's pouch, often staying inside the pouch for about six months.
>
> The koala lives in the tops of a few varietys of eucalyptus trees, easyly satisfying its hunger with young eucalyptus leaves and buds. The koala relys solely on this limited diet and seldom drinks water. It is a sluggish animal, sleeping lazyly during the day and moving in an unhurryed way from one eucalyptus tree to another.

1. _____   5. _____

2. _____   6. _____

3. _____   7. _____

4. _____

Noun Plurals

Name _____

Possible Score | 66 | My Score |

You can write the plural of most nouns by simply adding *-s*.

island + **s** = island**s**   muscle + **s** = muscle**s**   Smith + **s** = Smith**s**

Add *-es* to form the plural of nouns that end in *s, sh, ch, x,* and *z*.

campus + **es** = campus**es**   brush + **es** = brush**es**   Rodriguez + **es** = Rodriguez**es**

There are special rules for forming the plural of nouns ending in *y* and nouns ending in *o*. Add *-s* to nouns that end in *y* following a vowel.

survey + **s** = survey**s**   holiday + **s** = holiday**s**

For nouns that end in *y* following a consonant, change the *y* to *i* and add *-es*.

liberty + **es** = libert**ies**   diary + **es** = diar**ies**

Add *-s* to nouns that end in *o* following a vowel.

ratio + **s** = ratio**s**   rodeo + **s** = rodeo**s**   studio + **s** = studio**s**

Add *-s* to most nouns that end in *o* following a consonant. Such nouns include many musical terms.

alto + **s** = alto**s**   piano + **s** = piano**s**   Eskimo + **s** = Eskimo**s**
cello + **s** = cello**s**   soprano + **s** = soprano**s**   poncho + **s** = poncho**s**

For a few nouns that end in *o* following a consonant, add *-es*.

echo + **es** − echo**es**   tomato + **es** = tomato**es**   hero + **es** = hero**es**
veto + **es** = veto**es**   potato + **es** = potato**es**   lingo + **es** = lingo**es**

You may add either *-s* or *-es* to spell the plural of a few nouns that end in *o* following a consonant, like *tornado, banjo, cargo, zero,* and *mosquito*. Check your dictionary for the spellings of such nouns.

Practice 1

Each of the following nouns forms its plural by adding *-s* or *-es*. Write the plural of each noun.

1. coach _____   8. topaz _____

2. García _____   9. batch _____

3. garage _____   10. finch _____

4. trouble _____   11. specimen _____

5. dress _____   12. sneeze _____

6. magazine _____   13. box _____

7. tax _____   14. brush _____

UNIT 4   Improving Spelling Skills

15. judge _____

16. opinion _____

17. bonus _____

18. choice _____

19. nickel _____

20. crash _____

Practice 2

Write the plural of each noun below. Make any changes necessary to form the plural correctly.

1. cello _____

2. journey _____

3. radio _____

4. veto _____

5. pulley _____

6. earthquake _____

7. grocery _____

8. poncho _____

9. emergency _____

10. dish _____

11. Eskimo _____

12. barnacle _____

13. tomato _____

14. piano _____

15. inch _____

16. activity _____

17. chimney _____

18. shoe _____

19. address _____

20. potato _____

21. tendency _____

22. guest _____

23. atom _____

24. studio _____

25. industry _____

26. ability _____

27. guess _____

28. idea _____

29. Tanaka _____

30. buzz _____

31. search _____

32. axle _____

33. bench _____

34. hoax _____

35. chance _____

36. butterfly _____

37. colony _____

38. clock _____

39. beach _____

40. hero _____

41. computer _____

42. copy _____

43. monkey _____

44. flashlight _____

45. decoy _____

46. soprano _____

Name _____ Possible Score [20] My Score [ ]

Add -s to form the plural of most nouns that end in *f* and *fe*.

belief + **s** = belie**fs**	gulf + **s** = gul**fs**	chief + **s** = chie**fs**
proof + **s** = proo**fs**	roof + **s** = roo**fs**	safe + **s** = safe**s**
bluff + **s** = bluf**fs**	cliff + **s** = clif**fs**	giraffe + **s** = giraffe**s**

For a few nouns that end in *f* and *fe*, change the *f* or *fe* to *v* and add -*es*.

self + **es** = sel**ves**	loaf + **es** = loa**ves**	thief + **es** = thie**ves**
half + **es** = hal**ves**	leaf + **es** = lea**ves**	wife + **es** = wi**ves**
wolf + **es** = wol**ves**	calf + **es** = cal**ves**	knife + **es** = kni**ves**
shelf + **es** = shel**ves**	elf + **es** = el**ves**	life + **es** = li**ves**

A few nouns have irregular plurals. To form these plurals, you must make an internal spelling change or add an ending other than -*s* or -*es*.

wom**a**n—wom**e**n	t**oo**th—t**ee**th	m**ou**se—m**i**ce	ox—ox**en**
m**a**n—m**e**n	f**oo**t—f**ee**t	g**oo**se—g**ee**se	child—child**ren**

Some nouns have the same form for singular and plural. Note, for example, these names of animals and national groups.

sheep	moose	Chinese	Swiss	Spanish
swine	trout	Sioux	French	Japanese

Practice

Write the plural of each word below. Make any changes necessary to form the plural correctly.

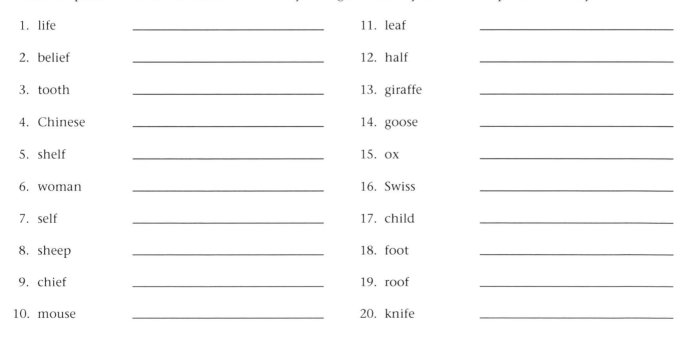

1. life _____
2. belief _____
3. tooth _____
4. Chinese _____
5. shelf _____
6. woman _____
7. self _____
8. sheep _____
9. chief _____
10. mouse _____

11. leaf _____
12. half _____
13. giraffe _____
14. goose _____
15. ox _____
16. Swiss _____
17. child _____
18. foot _____
19. roof _____
20. knife _____

Application

Name _____

Possible Score | 32 | My Score | |

Each of the following sentences has two or more singular words in parentheses. On the line beneath each sentence, write the plural forms of these words.

1. The (Ontiveroz) are growing their own (tomato) in the backyard this summer.

   _____

2. (Knife) and (poncho) are essential equipment for serious (backpacker).

   _____

3. On Wednesday night, the (man) of the square-dance group are preparing dinner for the (woman).

   _____

4. Dave announced, "My favorite (kind) of fruit are (peach) and (strawberry)."

   _____

5. Elsa and Justine enjoy (magazine) with science-fiction (story).

   _____

6. Growing (pumpkin) is just one of Jamie Kirkpatrick's (hobby).

   _____

7. Special memorial services will be observed in the (church) and in the (synagogue) next week.

   _____

8. Environmentalists insist that (wolf) as well as (sheep) are important in preserving the balance of nature.

   _____

9. Last week the union (leader) made several (speech) about current (wage).

   _____

10. The (Sioux) are sending a representative to Washington to discuss educational (policy).

    _____

11. The (child) in that tour group enjoyed watching the (monkey) more than the (moose).

    _____

12. In late September, the (leaf) on the willow (tree) began to turn yellow.

    _____

13. "Do you know whether (mouse) have sharp (tooth)?" asked Wendy.

    _____

14. The (geologist) took two (survey) of the area before they found the type of rock they were looking for.

Name _____   Possible Score `38`   My Score [ ]

Your means "belonging to you." *You're* is the contraction of *you are*.

> I hope **your** sore throat is better soon.
> I hope **you're** feeling better today.

Its means "belonging to it." *It's* is a contraction of *it is* or *it has*.

> Indonesia gained **its** independence in 1949.
> **It's** good to see you again. [it is]
> **It's** been a long time. [it has]

Whose means "belonging to whom." *Who's* is a contraction of *who is* or *who has*.

> **Whose** pen is this?
> **Who's** there? [who is]
> **Who's** been using my radio? [who has]

Their means "belonging to them." *There* may mean "at that place," or it may function as a sentence opener when the real subject follows the verb. *They're* is the contraction of *they are*.

> Anne and Jeff left **their** bikes in the garage.
> The baking dishes are over **there** by the cabinet.
> **There** was a telephone call for you last night.
> The band members are ready; **they're** waiting for you.

Practice

Underline the word in parentheses that correctly completes each of the following sentences.

1. (Their, There, They're) is probably a perfectly natural explanation.

2. "(Its, It's) a pleasure to see you again," said Ms. Wyatt.

3. The committee submitted (its, it's) report today.

4. I hope (their, there, they're) bus won't be late.

5. Jay hopes (their, there, they're) on time tomorrow.

6. Do you know (whose, who's) coming to the party this evening?

7. If (your, you're) going to the library, would you return my books?

8. (Whose, Who's) roller blades are in the closet?

9. (Your, You're) aquarium has many interesting saltwater fish.

10. (Their, There, They're) toy collie's name is Shep.

11. (Whose, Who's) stereo was playing so loudly last night?

12. (Your, You're) rent check was due last Thursday.

13. (Its, It's) getting too dark to play tennis.

14. Don saw a redheaded woodpecker over (their, there, they're).

15. Where did they dock (their, there, they're) boat?

16. (Whose, Who's) seen my bicycle key?

17. (Your, You're) the one who signed that shipping order.

18. That blackbird has hurt (its, it's) wing.

19. (Their, There, They're) bowling scores were quite high.

20. Brooke told me that (your, you're) planning to become a social worker.

21. She is the one (whose, who's) learning to play the violin.

22. The buffalo cares for (its, it's) young until they are about three years old.

23. (Their, There, They're) are twenty chemical engineers working at the factory.

24. (Whose, Who's) the new swimming instructor at the Deerfield Park District pool?

25. Cassie says that (its, it's) easy to jog five miles.

26. I haven't seen (your, you're) Siamese cat yet.

27. (Their, There, They're) wasn't any fruit left in the refrigerator.

28. (Whose, Who's) taken that course in marine biology?

29. (Their, There, They're) apartment is on the west side of Chicago.

30. Why don't you try waterskiing? (Its, It's) not as difficult as you think.

31. Is (your, you're) car parked in the Skokie Swift parking lot?

32. (Whose, Who's) sunglasses and sun visor are these?

33. The new seafood restaurant is over (their, there, they're) near the pier.

34. (Their, There, They're) going to open a joint savings account.

35. I'd like to know (whose, who's) been eating these sandwiches.

36. (Its, It's) leaves are broad and glossy.

37. (Its, It's) taken us several weeks to learn the latest dance steps.

38. Ask them if (their, there, they're) going to the movie with us.

Name _____ Possible Score | 29 | My Score | |

Compliment means "something good said about a person" or "to say something good." *Complement* means "something that completes" or "to complete."

> The speaker paid a **compliment** to her host.
> Did he **compliment** you on your work?

> Exercise is a necessary **complement** to a proper diet.
> In team teaching, the work of one teacher **complements** the work of the other.

All ready is a phrase meaning "completely ready." *Already* is a single word meaning "before a given time."

> Susana was **all ready** by lunchtime.
> They were **already** finished by lunchtime.

All together is a phrase that means "everyone together." *Altogether* is a single word that means "in all" or "wholly."

> The guests are **all together** in the main dining room.
> **Altogether**, there were twelve men and nine women.

Principal can be a noun meaning "a head person" or an adjective meaning "most important." *Principle* means "a rule or a code of conduct." Think of the letters *le*, which end both *princip**le*** and *ru**le***.

> The **principal** of our school plays the drums. [noun]
> Our **principal** reason for coming was to see you. [adjective]
> The **principle** underlying this activity is not clear.

Passed is the past-tense form of *pass*. The *-ed* ending signals that it is a verb form. *Past* can function as a noun, a preposition, or an adjective, depending on its use in a specific sentence.

> Joe **passed** his chemistry exam.
> Grandmother likes to tell us about the **past**. [noun]
> We drove **past** the new town hall today. [preposition]
> Sam has studied guitar for the **past** month. [adjective]

Practice

Underline the word in parentheses that correctly completes each of the following sentences.

1. Dad just (passed, past) the turnoff by mistake.

2. I think Eileen has (all ready, already) eaten dinner.

3. Timothy thinks that Jeanette's sense of humor (compliments, complements) her serious attitude toward studying.

4. (All together, Altogether), about thirty people couldn't get tickets.

5. For the (passed, past) semester, Lynn has been taking Russian as an elective.

6. Irving was pleased to receive a (compliment, complement) from his teacher.

7. (All together, Altogether), ten seals are sunning themselves on the rocks.

8. Both candidates were known to the community members as people of high ideals and firm (principals, principles).

9. They were (all together, altogether) in the judge's chambers.

10. The (principal, principle) of Oakton High School hopes to become a superintendent of schools next year.

11. The (principals, principles) of geometry are not difficult to understand.

12. The museum curator was (all ready, already) to attend the staff meeting.

13. They have (all ready, already) finished the new exhibit.

14. Those earrings (complement, compliment) your outfit.

15. In the (passed, past), sewage-treatment systems were less efficient.

16. The president of the club (complemented, complimented) the speaker on her excellent organization and presentation of the facts.

17. Their (principal, principle) concern was the investment of club funds.

18. Some people are embarrassed by (complements, compliments).

19. The players were (all ready, already) to begin the match.

20. (All together, Altogether) she has saved three hundred dollars.

21. During the (passed, past) weeks, the weather has been unusually cool and rainy.

22. We have (all ready, already) barbecued the chicken.

23. The team members were (all together, altogether) in the locker room.

24. They walked (passed, past) the doctor's office.

25. Our vacation time (passed, past) much too quickly.

26. Many people think that brown rice (compliments, complements) fish.

27. The textbook writers and the novelists were seated (all together, altogether) in one section of the auditorium.

28. The actors are (all ready, already) to begin rehearsing.

29. The tour group (passed, past) Tokyo's Imperial Palace.

Name _____

Possible Score | 33 | My Score | [ ]

Accept is a verb that means "to receive." *Except* is a preposition that means "excluding" or "leaving out."

Carmen will **accept** the award for the team.

All the books **except** those in boxes were damaged.

Thorough has two syllables. It is a modifier meaning "complete," "careful," or "detailed." *Through* has one syllable and rhymes with *blue*. It may indicate passage from one end of something to the other, or it may mean "finished."

Dr. Fong recommended that she have a **thorough** physical examination.

The nail went completely **through** the board.

We are finally **through** with that committee work.

Proceed means "to go forward" or "to continue." *Precede* means "to go in front of" or "to come before."

Proceed with your work; don't let me bother you.

The luncheon will **precede** the presentation of the awards.

Formerly means "previously" or "in earlier times." *Formally* means "in a formal, dignified manner."

Formerly, only seniors could take consumer education.

Ms. Gómez dressed **formally** for the dinner party.

Advice is a noun that rhymes with *precise*. It means "an opinion about what should be done." *Advise* is a verb that rhymes with *despise*. It means "to give advice to."

I wish I has some good **advice** for you.

Carl didn't **advise** me to take these courses.

Practice

Underline the word in parentheses that correctly completes each of the following sentences.

1. With only one lane open, traffic (preceded, proceeded) slowly across the bridge.

2. Veasna ate everything (accept, except) the dessert.

3. Our physical-education program was (formally, formerly) smaller than it is now.

4. Dee's (advice, advise) was to review the material carefully.

5. The driver of the pickup was stopped for going (thorough, through) a red light.

6. The seniors will (precede, proceed) the other classes marching into the gym.

7. The detective made a (thorough, through) search of the room for fingerprints.

8. Did the scientist (accept, except) the responsibility for the testing error?

9. Jo did (thorough, through) research before presenting her argument to the committee.

10. The invention of the riding plow (preceded, proceeded) the invention of the car.

11. You must dress (formally, formerly) for the prom.

12. The dolphin jumped (thorough, through) the hoop.

13. All of the dancers (accept, except) that one are wearing red headdresses.

14. Tom did not follow her (advice, advise).

15. They are (thorough, through) with their report.

16. Does that train pass (thorough, through) Death Valley?

17. The moderator suggested that we (precede, proceed) with the debate.

18. The Robinsons were (formally, formerly) residents of Davenport, Iowa.

19. We were (adviced, advised) to buy a Yorkshire terrier rather than a Great Dane.

20. Benita avoids giving unwanted (advice, advise).

21. All of the plays (accept, except) the last were comedies.

22. The use of chemotherapy in treating infectious diseases (preceded, proceeded) the discovery of insulin.

23. The Severskys dressed (formally, formerly) for the wedding.

24. Dr. Van Ness gave a (thorough, through) lecture on the properties of detergent.

25. Did Rosa Álvarez (accept, except) her party's nomination?

26. (Precede, Proceed) down the hall in single file.

27. We are almost (thorough, through) with our homework.

28. Hexachlorophene was (formally, formerly) used in deodorants and antiperspirants.

29. All of the campsites (accept, except) that one have been taken.

30. The school children walked (thorough, through) the factory, looking at everything and asking many questions.

31. The labor organizer (preceded, proceeded) with her speech.

32. The drugstore owner would not (accept, except) my check.

33. She was (formally, formerly) a landscape architect.

Name _____

Possible Score | 29 | My Score | [ ]

Personal means "relating or belonging to a person." *Personnel* means "a group of people," often "employees."

> These are my **personal** papers.
>
> All interviews are held at the **personnel** office.

Allusion means "an indirect reference." *Illusion* means "something that misleads or deceives."

> Did anyone understand the **allusion** to the book *Catch 22?*
>
> The fog gave the **illusion** that the road led right into the river.

Conscience is a noun that means "a sense of right and wrong." *Conscious* is an adjective that means "aware" or "awake."

> Dave's **conscience** made him stay to help the others.
>
> Sue was **conscious** of the change in Janie's attitude.
>
> Alan was stunned by the blow but still **conscious**.

Later means "after the usual time." *Latter* means "the second of two things mentioned."

> Should I take the earlier train or the **later** one?
>
> Glue or tape will do; the **latter** is easier to use.

Moral means "relating to ideas of right or wrong" or "conforming to a standard of right behavior." *Morale* means "the sense of well-being of a person or a group."

> Steve felt a **moral** obligation to help, although he had no legal responsibility toward them.
>
> The team's **morale** improved after the coach's talk.

Practice

Underline the word in parentheses that correctly completes each of the following sentences.

1. This essay is difficult to understand because there are so many (allusions, illusions) to literary figures.

2. All the tickets were sold (later, latter).

3. (Moral, Morale) has been low since Mr. Morelli resigned.

4. The new (personnel, personal) policy came as a surprise to many employees.

5. Having a local rather than a general anesthetic enabled Adrienne to remain (conscience, conscious) while the dentist pulled her tooth.

6. The hot air over the pavement created the (allusion, illusion) of a pool of water.

7. Your questions are much too (personal, personnel).

8. They adopted the most (moral, morale) course of action possible in the situation.

9. All (personal, personnel) will be expected to attend the company dinner.

10. You can take the old highway or the new bypass through the mountain; the (later, latter) is fifteen minutes faster.

11. The (allusion, illusion) to her finances made her uncomfortable.

12. A mirror, a piece of glass, and some tiny white lights had been used to create an interesting optical (allusion, illusion).

13. We will attend the career conference (later, latter).

14. The (personal, personnel) manager will begin interviewing for the job at 9 A.M.

15. The cultural building and the palace date from the 1700s. The (later, latter) is surrounded by hundreds of beautiful fountains.

16. Sofía was barely (conscience, conscious) after the car accident.

17. That book contains many historical (allusions, illusions).

18. After John cheated on the exam, his (conscience, conscious) began to bother him.

19. The drawing creates the (allusion, illusion) that this line is longer than that line.

20. The information in the folder is quite (personal, personnel).

21. The writer made many (allusions, illusions) to her early life.

22. Excessive gossip had weakened (moral, morale) to the point that the workers were unwilling to trust one another.

23. Ms. Gonzalez owns a car and a van; she drives the (later, latter) more frequently.

24. He carried his (personal, personnel) belongings in a small suitcase.

25. His (moral, morale) improved as he began to regain his health.

26. Won't you join us for dinner (later, latter)?

27. We were not (conscience, conscious) of the demands the job had placed upon him.

28. Mr. Gianapolos told Laurie, "Let your (conscience, conscious) guide you in making the decision."

29. The manager's irresponsible behavior filled them with (moral, morale) indignation.

Application

Name _____

Possible Score 49   My Score ☐

Underline the word in parentheses that correctly completes each of the following sentences.

1. (Its, It's) almost time for the concert to begin.

2. The mayor made many (allusions, illusions) to the policies of her predecessor.

3. By the time we got to the car, the rain had (all ready, already) stopped.

4. The astronauts received (thorough, through) instructions.

5. Shelly is studying the (principals, principles) of astronomy.

6. Bernie has been watching that show every night for the (passed, past) week.

7. All (personal, personnel) received notification of the new sick-day policy.

8. The cat refused to eat (its, it's) food.

9. Both the telephone and the phonograph were invented in the late 1800s; the (later, latter) was invented in 1877.

10. The researchers are (all together, altogether) in the laboratory.

11. In the (passed, past), roller skates worn outdoors usually had steel wheels.

12. The messenger will deliver the advertisements (later, latter) this afternoon.

13. I hope (your, you're) coming with us.

14. Their (principal, principle) aim was to make sure the children were safe.

15. Did Marie (accept, except) the responsibility?

16. The seaweed soup (complemented, complimented) the main course.

17. Jason was (thorough, through) with the exam an hour ago.

18. The (principal, principle) of our school is organizing a work-study program.

19. (Your, You're) new ski jacket looks warm.

20. (Precede, Proceed) into the garden; the ceremony is about to begin.

21. Jake is embarrassed whenever someone pays him a (compliment, complement).

22. We walked right (passed, past) the drugstore.

23. The (advice, advise) they gave you was sound.

24. (Whose, Who's) notebook is this?

25. Everyone (accept, except) Dee enjoyed the tour of Rome.

26. Deciding what we can afford is (all together, altogether) a different problem.

27. The basketball player threw the ball (thorough, through) the hoop.

28. I can't (advice, advise) you what to do.

29. (Whose, Who's) seen my sunglasses?

30. Juanita (preceded, proceeded) Paul as president of the chemistry club.

31. The construction workers were (all ready, already) to begin paving the road.

32. They (passed, past) the civic center on the way to the theater.

33. The board members dressed (formally, formerly) for the ceremony.

34. This notebook is my (personal, personnel) property; don't touch it.

35. A mirrored wall often creates the (allusion, illusion) of more space.

36. (Their, There, They're) are a hammer and some nails behind the furnace.

37. She felt a (moral, morale) obligation to find the missing jewelry.

38. Beth wants to know if (your, you're) going to lend us the TV.

39. Alejandro was not (conscience, conscious) of the problems his proposal presented.

40. (Its, It's) nearly five o'clock.

41. Vanessa was weak but (conscience, conscious).

42. Their (principal, principle) aim was to gain equal pay for equal work.

43. (Moral, Morale) fell when the project director announced her resignation.

44. She was (all ready, already) to leave at noon.

45. (Their, There, They're) not planning to take a vacation this summer.

46. His (conscience, conscious) would not permit him to take the money.

47. (Their, There, They're) apartment was painted yesterday.

48. Gary and Kathy want to go to Knott's Berry Farm (later, latter).

49. Employee (moral, morale) was much better than it had been a month before.

Name _____

Underline the word or phrase in parentheses that correctly completes each of the following sentences.

1. By predicting earthquakes, geologists can prevent (disasterous, disastrous) loss of life.

2. Meet us at the main (enterance, entrance) at two o'clock.

3. After a month, Bob decided that the new job was not very (different, diffrent) from the old one.

4. There is an (elementary, elementry) school on the corner of Oglesby Avenue and Sixth Street.

5. (Releif, Relief) organizations are sending food and medicine to the flood victims.

6. Since she wrote last month, Carol should (receive, recieve) news of her job application soon.

7. They seem quite (conceited, concieted).

8. The (neighbors, nieghbors) were upset by the noisy crowd that attended the concert.

9. The workers (confered, conferred) with the grievance committee about the new parking restrictions.

10. Felix felt a (commitment, committment) to plan the exhibit.

11. You have (omited, omitted) the answer to the fifth question.

12. We hadn't (planed, planned) to drive all the way to Chicago.

13. They keep (forgeting, forgetting) to bring enough money for lunch.

14. Ms. Plunkett is the new (guidance, guideance) counselor at our school.

15. Nancy and Erich were (extremely, extremly) tired after volunteering at the hospital all day.

16. This blend of cotton and wool is especially (servicable, serviceable) for work clothes.

17. The (courageous, couragous) girls piloted the boat to safety.

18. Because no one thought we could succeed, we worked (doublely, doubly) hard.

19. Mrs. Thorndike moved (easily, easly) into the new routine of working two jobs.

20. You are (luckier, luckyer) than you think.

21. Does Mara have the (daily, dayly) paper delivered to her office?

22. That (familie's, family's) camper is parked near the creek.

23. Foxes are known for their cunning and (sliness, slyness).

24. (Shellacing, Shellacking) and sanding the old chair four times gave it a smooth finish.

25. The entire class (picniced, picnicked) in Harms Woods.

26. Arden is majoring in (political, politickal) science.

27. I don't approve of your (tacticks, tactics), but you certainly have done an excellent job.

28. The (iregular, irregular) pattern of the wallpaper made Doug feel dizzy whenever he looked at it.

29. The Fitzpatricks asked the realtor whether the house had a (subasement, subbasement).

30. Have they (discovered, disscovered) a secret panel?

31. Those diplomats recently signed an important (interAmerican, inter-American) trade agreement.

32. Naomi is taking an accelerated program so that she can be (selfsupporting, self-supporting) by next year.

33. The (taxes, taxs) and assessments amount to $250 a month.

34. The (monkeys, monkies) in the cage chattered noisily when the zoo keeper brought them their food.

35. The Kaplan Community Center provides various athletic and social (activities, activitys) for children, teenagers, and adults.

36. Sally has entered the bareback-riding competition in several (rodeoes, rodeos).

37. (Potatoes, Potatos) grow best in the northern and western portions of the United States.

38. The (cliffs, clives) rose sharply from the valley floor.

39. Air pollution regulations now prohibit the burning of (leafs, leaves) in most urban areas.

40. Two (mans, men) have recently joined our investment club.

41. I don't think (its, it's) a good idea to hike through the woods alone, Ted.

42. (Their, There, They're) were thousands of people at the lakefront festival on Sunday.

43. No one knows yet (who's, whose) going to handle the travel arrangements for the group.

44. We (complemented, complimented) the account executives on the successful advertising campaign.

45. Is Mannie (all ready, already) to take the math test?

46. The time (passed, past) quickly once Anna's friends arrived to keep her company.

47. Shandra checked everything in the car (accept, except) the fluid in the windshield-washer tank.

48. The new mayor of Edgewood was (formally, formerly) an architect specializing in city planning.

49. The (personal, personnel) gathered in the company cafeteria to discuss the new bonus plan.

50. This novel contains many (allusions, illusions) to recent social and political trends in Africa.

Name _____   Number Correct × 5 = ☐

Each numbered sentence contains an underlined word. Select the correct definition for the underlined word from choices *A,B*, or *C* and circle the letter of your choice.

1. Since Mozart played his first concert at age five, it's not surprising that many considered him a <u>virtuoso</u> when he reached adulthood.
   A. a highly skilled musician   C. a musical prodigy
   B. an amateur musician

2. Jim is one of those <u>laconic</u> cowboy types—you practically have to hold a gun to his head before he'll say anything.
   A. talkative   C. fond of the outdoors
   B. using few words

3. The boss gave a <u>succinct</u> reply to my request for a raise: "No!"
   A. complicated and wordy   C. brief and clear
   B. lengthy and confusing

4. The principal <u>reproached</u> the student council, expressing her disapproval of how it had handled the class elections.
   A. praised and congratulated   C. came up to again
   B. criticized

5. Although the brokers were joking among themselves in the morning, there was a <u>dearth</u> of humor in the afternoon when word of the stock-market crash came over the ticker tape.
   A. an absence or scarcity   C. a moderate amount
   B. an abundance

6. Mary was <u>dejected</u> about having to postpone her wedding, but she cheered up considerably when her mother found another hall where they could hold the reception.
   A. extremely angry   C. depressed, in a low mood
   B. secretly glad

7. The value of that stock <u>fluctuates</u> widely—for example, it was worth $35.42 on Monday, $31.13 on Wednesday, and $46.75 today.
   A. remains stable   C. increases greatly
   B. shifts back and forth

8. Old man Tucker will often <u>digress</u>, or ramble, if you ask him about his experiences during the thirties.
   A. tell just the relevant facts   C. stray from the main point
   B. exaggerate, boast

9. When the tear-gas grenade went off, the crowd <u>dissipated.</u>
   A. scattered, broke up
   B. was extravagant in pursuit of pleasure
   C. used up foolishly

10. Critics agree that Macbeth's main <u>fault</u> was overreaching ambition.
    A. a crack in the earth
    B. the responsibility for doing wrong
    C. a flaw, weakness

11. Although the <u>strident</u> chants of the striking postal employees could be heard for several blocks, they were apparently ignored by the new postmaster.
    A. calm, gentle
    B. harsh, insistent
    C. soft, melodic

12. In spite of his generous, open nature, Jeff was always <u>frugal</u> when it came to money—never spending more than he had to.
    A. thrifty
    B. reckless
    C. daring

13. After putting on his white clown's makeup; a bulging, red nose; and an orange wig, Albert looked <u>ludicrous</u>.
    A. serious
    B. sad
    C. ridiculous

14. Even in the face of the most maddening complications, Mary Beth always manages to remain collected, calm, and <u>affable</u>.
    A. easily excited
    B. friendly, gracious, at ease
    C. nervous

15. When it was discovered that the mail-order house had no merchandise to deliver, the judge determined that its intention was to <u>defraud</u> the public.
    A. cheat, to deceive
    B. serve
    C. welcome

16. If *emancipate* means "to set free," then <u>emancipator</u> must mean
    A. a person who sets free.
    B. the setting free of.
    C. in the manner of setting free.

17. If *determine* means "to figure out," then <u>predetermine</u> must mean
    A. not able to figure out.
    B. to figure out before.
    C. to figure out afterward.

18. If *cast* means "to assign parts in a play," then <u>miscast</u> must mean
    A. to assign parts in a play wrongly or badly.
    B. to assign parts in a play before the auditions are held.
    C. not to assign parts in a play.

19. If *fantasy* means "something created by one's imagination," then <u>fantasize</u> must mean
    A. not created by the imagination, real.
    B. to create in the imagination.
    C. persons who create in their imaginations.

20. If *ubiquitous* means "existing everywhere at the same time," then <u>ubiquitousness</u> must mean
    A. something that exists everywhere at the same time.
    B. the state of existing everywhere at the same time.
    C. able to exist everywhere at the same time.

Context Clues to Word Meanings

Name _____

Possible Score **20**

My Score ☐

When you come across an unfamiliar word in a sentence, don't just skip over it. Think about the context in which the word appears—that is, the other words that surround it. First, consider the general subject of the sentence. For example, what is the general subject of the following example sentence? And what does *pseudonym* mean?

> Some women writers in the 1800s used a man's name as a **pseudonym** so that readers would not know that the author was a woman.

You might decide that the general subject of this sentence is writing. Next, look for other words in the sentence that may explain the meaning of the unfamiliar word even further. The words *women writers...used a man's name* give you additional clues that *pseudonym* might have something to do with using a false name when writing. You might decide that *pseudonym* means "a false name" or "a pen name." You can't be positive, but you can make an educated guess.

Sometimes, the sentence in which an unfamiliar word appears does not provide helpful clues to the meaning of the word. In such cases, other sentences in the paragraph may help. Here is an example in which the meaning of an unfamiliar word is cleared up in a following sentence.

> My first attempt at skiing was a **fiasco**. Not only did I fall, but I couldn't even get back up on my skis without help.

The first sentence tells you that attempting to ski is the general subject. But what, in this context, is a *fiasco*? The second sentence gives you clues with words like *fall, couldn't get back up...without help*. Clearly, the first attempt at skiing was not even partly successful. So, you could reasonably decide that *fiasco* means "not successful" or "a complete failure." But if you are still in doubt about the meaning of a word when you finish reading a paragraph, consult your dictionary.

Practice 1

Use context clues to help you decide which of the four choices following each sentence below is closest to the meaning of the word in bold type. Circle the letter of that choice.

1. After the strong winds of the week before, everyone welcomed the softly blowing **zephyr**.

   a. a heavy rain   b. a gentle breeze   c. a hot spell   d. a hurricane

2. Connecting the two land masses is a narrow **isthmus** that separates the Atlantic and Pacific Oceans.

   a. a strip of land with water on two sides   b. a cliff   c. an island   d. a valley

3. Cattle, deer, and many birds are **herbivorous**. They cover large areas in search of grasses and seeds.

   a. wild   b. meat eating   c. plant eating   d. tame

4. Pablo Casals played the cello so expertly that he was widely recognized as a **virtuoso**.

   a. a spectator   b. an amateur musician   c. a singer   d. a skilled musician

5. It was hard to ignore the **strident** voices of the protesters as they shouted their demands.

   a. harsh, insistent   b. pleasant   c. soft, gentle   d. melodic

6. There was a **hiatus** in the hostilities. Both sides had agreed to a temporary cease-fire.

   a. a gap or break   b. a continuation   c. a beginning   d. a final ending

UNIT 5 Building Vocabulary

7. The Riveras combined Spanish-American, Victorian, and modern furniture, achieving a pleasing, **eclectic** style.

   a. unattractive   b. the best from one source   c. disagreeable   d. the best from various sources

8. Although neither one said anything, agreement was **implicit** in the smiles and handshakes of the two men.

   a. stated, plainly expressed   b. doubtful   c. implied, not directly expressed   d. broken

9. Ms. Jensen never used more words than she needed. In fact, she was **laconic** even with her best friends.

   a. sarcastic   b. using many words   c. untruthful   d. using few words.

10. My father, who grew up in a large, poor family, learned as a boy how to save and to be **frugal**.

   a. reckless   b. thrifty   c. wasteful   d. indifferent

Practice 2

Use context clues in each of the following sentences to find the word in bold type that best completes each sentence. Write the word in the space provided.

Regale: to entertain, to give pleasure or amusement   **Affable:** friendly, gracious, at ease

Scrutinize: to examine closely   **Upbraid:** to scold angrily

Voracious: greedy, having a huge appetite   **Erratic:** having no regular course, wandering

Malcontent: discontented person, a rebel   **Anthology:** a collection of literary pieces

Litigation: a lawsuit   **Lethargic:** lacking in alertness or activity, sluggish

Excise: to remove by cutting out   **Nocturnal:** of, or relating to, the night

1. Tim's _____ behavior made his parents suspect that he was not getting enough sleep.

2. The committee members promised to _____ the school-expansion plans carefully.

3. The lawyers announced to the eager reporters that the disagreement would be settled out of court, without _____ .

4. Ms. Terlecki was _____ and courteous as she greeted the newcomers.

5. Mr. O'Brien liked to _____ his friends with stories about his years on the stage.

6. His _____ tee shots—some veering off to the left, others slicing to the right—cost him the tournament.

7. Bats are _____ creatures, sleeping during the day and venturing out only after the sun has set.

8. John was labeled a _____ because he was always complaining.

9. This new _____ contains the best short stories of the last five years.

10. The doctor will _____ the tumor with the utmost caution.

Name _____   Possible Score [20]   My Score [ ]

One way to arrive at the meaning of an unfamiliar word in a sentence is to look for other words in the sentence whose meaning you already know. Then see if the familiar words can be linked to the unfamiliar word in such a way as to provide clues to its meaning.

For example, the unfamiliar word may be one of several words in a series of synonyms—words with similar meanings. If you know the meaning of at least one of the synonyms in the series, you should be able to guess at the meaning of the unfamiliar word. What words give you clues to the meaning of *staid* in this sentence?

> The **staid**, serious, and self-restrained manner of the judge always had a steadying effect on people.

Because the unfamiliar word *staid* is linked with *serious* and *self-restrained* in a series, you could reasonably assume that it is close to these two words in meaning. So, you might decide that *staid* means "serious, composed, steady."

Sometimes, an unfamiliar word is linked to a familiar word by *and*. Suppose you don't know the meaning of the word *defraud*. What clue to its meaning can you find in this sentence?

> The store owner's attempt to deceive and **defraud** his customers put him in serious trouble.

Because *defraud* and *deceive* are joined by *and*, you can assume that the two words are probably close in meaning. So, you might decide that *defraud* must mean something like "to deprive someone of something by deceit; to cheat."

Sometimes, a word group, rather than a single word, has the same meaning as an unfamiliar word in the same sentence. What clue do you find to the meaning of *officiously* in the word group that follows it?

> Diane thought her neighbor acted **officiously**, giving advice that was not asked for and not needed.

The word group *giving advice that was not asked for and not needed* describes how the neighbor acted. Since *officiously* also describes how the neighbor acted, you can assume that it means "in an interfering, nosy manner."

Remember, to make an educated guess about the meaning of an unfamiliar word in a sentence, look for other words whose meaning you already know and that are linked to the unfamiliar word. To make certain your guess is correct , check the word in your dictionary.

Practice 1

In each sentence, look for the word or words that probably have a similar meaning to the word in bold type. Then from the four choices given after each sentence, pick the one that is closest in meaning to the word in bold type. Circle the letter of your choice.

1. The children, **restive** and uneasy, were still trying to challenge the new bedtime rules.

   a. happy, unconcerned   b. easy to manage   c. calm, relaxed   d. hard to manage

2. The meal was dull and **insipid**, and unfortunately so was the conversation.

   a. exciting, lively   b. flat, flavorless   c. spicy, hot   d. interesting, flavorful

3. The treasurer's report was short, simple, and **succinct**.

   a. brief and clear   b. vague and rambling   c. complicated and wordy   d. lengthy and confusing

4. The coach **reproached** the team, expressing her displeasure at the way they had played.

   a. praised   b. criticized   c. congratulated   d. joked with

5. Luis was **adamant**, firm, and completely unyielding in his opposition to our suggestions.

    a. flexible   b. relaxed   c. inflexible   d. undecided

6. The wheat crop was **copious**, yielding an abundance of low-priced flour and animal feed.

    a. insufficient   b. expensive   c. plentiful   d. delicious

7. The conservation group will remain **vigilant**, checking carefully for any signs of water pollution.

    a. indifferent   b. unconcerned   c. contented   d. watchful

8. The committee promised to examine the situation carefully, to **probe** any suggestion of misconduct.

    a. ignore completely   b. investigate thoroughly   c. encourage fully   d. enjoy briefly

9. The guard was considered **remiss** and careless for sleeping while at work.

    a. neglectful of duty   b. thoughtful   c. concerned   d. attentive to duty

10. The clown's **ludicrous**, comical behavior brought waves of laughter from the crowd.

    a. sad   b. angry   c. ridiculous   d. serious

Practice 2

Answer each of the following questions *yes* or *no* according to your understanding of the word in bold type. Use a dictionary if you need help with any of the meanings.

1. _____ Would you want to go to a movie that had an **insipid** plot?

2. _____ Should a crossing guard at an elementary school be **vigilant**?

3. _____ Does a person who speaks **succinctly** take a lot of time and use many words to say something?

4. _____ Would you expect a doctor to **probe** for symptoms of illness in a patient?

5. _____ If you made a **ludicrous** statement, would you expect your friends to laugh?

6. _____ If a student takes **copious** notes, would you expect him or her to use a lot of paper?

7. _____ Would a person who was **remiss** in his or her duties make a good baby-sitter?

8. _____ Would you expect students who were **restive** about a regulation to want to speak to the principal about it?

9. _____ Is it easy to talk to people who are always **adamant** in their opinions?

10. _____ If your brother borrowed your bike and left it out in the rain, would you **reproach** him?

Possible Score 18   My Score ☐

A. The following is a list of some of the words that appeared in bold type in the previous two lessons. Choose ten of these words and write a sentence for each one. Be sure your sentences show that you understand the meanings of the words you have chosen.

herbivorous	strident	frugal	ludicrous	regale
staid	succinct	copious	scrutinize	probe
hiatus	lethargic	adamant	affable	fiasco

1. _____

_____

_____

2. _____

_____

_____

3. _____

_____

_____

4. _____

_____

_____

5. _____

_____

_____

6. _____

_____

_____

7. _____

_____

_____

UNIT 5   Building Vocabulary

8. _____

_____

_____

9. _____

_____

_____

10. _____

_____

_____

B. Read each of the following sentences and use context clues and similar word clues to determine the probable meaning of the word in bold type. Write the meaning in the space provided.

1. Claire's grace and **dexterity** helped her to ski through the twisting slalom course with ease. _____

_____

2. Mr. Johnson **enlivened** the party with his humorous stories and enthusiastic manner. _____

_____

3. The retired colonel led a quiet, uneventful life—a **sedentary** existence. _____

_____

4. The minister's **homily** was the best sermon I've heard in a long time. _____

_____

5. The firefighter **jeopardized** her life by running back into the burning building. _____

_____

6. Both the defense lawyers and the prosecuting attorney agreed that the jury's decision was fair, unprejudiced,

and **impartial**. _____

_____

7. Roger was a **miserly** man—refusing to spend his money even on the necessities of life. _____

_____

8. She reminded us that we had been **forewarned** of the danger before we left for the mountains. _____

_____

Name _____ Possible Score 15 My Score ☐

Finding clues to what an unfamiliar word does *not* mean can sometimes be the best way to determine what it *does* mean. If you come across an unfamiliar word in a sentence, see if there is a familiar word nearby that contrasts with it, that has an opposite meaning. Since you know what the familiar word means, the contrast will give you a clue to the meaning of the unfamiliar word.

In the following sentence, what clues are there to the meaning of *ornate*?

> The restaurant was **ornate**, not plain and simple as we had expected.

The word *ornate* is contrasted with the words *plain* and *simple*. The word that signals the contrast is *not*. If *plain* and *simple* both mean "without decoration," then *ornate* probably means the opposite. You could assume that *ornate* must mean "heavily decorated" or "elaborate."

Besides *not*, other words that may signal contrast are *although, however, but,* and *nevertheless*. What word signals contrast in the example sentence that follows? How can you figure out what the word *dearth* means?

> Although the hikers started out in a happy and talkative mood, there was a **dearth** of laughter and conversation when they returned twelve hours later.

In this sentence, the word *although* signals a contrast between the two moods of the hikers. They started out happy and talkative and returned in the opposite mood, with a *dearth* of laughter and conversation. So, you could decide that *dearth* must mean "an absence or scarcity."

Sometimes when there is a contrast in a sentence, the contrasting words may not be exactly opposite in meaning. For instance, in the following sentence, does *tepid* mean "cold," the exact opposite of *hot*?

> At lunch, our soup was **tepid**, not hot.

The word *tepid* is not the exact opposite of *hot*. It does not mean "cold" but rather "moderately warm" or "lukewarm." Unfortunately, you can't tell from the example sentence what the exact meaning of *tepid* is. The most you can tell is that something *tepid* is "not hot." You need your dictionary to find out the exact degree of heat *tepid* represents.

Finding a word or two with a contrasting meaning can help you to make an educated guess about an unfamiliar word in a sentence. You should remember, however, that contrast clues may not tell you exactly what a word means. If you are still in doubt about an unfamiliar word after considering the words with contrasting meaning, use your dictionary to pin down the exact meaning.

Practice 1

Use contrast clues in each of the following sentences to determine the meaning of the word in bold type. Then from the four choices given after each sentence, pick the one that is closest in meaning to the word in bold type. Circle the letter of your choice.

1. Although campers are free to choose most activities, the swimming classes are **compulsory**.

    a. not required   b. required   c. easy   d. tiring

2. The supervisor claimed she was **flexible**; nevertheless, she refused to consider a new work schedule.

    a. very unhappy   b. rigidly firm   c. always impatient   d. capable of change

3. The young lawyer began by **advocating** passage of the new bill, but she ended by arguing against it.

    a. pleading for   b. disapproving of   c. not supporting   d. resisting

UNIT 5 Building Vocabulary

4. Ben was **abstemious** at dinner last night; however, today he returned to his habit of eating everything in sight.

   a. hungry   b. greedy   c. restrained   d. sloppy

5. Although Joe lacked formal training, his experience made him **competent** to handle the job.

   a. qualified   b. eager   c. unwilling   d. unfit

6. Ms. Gibson liked to **improvise**, not to make precise arrangements or to prepare her remarks in advance.

   a. plan carefully   b. joke   c. do without planning   d. sing

7. A **lucrative** summer job is best; nevertheless, even work with little or no pay is useful experience.

   a. easy   b. interesting   c. enjoyable   d. profitable

8. Although Marie worked hard to give an excellent report, her lack of information made it only **mediocre**.

   a. of high quality   b. of ordinary quality   c. amusing in tone   d. angry in tone

9. Art is **pessimistic** about tomorrow's game, but the other members of the team remain hopeful.

   a. expecting a bad result   b. expecting a good result   c. in a happy mood   d. in a calm mood

10. Runners with **stamina** finished easily; however, others tired quickly and fell out of the race.

    a. loss of appetite   b. poor training   c. no money   d. staying power

Practice 2

In each of the following sentences, find the words that contrast in meaning with one of the words in bold type that follows. Fill in the blank with the word in bold type.

Evasive: indirect, avoiding a straightforward answer
Imperceptible: not capable of being seen or touched
Elated: in a joyous mood, marked by high spirits
Contemporaries: people living at the same time
Tangible: real, capable of being seen or touched

Dejected: in a low mood, depressed
Posterity: descendants, future generations
Facilitate: to make easier
Complicate: to make complex or difficult
Candid: straightforward, honest, frank

1. Joanie was trying to _____ the preparations for the party; nevertheless, her trying to do everything herself only served to make things harder.

2. The biologist, in his speech to the citizens' group, warned, "Although the present generation is safe, we must act now to protect _____ ."

3. At first Mark felt _____ about missing the game, but later the coach's visit cheered him up.

4. Rita wants _____ proof of the existence of flying saucers; however, she has never touched or even seen one.

5. Mr. Ryan was always _____ when he counseled students; he didn't beat around the bush.

Explanations as Meaning Clues

Name _____ Possible Score [25] My Score [ ]

At times, a writer must use a word or a meaning that is unfamiliar to some readers. A careful writer in such cases will supply an explanation to make certain that readers understand the word or the special way it is used. Then, it is up to the careful reader to recognize and apply the explanation as a clue to word meaning. For instance, in this sentence what tells you the meaning of the word *cinch?*

As we saddled our horses, Mr. Gomez told us to make the **cinch**, or bellyband, as tight as we could.

The explanatory phrase *or bellyband* briefly defines the word *cinch*. If a word has several meanings, as *cinch* does, such an explanation will tell you which meaning the writer intends.

There is more than one way to include an explanation in a sentence. Occasionally, a writer will tell you exactly what meaning is intended.

By **predator**, I mean any animal that hunts and kills other animals for food.

The word **reconcile** is used here in the sense of "restore to friendship or harmony."

More often, a phrase like *that is, in other words,* or *for example* will precede the explanation.

Citizens responded to the news with **apathy**—that is, with complete indifference.

Sometimes, the explanation has no introductory words but is simply set off from the unfamiliar word by commas or dashes.

The guide warned that a **tyro**, a beginner, should not attempt rock climbing alone.

My interest in education reached its **nadir**—the lowest point—when I had to repeat algebra.

Sometimes, the explanation is a word or a phrase preceded by the word *or.*

Mr. Rubin had a tendency to **digress**, or get off the subject, whenever he talked about the 1960s.

And sometimes the explanatory word or phrase will come first, and the unfamiliar word will *follow.*

The lawyer's manner struck us as being both secret and sly—in short, **furtive.**

Practice 1

Each of the following words in bold type is followed by two words or phrases. One is close in meaning to the word in bold type. The other is opposite in meaning. Circle the word or phrase that is closest in meaning to the word in bold type.

1. **tyro:** beginner, expert

2. **arduous:** easy, difficult

3. **tenacious:** weak, firm

4. **turmoil:** confusion, calm

5. **nadir:** lowest point, highest point

6. **apathy:** indifference, concern

7. **slovenly:** neat, careful, untidy, careless

8. **divulge:** hide, reveal

9. **digress:** remain on subject, stray from subject

10. **augment:** decrease, increase

11. **vindicate:** defend, blame

12. **furtive:** sincere, sly

13. **dilemma:** difficult problem, simple problem

14. **reconcile:** restore to harmony, destroy harmony

15. **fluctuate:** remain stable, change

Practice 2

Each of the following sentences contains a word in bold type and an explanation of that word. Use the explanation to determine the meaning of the word in bold type. Then choose the definition from the list that is closest in meaning to the word in bold type and write both the word and the definition in the space provided.

to shift back and forth   firm in resisting or enduring

requiring care and hard work   to prove to be right or reasonable

to make something greater   disturbance, confusion

the way a person acts   problem requiring a difficult choice

not neat or careful   to make public, disclose

1. The puppy was stubborn and persistent—really **tenacious**—in holding the slipper in its jaws. _____

   _____

2. Our club tried to **augment**, or increase, its funds by raising the monthly dues to five dollars. _____

   _____

3. Tom thought his younger brother was untidy, careless, and sloppy—in short, **slovenly**. _____

   _____

4. The candidate tried to **vindicate** her view on foreign aid—that is, to justify it. _____

   _____

5. By **turmoil**, I mean commotion, agitation, and disorder. _____

   _____

6. The temperature **fluctuates** widely—for example, it may vary as much as thirty degrees in one day. _____

   _____

7. The reporter refused to **divulge**, or reveal, the source of his information. _____

   _____

8. The problem seemed to present two solutions, each equally unsatisfactory—a true **dilemma**. _____

   _____

9. Callie found backpacking enjoyable but also **arduous**—a difficult and strenuous pastime. _____

   _____

10. Rachel's **demeanor**, or manner, was straightforward and honest. _____

    _____

Application

Name _____

A. The following is a list of some of the words that appeared in bold type in lesson 81. Choose seven of these words and write a sentence for each. Be sure each sentence contains a contrasting word clue to help the reader understand the meaning of the word you have chosen.

elated	compulsory	stamina	competent	candid
lucrative	ornate	flexible	tangible	evasive
improvise	mediocre	dejected	pessimistic	facilitate

1. _____

_____

_____

2. _____

_____

_____

3. _____

_____

_____

4. _____

_____

_____

5. _____

_____

_____

6. _____

_____

_____

7. _____

_____

_____

B. The following is a list of some of the words that appeared in bold type in lesson 82. Choose seven of these words and write a sentence for each. Be sure each sentence contains an explanation clue to help the reader understand the meaning of the word you have chosen.

reconcile	tenacious	augment	furtive	turmoil
tyro	digress	slovenly	dilemma	nadir
arduous	apathy	divulge	vindicate	fluctuate

1. _____

_____

_____

2. _____

_____

_____

3. _____

_____

_____

4. _____

_____

_____

5. _____

_____

_____

6. _____

_____

_____

7. _____

_____

_____

Name _____ Possible Score | 16 | My Score | |

You can sometimes figure out the general meaning of an unfamiliar word by paying close attention to the other words in the sentence—that is, by using clues found in the word's context. But to get the exact definition of a word, you must look it up in a dictionary. Even then, you'll still need to use context clues. Remember, a word may have several definitions. So, don't stop after reading the first definition. You must find the one that best fits the context in which the word appears.

For example, suppose you read a sentence that contains the word *facade*, and you decide to look the word up. First, think about the context in which the word appears—that is, the meaning of the other words in the sentence.

> Judy tried to hide her disappointment behind a **facade** of carefree indifference.

You'll probably decide that in this context *facade* has something to do with appearance and behavior—how Judy looked and acted. Now, when you check *facade* in a dictionary, you'll be able to decide which of the two definitions listed there best fits the context.

1. the front of a building
2. a false, superficial, or artificial appearance

Clearly, the second meaning of *facade* is the one you want.

Once you have found the meaning that fits a word in a particular context, be sure to read the other meanings, too. Then you'll understand the word when you find it used in other contexts. For example, after checking both meanings of **facade**, suppose you later find this sentence in a description of an old town hall:

> The **facade** was partially replaced and remodeled after a fire in 1989.

Remembering that one meaning of **facade** is "the front of a building," you'll know right away what the writer meant.

Often, the context of a word includes not only the surrounding words but also the time during which the word was used or the place where it was used. Even familiar words may have special meanings that were used during particular historical periods or in particular countries.

The dictionary has special labels that identify definitions influenced by time or place. It may use the label *obsolete* for a meaning no longer used today and *archaic* for a meaning rarely used. If a word meaning is not common to all English-speaking countries, labels like *British* or *Australian* show where a word carries that meaning. Suppose that you are reading *King Lear* and find Shakespeare's reference to "...mice, rats, and such small deer...." You might be confused to see mice and rats referred to as deer. But remember that Shakespeare wrote during the seventeenth century. If you check a dictionary, you'll find that one meaning of *deer* has a special label.

> **deer** 1. *archaic:* animal, especially a small mammal.

So *deer* in this seventeenth-century context simply means any small mammal, not the larger animal with hooves and antlers that people call a deer today.

Practice 1

Read the following sentences, each of which contains a word in bold type. Look up each of these words in a dictionary and choose the definition that best fits the word's context. Write that definition in the space provided.

1. Tina's only **fault** is that she doesn't know when to stop joking.

_____

2. The San Andreas **fault** in California caused the great San Francisco earthquake in 1906.

_____

3. Fire inspectors agreed that a highly **volatile** gas had been the cause of the explosion and fire.

_____

4. Inna's **volatile** disposition made it hard for her to settle down to any project for a long time.

_____

5. Our neighbor, who grew up in England, still refers to the **bonnet** of his car.

_____

6. Sandy found that an old-fashioned **bonnet** gave her good protection from the hot summer sun.

_____

Practice 2

Read the two definitions given for each of the following words. Then read the sentences, each of which contains one of the words defined. Decide which of the two meanings is intended in each sentence and write the number of that meaning in the space before each sentence.

Dissipate: 1. to scatter, to cause to disappear   **Starve:** 7. to die of hunger
            2. to use up foolishly or heedlessly   8. _obsolete:_ to die

Nice: 3. pleasing, agreeable, kind   **Florid:** 9. flowery in style, ornate
            4. exact, precise, particular   10. tinged with red, ruddy

Nurture: 5. to further the development of
                 6. to nourish, to feed

_____ 1. Wild grasses and grains were sown to **nurture** the hungry geese on their journey south.

_____ 2. Flood victims may **starve** if food doesn't arrive soon.

_____ 3. The brothers **dissipated** the family fortune by gambling.

_____ 4. Not everyone enjoys that writer's **florid** prose.

_____ 5. Mrs. Nelson likes to point out **nice** distinctions between words like _wise_ and _knowledgeable._

_____ 6. In Chaucer's _Troilus and Criseyde,_ written in about 1385, Troilus promises to "live and **starve**" faithful to his love Criseyde.

_____ 7. Ann tried to act as if she were having a **nice** time.

_____ 8. The strong wind rapidly **dissipated** the clouds of smoke.

_____ 9. One purpose of the pilots' survival course was to **nurture** self-reliance and endurance.

_____ 10. The farmer had a healthy, **florid** complexion from working outdoors all year round.

Name _____

Possible Score | 56 | My Score | ☐

Often, you can guess the meaning of a word by its context. But what do you do if an unfamiliar word is standing alone or if its context gives you no help? In these cases, the *form* of the word—how the word is put together—will often give you clues to its meaning.

To find meaning clues in the form a word takes, you must break the word down into its parts. Some words, like *work* have only a single part. But many other words, like *unworkable*, are combinations of word parts.

The Base The part of the word that carries the principal meaning is called the *base*. The base of *unworkable* is *work*. Some bases, like *work*, can stand by themselves as words. Many others, however, must be combined with at least one other word part before they make sense as words. For example, *-ceive* is the base of the word *receive*. Bases like *-ceive* are often difficult to recognize because they are word parts borrowed from Latin or Greek.

The Prefix The part of the word that comes before the base is called the *prefix*. The prefix in *unworkable* is *un-*. Because prefixes have meanings of their own, they change the meanings of the bases to which they are attached. Since *un-* means "not," *unworkable* must mean "not workable." Being able to recognize prefixes can help you figure out the meanings of unfamiliar words. You probably already know the meanings of many prefixes.

impossible = **not** possible

reheat = heat **again**

antiaircraft = **against** aircraft

predetermined = determined **before**

semicircle = **half** circle

subhuman = **under, below** the human

The Suffix The part of the word that comes after the base is called the *suffix*. The suffix in *unworkable* is *-able*. Suffixes also have meanings of their own, and thus, like prefixes, they change the meanings of the bases to which they are attached. Since *-able* means "capable of," anything that is *workable* is capable of working or of being worked. You probably know the meanings of many suffixes already.

connect**or** = **thing that** connects

chem**ist** = **one who** knows chemistry

repair**able** = **able** to be repaired

hope**ful** = **full of** hope

beaut**ify** = **to make** beautiful

union**ize** = **cause to become** a union

Therefore, a good way to guess at the meaning of an unfamiliar word is to see how it is put together. Look at the word carefully. Can it be divided into prefix, base, and suffix? If it can, what clues to the meaning of the whole word do the meanings of its parts give you?

Practice 1

Circle the prefix in each of the following words. If you can guess what the prefix means, write your guess in the space after the word. Otherwise, check the definition of the prefix in your dictionary and write that definition. If a word has no prefix, write *none* after the word.

1. regressive _____

2. semitone _____

3. ocean _____

4. indecisive _____

5. incredible _____

6. enlist _____

7. slothful _____

8. disassemble _____

9. subservient _____

10. preeminent _____

11. antithesis _____

12. financier _____

13. encode _____

14. score _____

Practice 2

Circle the suffix in each of the following words. If you can guess what the suffix means, write your guess in the space after the word. Otherwise, check the definition of the suffix in your dictionary and write that definition. If a word has no suffix, write *none* after the word.

1. wrathful _____

2. apologist _____

3. amplify _____

4. exclude _____

5. incongruous _____

6. defection _____

7. edible _____

8. epoch _____

9. supplicate _____

10. bearable _____

11. arbiter _____

12. sensuous _____

13. switch _____

14. beautify _____

Name _____

A. In the space after each word, write both the prefix and a short definition of the word. Then use the word in a sentence of your own.

1. antisocial _____

_____

_____

2. unnecessary _____

_____

_____

3. circumnavigate _____

_____

_____

4. transcontinental _____

_____

_____

5. television _____

_____

_____

6. illiterate _____

_____

_____

7. reform _____

_____

_____

8. imperfect _____

_____

B. In the space after each word, write both the suffix and a short definition of the word. Then use the word in a sentence of your own.

1. salable _____

   _____

   _____

2. sensitize _____

   _____

   _____

3. Chicagoan _____

   _____

   _____

4. dentist _____

   _____

   _____

5. independence _____

   _____

   _____

6. romantic _____

   _____

   _____

7. actor _____

   _____

   _____

8. specify _____

   _____

   _____

Name _____ Possible Score 40 My Score

It's not very helpful to think of an unfamiliar word as a solid unit, as something that cannot be divided. Instead, think of the unfamiliar word, especially if it's a long word, as being a combination of parts. Then, you will be better able to guess its meaning. Here's a long word that's been divided into parts:

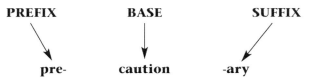

PREFIX	BASE	SUFFIX
pre-	caution	-ary

When you come across an unfamiliar word like *precautionary*, try breaking it up into parts you can recognize. If you know *caution* means "carefulness," *pre-* means "before," and *-ary* means "something connected with," you could guess that *precautionary* might mean "something connected with carefulness beforehand." Even though this guess is not the exact dictionary definition, it should help you read the sentence with better understanding.

Only **precautionary** steps like boiling the drinking water kept the epidemic from spreading.

To get at the meaning of an unfamiliar word, see if it can be divided into parts—prefix, base, and suffix. First, locate and try to define its base, the main part of the word. You'll recognize some bases immediately. In *replay*, for example, you find the familiar word *play*. You probably know that the prefix *re-* means "again." So you can guess the meaning of *replay* easily.

But what about a word like *reduce*? One difficulty in trying to figure out the meaning of an unfamiliar word by breaking it down into its parts is recognizing those parts. Does the base of *reduce*, *-duce*, mean anything to you by itself? It probably doesn't because *-duce* is not a word in English. It's a base borrowed from the Latin word *ducere*. Following is a list of common bases. Many of them stem from Latin and Greek words. And most of these bases are like *-duce*—that is, they can't stand alone as English words. Try to learn the meanings of as many bases from the following list as you can. Knowing these bases and their meanings will help you to figure out the meanings of many unfamiliar words.

Base	Meaning	Example
anthrop	man	**anthrop**ology
arch, archi	rule, govern, first in importance	mon**arch**
capt, cept, ceive, cap, cip, ceit	take, seize	re**ceive**, **capt**ure
cogn	know	re**cogn**ize
cred	belief, trust	**cred**itable
duc, duct	lead, make	con**duct**
fact, fect, fic, fac	do, make	de**fect**, **fact**ory
fer	bear, carry	of**fer**
graph, gram	write	auto**graph**
jud	judge	pre**jud**ice
log, logy	word, study	ana**logy**
mit, miss	send	e**mit**
plic, ply, plex	fold, bend, twist	com**plic**ated
pone, pos	place, put	post**pone**

Base	Meaning	Example
psych	mind, soul	**psych**ology
scrib, script	write	de**scrib**e
sist, sta	stand, endure	per**sist**
soph	wise, wisdom	**soph**isticated
spect, spec, spic	look	con**spic**uous
tain, ten, tin	hold, have	re**tain**
tend, tens, tent	stretch	ex**tens**ion
vol	wish	bene**vol**ent

Practice

Find the base in each of the following words. Then write the base and its definition in the space provided. Use the definitions in the base list in this lesson.

1. inscription _____

2. incredible _____

3. telegram _____

4. manufacture _____

5. permit _____

6. inspector _____

7. facile _____

8. except _____

9. spectator _____

10. distend _____

11. transfer _____

12. remit _____

13. grammar _____

14. logic _____

15. interpose _____

16. despicable _____

17. inscribe _____

18. dismiss _____

19. confer _____

20. emissary _____

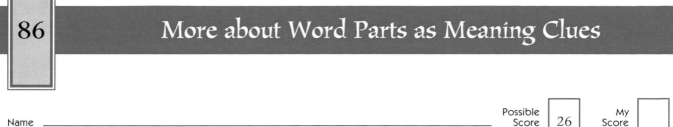

Name _____   Possible Score | 26 | My Score | |

Dividing a word into its parts—prefix, base, and suffix—can help you to make an educated guess about the meaning of an unfamiliar word. But this method for defining words isn't always foolproof. For one thing, words sometimes change in meaning as time goes by. Another problem is that the literal meaning of the parts of a word may not always add up to the meaning of the whole word.

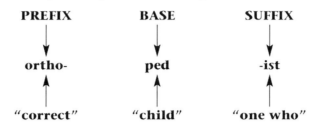

PREFIX	BASE	SUFFIX
ortho-	ped	-ist
"correct"	"child"	"one who"

You might assume that an orthopedist is a "person who corrects children." But an orthopedist is actually a doctor who specializes in correcting bone deformities. If all you had to go on in defining *orthopedist* were the separate meanings of its parts, you wouldn't be able to figure out its real meaning.

Still, knowing the meaning of common prefixes, bases, and suffixes can help you figure out the meanings of many unfamiliar words. Following are two lists—one of prefixes and their meanings and one of suffixes and their meanings. Try to learn the meanings of as many word parts from these lists as you can.

Prefix	Meaning	Example
a-	lacking, without	**a**moral
anti-	against	**anti**war
bi-	two	**bi**centennial
circum-	around	**circum**vent
contra-, contro-	against	**contro**versy
de-	away, from, off, down	**de**cline, **de**duce
dis-, dif-	away, off, opposing	**dis**traction
eu-	good, pleasant	**eu**genics
ex-, ef-, e-	away from, out	**ex**ternal
il-, ir-	not	**il**legal
in-, im-	not, in, into	**in**ject
inter-	between, among	**inter**vene
mal-	bad	**mal**ice
mis-	badly, poorly, not, hate	**mis**use, **mis**anthrope
post-	after	**post**script
pre-	before	**pre**cede
pro-	before, in place of	**pro**ceed
re-	again, back	**re**submit
semi-	half	**semi**circle
sub-, suf-, sum-, sus-, sup-	under, beneath	**sub**marine, **sus**pended
syn-, sym-, syl-, sys-	together, with	**sym**pathy, **syn**onym
tele-	far, distant	**tele**scope
trans-	across, beyond	**trans**late
ultra-	beyond, excessively	**ultra**modern
un-	not, opposing	**un**true

UNIT 5 Building Vocabulary

Suffix	Meaning	Example
-able, -ible	able, likely	vis**ible**
-an, -ian	one belonging to, pertaining to	Republic**an**, mart**ian**
-ance, -ancy, -ence, -ency	act of, condition, fact	venge**ance**, presid**ency**
-ant, -ent, -dom	actor, agent, showing state of, rank, condition	ten**ant**, duke**dom**
-er, -or, -eer	doer, maker, dealer in, worker at, one who	lectur**er**, engin**eer**
-fy, -ify	make, cause to have	cod**ify**
-ic	dealing with, caused by, person or thing showing	automat**ic**, psych**ic**, fanat**ic**
-ist	doer, believer	public**ist**
-ize	make, cause to be	demoral**ize**
-ous, -ose	marked by, given to	fam**ous**

Practice 1

Using the list of prefixes in this lesson, find the correct prefix for each defintion given in parentheses. Then write the word that results when the prefix is added to its base.

1. (again) + play _____

2. (away from) + pulsion _____

3. (down) + tain _____

4. (hate) + anthropic _____

5. (after) + script _____

6. (against) + dict _____

7. (away from) + plode _____

8. (half) + annual _____

9. (far) + vision _____

10. (not) + fair _____

11. (not) + visible _____

12. (two) + weekly _____

13. (good) + thanasia _____

14. (against) + biotics _____

15. (together) + onym _____

16. (across) + mit _____

Practice 2

Using the list of suffixes in this lesson, find the correct suffix for each definition given in parentheses. Then write the word that results when the suffix is added to the word in bold type.

1. **wise** + (state of) _____

2. **oversee** + (worker at) _____

3. **transfer** + (act of) _____

4. **fertile** + (cause to be) _____

5. **pore** + (marked by) _____

6. **supervise** + (one who) _____

7. **notice** + (able) _____

8. **Darwin** + (pertaining to) _____

9. **Mexico** + (one belonging to) _____

10. **notice** + (cause to have) _____

Application

Name _____

Possible Score | 75 | My Score |

A. Using the list of prefixes in lesson 86, find the definition of each prefix below and write it in the space before the prefix. Then, in the spaces labeled *a, b,* and *c,* write three words that begin with each prefix. Finally, use one of the words in a sentence.

_____ 1. **dis-** a. _____ b. _____

c. _____ _____

_____

_____ 2. **in-** a. _____ b. _____

c. _____ _____

_____

_____ 3. **mis-** a. _____ b. _____

c. _____ _____

_____

_____ 4. **trans-** a. _____ b. _____

c. _____ _____

_____

_____ 5. **pro-** a. _____ b. _____

c. _____ _____

_____

B. Using the list of bases in lesson 85, find the definition of each base below and write it in the space before the base. Then, in the spaces labeled *a, b,* and *c,* write three words that contain each base. Finally, use one of the three words in a sentence.

_____ 1. **mit** a. _____ b. _____

c. _____ _____

_____

_____ 2. **spect** a. _____ b. _____

c. _____ _____

_____

_____ 3. **cred** a. _____ b. _____

c. _____ _____

_____

_____ 4. **script** a. _____ b. _____

c. _____ _____

_____

_____ 5. **tain** a. _____ b. _____

c. _____ _____

_____

C. Using the list of suffixes in lesson 86, find the definition of each suffix below and write it in the space before the suffix. Then, in the spaces labeled *a, b,* and *c,* write three words that end with each suffix. Finally, use one of the three words in a sentence.

_____ 1. **-able** a. _____ b. _____

c. _____ _____

_____

_____ 2. **-ance** a. _____ b. _____

c. _____ _____

_____

_____ 3. **-or** a. _____ b. _____

c. _____ _____

_____

_____ 4. **-ist** a. _____ b. _____

c. _____ _____

_____

_____ 5. **-ous** a. _____ b. _____

c. _____ _____

_____

Name _____   Possible Score 7   My Score

Breaking down an unfamiliar word into familiar word parts can sometimes help you guess its meaning. But deciding the meaning of a word by adding up the meanings of its parts doesn't always work. Suppose, for example, that you don't know the meaning of *preclusion* in this sentence.

> An investigation of the senator's involvement in the bank scandal led to his **preclusion** from the ballot.

Even if you recognize *pre-* as a prefix meaning "before," that isn't much help if you don't know what the base, *clus,* means or if you forget that *-ion* is a suffix. So, there is only one thing to do: look up the word in a dictionary. But even then you'll still find that you need a knowledge of word parts and their meanings.

If, as is likely, you're using a desk dictionary, you won't find *preclusion* listed as a main entry by itself. Instead, you'll probably find it listed as part of another entry, like this:

> **preclude** (pri-klo͞od′) *vt* **-cluded; -cluding. 1.** To make impossible by previous action; to prevent. **2.** To bar (a person) from something.—**preclusion** *n*—**preclusive** *adj*—**preclusively** *adv*

The noun *preclusion* appears near the end of the entry as a word built from the verb *preclude.* Although the dictionary has given you the meaning of *preclude,* you'll have to determine the meaning of *preclusion* yourself. Here's how:

First, look up the meaning of the suffix *-ion.*

> **-ion** *n suffix* **1.** An act or process, or the outcome of an act or process. **2.** A state or condition

Then, combine the meaning of *preclude* and the meaning of *-ion* that best blends with the context of the sentence in which *preclusion* appears. In this way you can determine that, in this sentence, *preclusion* must mean "the act of barring a person from something."

Practice

Look up each of the following words in a dictionary. If you can't find a word listed as a main entry, first look up the meaning of the part of the word that is in bold type. Then, look up the meanings of the other parts of the word. Combine these meanings to arrive at a definition for the whole word, and write that definition in the space provided.

1. **deferential**ly _____

2. re**investig**ative _____

3. non**biodegradable** _____

4. un**inhabit**able _____

5. **rigorous**ness _____

6. **depreciat**ion _____

7. **corroborat**ion _____

Application

Name _____

Here is a list of ten words followed first by definitions of suffixes and prefixes and then by definitions of words closely related to the list words. Use these definitions to determine the meanings of the ten list words. Then write each list word and its meaning in the space provided.

1. disparagement   3. reescalation   5. captivator   7. extraneously   9. chronologically
2. ubiquitousness   4. nonshrinkable   6. cataclysmic   8. ineptitude   10. perpetuation

-or, er one who   **-ly**   in a specified manner   **non-**   not
-ence act or process,   **-able** capable of   **-ment**   an action or result of an action
-ation state or condition **-tude** state or condition,   **-ic**   tending to produce, caused by
-ion   **-ness** quality   **re-**   again

Chronological: arranged according to the order of time
Captivate: to influence by charm, art, or great appeal
Ubiquitous: existing everywhere at the same time, widespread
Cataclysm: violent change, momentous event marked by upheaval and destruction
Disparage: to degrade or belittle, to speak slightingly about
Extraneous: coming from the outside, not belonging, not relevant
Perpetuate: to cause to last indefinitely
Inept: unfit, incompetent, inappropriate
Shrink: to contract, to become smaller
Escalate: to increase, to expand

1. _____

2. _____

3. _____

4. _____

5. _____

6. _____

7. _____

8. _____

9. _____

10. _____

Name _____   Number Correct × 5 = ☐

Each numbered sentence contains an underlined word. Select the correct definition for the underlined word from choices *A, B,* or *C* and circle the letter of your choice.

1. The expert put on an eyepiece and <u>scrutinized</u> the newly discovered Rembrandt, looking for signs of forgery.
   A. examined closely
   B. glanced over
   C. glared at

2. Uncle Max, who spent thirty-five years in the Navy, loved to <u>regale</u> us with lively stories about his travels.
   A. bore
   B. entertain, amuse
   C. tell from memory

3. The teacher in charge of the playground was considered <u>remiss</u> and careless after the first-grader broke a leg.
   A. neglectful of duty
   B. thoughtful, considerate
   C. attentive to the requirements of the job

4. Even after the woman was offered a fair price, she remained <u>adamant</u> and completely unyielding on the subject of selling.
   A. willing to change
   B. undecided
   C. firm, resistant to change

5. Although I'd like a <u>lucrative</u> job, I'd settle for one with a low salary if it gave me a chance to meet people.
   A. menial, low paying
   B. interesting, stimulating
   C. profitable, high paying

6. Dee was <u>elated</u> when she broke the school record, but she felt depressed and sad later when she found out she had eliminated her best friend from the finals.
   A. joyful, in high spirits
   B. dejected, in a bad mood
   C. frank, straightforward

7. You can do a lot to <u>augment</u> your income—for example, take on an extra job, invest in the stock market, or win the lottery.
   A. increase
   B. lessen
   C. modify

8. There has been a lot of pressure on politicians to make them <u>divulge</u>, or reveal, their incomes and assets.
   A. keep secret
   B. disclose, make public
   C. keep records of

9. Ms. Cohen made a <u>nice</u> distinction between *excuses* and *reasons*.
   A. pleasing, agreeable, kind
   B. exact, precise, particular
   C. socially acceptable

10. Nick was so <u>volatile</u> that he could hardly sit still and concentrate for one class period.
    A. having the power to fly
    B. explosive, tending to erupt into violence
    C. unable to hold one's attention fixed, changeable

11. Although she tried her best and practiced long and often, María's attempt at learning to play the trombone was a <u>fiasco</u>.
    A. not successful, a complete failure   C. an enjoyable experience
    B. a happy time

12. After three weeks of camping in the mountains and cooking his own food, Julio came home with a <u>voracious</u> appetite.
    A. small   C. picky
    B. huge, greedy

13. Mary's wildly impulsive behavior has always been in sharp contrast to her younger sister's <u>staid</u> nature.
    A. reckless   C. serious, composed, steady
    B. flighty

14. The <u>ornate</u> furniture seemed out of place in such a small, simple house.
    A. plain   C. heavily decorated, elaborate
    B. clean

15. At one time, a coat and tie were <u>compulsory</u> in that restaurant, but now the restaurant accepts casual dress.
    A. optional   C. required
    B. outlawed

16. If *harmony* means "internal calm, peace," then <u>harmonious</u> must mean
    A. to make calm or peaceful.
    B. having internal calm, peaceful.
    C. not calm, upset.

17. If *stratum* means "a layer," then <u>substratum</u> must mean
    A. to make into layers.
    B. a person who does layering.
    C. a layer below the stratum.

18. If *venin* means "snake poison," then <u>antivenin</u> must mean
    A. something for use against snake poison.
    B. a snake charmer.
    C. a nonpoisonous snake.

19. If *oversee* means "to supervise," then <u>overseer</u> must mean
    A. a fortune-teller.
    B. a person who supervises.
    C. to supervise more.

20. If *inept* means "awkward," then <u>ineptitude</u> must mean
    A. not awkward.
    B. the quality of being awkward.
    C. a person who is awkward.

UNIT 6

APPLYING WRITING SKILLS

Pretest

Name _____   Number Correct × 5 = [ ]

Read the two partial paragraphs that follow and the sentences that come after each. Then, in the space provided, write the letter of the sentence that would make the best topic sentence for each paragraph. The topic sentence comes first in these paragraphs.

_____ 1. They wear T-shirts identifying themselves as members of a particular club or crew. The license plates on their cars read BALLOON. And the horns on many balloonists' cars play the first few notes of the song "Up, Up, and Away in My Beautiful Balloon."

   A. Balloonists are no different from other people.
   B. Even down to earth, balloonists tend to stand out.
   C. Balloonists really enjoy their sport.
   D. Balloonists drive very unusual cars.

_____ 2. Then, to most people it probably seemed a good way to distinguish themselves from others with the same surname. Later, to politicians, it became something else; an oratorical asset. A speaker could heighten the dramatic effect by rolling out the *Jennings* in *William Jennings Bryan* or the *Delano* in *Franklin Delano Roosevelt.*

   A. The middle name didn't become important until about the time of the Civil War.
   B. "What's in a name?" Shakespeare asked.
   C. Middle names always have been of great importance.
   D. At one time middle names were important, but not anymore.

Read the two paragraphs that follow. Find the one sentence in each that does not support the topic sentence and that should thus be removed to give the paragraph unity. Write the letter of this sentence in the space provided.

_____ 3. A. Personality is reflected in the tempo of one's speech. B. A stubborn person bites off each word with clipped determination. C. A meek individual shyly punctuates thoughts with "ah's," "uh's," and "and's." D. Many meek people are very good company. E. A pedant uses long-winded sentences stuffed with polysyllabic words. F. The aged speak slowly, while the very young gush forth.

_____ 4. A. Now you can buy a whole restaurant in kit form. B. A firm in Hong Kong designs, builds, and packages Chinese restaurants and ships them all over the world. C. One such restaurant arrived in New Orleans recently in twelve containers. D. The containers were made of low-grade plywood. E. They held everything from stone lions to toothpicks to a solid brass dance floor that weighed a ton and a half. F. It took a dozen carpenters three months to assemble the restaurant. G. The price of the kit was one million dollars.

The following group of sentences can be used to make a paragraph. These sentences, however, are not in logical order. Read the sentences and put them in order by writing the letters *A* through *F* in the spaces provided.

_____ 5. A. Lemon, knowing that Palmer's curve wasn't working, looked for another fastball on the second pitch.

_____ 6. B. The Oriole defense steadied itself for a play at any base.

_____ 7. C. And some lucky fan in the left-field upper deck got a five-hundred-foot souvenir.

_____ 8. D. Lemon came to bat with the bases loaded.

_____ 9. E. He got it.

_____ 10. F. The first pitch from Palmer was a strike—a fastball right down the middle.

Arrange these sentences into a logical paragraph by writing the letters *A* through *F* in the spaces provided.

_____ 11. A. By the time the fire department arrived, the whole house was in flames.

_____ 12. B. The fire started in the basement.

_____ 13. C. The fire spread quickly through the basement and up to the first floor.

_____ 14. D. It apparently began in a pile of rags and old newspapers near the furnace.

_____ 15. E. Two hours later, all that remained of the Peterson home was a mound of smoking black ash.

_____ 16. F. The firefighters struggled bravely, but in vain.

Find the word or phrase that best completes or answers each of the following four statements or questions and write its letter in the space provided.

_____ 17. In a sentence outline, all —.

   A. the major headings are written as sentences   C. the subheadings are written as sentences

   B. the parts are written as dependent clauses   D. the parts are written as sentences

_____ 18. Which of the following outlines has the correct form—A, B, or C?

A. I. _____
    A. _____
    B. _____
      1. _____
  II. _____
      1. _____

B. I. _____
    A. _____
  II. _____
    B. _____
  III. _____
    C. _____

C. I. _____
    A. _____
    B. _____
  II. _____
    A. _____
    B. _____

_____ 19. Which of the following greetings would you expect to find in a personal letter?

   A. Dear Peter,   C. Dear Peter;

   B. Dear Peter.   D. Dear Peter:

_____ 20. In a business letter, the part that occurs directly above the signature is called the—.

   A. closing   C. heading

   B. inside address   D. body

Name _____ Possible Score │ 10 │ My Score │ │

Most paragraphs contain a sentence that answers the question "What is this paragraph about?" See if you can find such a sentence in each of the following paragraphs:

> The clouds in the distance looked ominous. I had never before seen thunderheads that hung so low in the sky yet whose tops towered to such great heights. They were colored a muddy greenish-gray. Slashes of blue-white lightning creased their dark folds.

> The once-beautiful collie was a sad sight. She had been wandering for several weeks, trying to find her way home, and now her fine, golden coat was matted and dirty. Her eyes, usually so bright and alert, were clouded with infection. She was near starvation.

The first sentence in each of these paragraphs tell what the paragraph is about. The sentence *The clouds in the distance looked ominous* tells the reader that this paragraph will describe how the sky looked before a thunderstorm. The sentence *The once-beautiful collie was a sad sight* tells the reader that the paragraph will describe the collie's appearance. Sentences like these are called *topic sentences*. The rest of the sentences in each paragraph develop the topic sentence with details.

Topic sentences are useful for two reasons: First, they give the reader a clear idea of the subject of each paragraph. Second, they can be used by the writer as a guide for selecting details.

The usual place for a topic sentence is at the beginning of a paragraph, but a topic sentence may also be placed at the end of a paragraph or even in the middle. See if you can find the topic sentence in the following paragraph:

> The roof of Mr. Sutter's house had been blown away, causing one of the walls to collapse. Power lines were down, their still-live wires arcing and hissing on the wet pavement. A towering oak tree, its trunk split by lightning, stood ablaze on the corner. Shards of glass from blown-out car windows littered the sidewalks. The street looked like a battle scene from an old war movie.

In this paragraph the last sentence is the topic sentence. It summarizes, rather than introduces, the paragraph. Yet in either position, the function of the topic sentence is the same: it states the subject of the paragraph.

Practice 1

Read each of the following paragraphs. Then choose the better topic sentence, *A* or *B*, to introduce or summarize each paragraph. Write the letter of your choice in the blank provided.

_____ 1. His eyes were outlined in dark gray circles. His nose was a shiny pink ball. A smile was painted around his mouth in vivid purple. Atop his head sat an electric-orange fright wig.

         A. The clown had a funny face.   B. The clown's face was a rainbow of colors.

_____ 2. It left the quarterback's hand in a perfect spiral. The ball floated down the field, just above the outstretched hands of the defenders. The receiver, running at full stride, looked up at the last moment. Looping downward, the ball nestled softly in his hands. The crowd roared as the referee signaled a touchdown.

         A. The pass was picture-perfect.   B. Our team scored a touchdown.

UNIT 6 Applying Writing Skills

_____ 3. The silence is almost total, broken only rarely by the chilling cry of a solitary animal. The whistles and screeches of the birds exist only in the memory now. And even when the sun-warmed snow at the top of a pine tree comes cascading down to the forest floor, even this is a muffled crash.

    A. The animals are all hibernating.   B. The winter forest is a quiet place.

Practice 2

Assume that each of the following sentences is a topic sentence beginning a paragraph. In the space after each sentence, write a brief description of what you think the paragraph will be about. Include some specific details.

1. After a smooth takeoff, our flight took on all the thrills of an amusement-park ride. _____

_____

_____

2. The rescue of the child from the burning building was daring and dramatic. _____

_____

_____

3. Mr. Rumple's costume was at once both comical and ingenious. _____

_____

_____

4. The snow was deeper than I had ever seen it. _____

_____

_____

5. My problems began the minute I boarded the bus. _____

_____

_____

6. The horse race ended in confusion. _____

_____

_____

7. I'll never forget the look on his face when I told him the news. _____

_____

_____

Name _____   Possible Score `12`   My Score `☐`

The topic sentence tells what a paragraph is about. The other sentences in a paragraph should relate directly to the topic sentence, adding details. In the following paragraph, the topic sentence comes first. As you read this paragraph, determine whether the other sentences relate directly to the topic sentence.

> The empty house on Eddy Street showed the neglect of twenty years. The sidewalk leading up to the spacious front porch was cracked and buckled. Weeds seemed to grow right out of the concrete. The porch sagged away from the house, and the hand-carved railing that encircled the house was missing in spots. Those shutters that had not already fallen to the ground hung at odd angles from the sides of the windows. For the last ten years the house had remained unsold. And there wasn't an unbroken pane of glass in the entire structure.

The sentence about the house remaining unsold for ten years relates only in an indirect, very general way to the topic sentence. It has the same subject as the topic sentence—the house on Eddy Street. But it doesn't tell you what the house looked like, as all the other sentences in the paragraph do. The paragraph would be more unified without this sentence.

As your write or revise what you have written, make sure the sentences in your paragraphs relate to the topic sentences. Sometimes, you'll find that a sentence doesn't fit in a paragraph because it really belongs in another. At other times, a particular sentence may not belong in any paragraph and should be dropped.

Practice

The topic sentence in each of the following paragraphs appears in bold type. As you read each of these paragraphs, draw a line through any sentence that does not relate to the topic sentence. If all the sentences in a paragraph do relate to the topic sentence, write the word *unified* immediately after the paragraph.

1. **It was a perfect day for the beach.** A few small clouds drifted across the deep blue sky. The sun was warm but never burning hot. A cool breeze blew in across the lake. The lake is one of the largest bodies of fresh water in the world. The water temperature was a delightful seventy degrees.

2. **Our new house is a model of energy efficiency.** It stands on the corner of Elm and Oak streets. The walls are fitted with a double thickness of insulation. The roof is covered with a series of twenty solar panels. In place of an air conditioner, we have a heat-exchange unit that keeps the temperature stable in both winter and summer.

3. **The initiation ceremony was stranger than I had imagined.** First, we all had to stand in a circle. Then black hoods were placed over our heads. Someone came by and painted a large *X* on our backs. Then we each had to recite the loyalty pledge while holding a live chicken. My Aunt Helen is allergic to chicken feathers. We were all relieved when the ceremony was finally over.

4. **The police questioned a variety of suspects about the crime.** There was Mr. Ellis Reed, a retired LaSalle Street banker. John Malina, an accountant, was also questioned. Another suspect was Louise Gulch, a waitress at a nearby restaurant. In all, the police talked to at least ten people.

5. **The flower vendor's stand was a riot of colors.** To one side stood a tall vase filled with pink and orange gladiolas. Yellow tea roses were bound together in small bouquets. Golden mums and red impatiens were arranged on a high shelf. Deep-purple lilacs gave off an intoxicating perfume. There were blue daisies, green carnations, and rare, white tulips.

6. **Ms. Jackson's class was the noisiest I had ever visited.** In one corner, a small group of students was debating the character of Shakespeare's villain Iago. In another corner, Cecilia Cortez was reciting one of her poems. Cecilia is thirteen years old and is considered a very good writer. Another group of students was doing a choral reading of Poe's "The Raven." At times, it seemed as if each group was vying to see which could be the loudest.

7. **The Chicago skyline boasts some of the world's tallest buildings.** There is the John Hancock Center, the tallest office/residential building in the world. And the Standard Oil building is the tallest marble-clad structure in the world. The biggest of them all, the Sears Tower, is officially the tallest building of any kind in the world. Chicago is also the third largest city in the United States.

8. **Our dog Penny has some pretty odd habits.** She has been known to growl for hours at nothing more menacing than a cardboard box. The vacuum cleaner sends her into a frenzy of leaping and barking. Whenever my father puts on his reading glasses, Penny slinks off and refuses to go near him. But her strangest behavior is reserved for my little sister's stuffed monkey, which Penny has buried five times in our backyard.

9. **In motion pictures, actors do not go through a play as stage actors do.** Instead, they rehearse and photograph each scene before going on to the next one. The scenes aren't always taken in story order. Often, actors begin work on the final scenes before starting the opening ones. Actors in movies are usually paid more than stage actors.

10. **Many unusual hiring practices still exist.** There's an executive in the Midwest, for example, who insists on inspecting the glove compartment of any prospect's car. Another won't hire anyone whose zodiac sign is not in harmony with her own. Zodiac signs were developed over two thousand years ago by astrologers. Still another employer, who stands five feet seven inches, will not hire anyone taller than he.

11. **The statues of generals on horseback carry a meaning often missed by many people.** If the front hooves of the horse are raised from the ground, this means that the general died in battle. If one hoof is raised, the general died from wounds received in battle. However if all four hooves are firmly planted on the ground, then the general probably died in bed.

12. By the time he met the German scientist Steinmetz, Edison was nearly totally deaf. Steinmetz communicated with Edison by tapping out messages in Morse code on his knee. Edison told Steinmetz that deafness had increased his powers of concentration. **Edison was one of those people who seem to profit by their handicaps.**

Name _____   Possible Score | 15 | My Score | |

In a unified paragraph, all the sentences relate directly to the topic sentence. But a unified paragraph may not necessarily be a coherent paragraph. A paragraph is coherent only if the sentences in it are arranged in a logical order, an order that enables a reader to move easily from one idea to the next. The simplest way to achieve coherence is to tell things in the order in which they happened. The order of the sentences in the following paragraph is purposely scrambled:

> The quarterback took the snap from the center and faked a handoff to the fullback. The offense wound up with a fifteen-yard gain. The play worked exactly as the coach had diagrammed it. As the defense tackled the fullback, the quarterback lofted a pass to the waiting halfback. While this phoney handoff was being executed, the halfback sneaked across the line of scrimmage.

The above paragraph lacks coherence because the sentences are not arranged in a logical order. But these same sentences can be rearranged so that the ideas they represent are clearly understood:

> The play worked exactly as the coach had diagrammed it. The quarterback took the snap from the center and faked a handoff to the fullback. While this phony handoff was being executed, the halfback sneaked across the line of scrimmage. As the defense tackled the fullback, the quarterback lofted a pass to the waiting halfback. The offense wound up with a fifteen-yard gain.

Practice

The sentences in the following paragraphs have been scrambled. Rewrite each paragraph, arranging the sentences in a logical order. The topic sentence may be placed first or last in each paragraph.

> Then the colonial forces counterattacked from their hideouts in the forest. The battle was a clear victory for the colonists. When the Redcoats wheeled around to face the colonists' ambush, they realized they were surrounded. The British attacked first, engaging a small band of colonists at the base of the hill. Surrender came quickly.

_____

_____

_____

_____

_____

_____

_____

_____

_____

_____

UNIT 6 Applying Writing Skills

The counterthrust maneuver brought the spacecraft under control just before the mission would have had to be aborted. The problem began shortly after the spacecraft reached orbit. Then the spacecraft began rolling at an ever increasing rate. A red light on the control panel told the astronauts that one of the control thrusters was stuck in the "on" position. In an effort to halt the motion, the astronauts began applying counterthrust.

_____

_____

_____

_____

_____

_____

_____

_____

_____

He decided he would have to rent the equipment when we reached the lake. And finally, to cap things off, it began to rain. After we were back on the road, Jack realized he had left his fishing gear in the garage back home. First, the car broke down, and we spent four hours getting it fixed. Our troubles began as soon as we left the city.

_____

_____

_____

_____

_____

_____

_____

_____

_____

Application

Name _____   Possible Score 10   My Score ☐

In both of the following two paragraphs, the original order of the sentences has been scrambled. Read each paragraph carefully. Then rewrite each paragraph, arranging the sentences in a logical order. Be sure to put the topic sentence first in each paragraph.

The president had been warned against such a public reception by his secretary and the Secret Service. The sun was boiling hot that day at the Pan-American Exposition in Buffalo. But President McKinley enjoyed meeting people and, most of all, shaking hands. Only President McKinley seemed cool and energetic as he stood shaking hands with the public in the Temple of Music. All the people had their handkerchiefs out in an effort to soak up some of the heat.

_____

_____

_____

_____

_____

_____

_____

_____

_____

_____

_____

_____

_____

_____

_____

_____

_____

_____

UNIT 6 Applying Writing Skills

Turn the page. **215**

A week later, McKinley was dead, the third president of the United States to be assassinated. The first bullet was deflected by a button on McKinley's vest; the second went deep into his body. McKinley noticed that the right hand of the next man in line was wrapped up in a handkerchief. As he was about to shake the man's hand, two shafts of fire darted out from the bandaged hand, striking the president in the chest. So he shifted his position to reach for the man's left hand.

Outlining

Name _____ Possible Score | 16 | My Score | |

Before you write a report, an explanation, or even an editorial, you should make an outline. Making an outline can help you to organize your notes and to focus clearly on what you want to say. Basically, an outline is a plan for a piece of writing. Here is an outline for a report on making bricks. As you read it, notice how the headings are marked off and arranged.

How Bricks Are Made
I. Forming the bricks
   A. Stiff-mud process
      1. Has most water added to clay
      2. Used for back-of-wall bricks
      3. Used for machine-made bricks
   B. Soft-mud process
      1. Has less water added to clay
      2. Used for handmade bricks
   C. Dry-press process
      1. Has least water added to clay
      2. Used for face bricks
II. Drying the bricks
   A. Heated to remove water
   B. Heated from one day to six weeks
III. Firing the bricks
   A. Stacked in kiln
   B. Burned to make brick strong

You will notice that an outline has several parts: a title; main headings, which are preceded by roman numerals; major subheadings, which are preceded by capital letters; and minor subheadings, which are preceded by arabic numerals. The first word in each heading is capitalized. Headings that are parallel in importance are indented the same. Each heading should be indented as shown in the outline above. Each subdivision must have at least two parts. You can't divide something into only one part.

There are two types of outlines: topic outlines and sentence outlines. In a topic outline, each heading is a word, a phrase, or a dependent clause. The outline above is an example of a topic outline. In a sentence outline, each heading is a complete sentence. Here is the same outline again, this time written as a sentence outline.

How Bricks are Made
I. Bricks are formed by three processes, which vary according to how much water is added to the clay.
   A. The stiff-mud process requires the most water.
      1. Water is added to the clay to make a stiff mud.
      2. This process is used to make bricks that are used in the backs of walls.
      3. This process is used to make bricks by machine.
   B. The soft-mud process requires less water than the stiff-mud process.
      1. Water is added to the clay to make a soft mud.
      2. This process is used to make handmade bricks.
   C. The dry-press process requires the least water.
      1. Just enough water is added to make the clay damp.
      2. This process is used to make face bricks.

UNIT 6 Applying Writing Skills

II. The bricks are dried.
    A. The bricks are heated to remove excess water.
    B. This process takes from one day to six weeks.
III. The bricks are fired.
    A. The bricks are stacked in a kiln.
    B. The bricks are burned to make them hard and strong.

Practice 1

Look carefully at the sample outlines below. Decide which of the three has the correct form and draw a box around it.

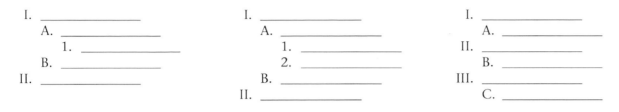

Practice 2

The title, main headings, and subheadings of a topic outline are listed below in their proper order. In the space provided, write them in outline form. Be sure to follow the rules for labeling, indenting, and capitalizing the main headings and the subheadings.

two classes of bees   _____

social bees   _____

live in colonies   _____

three main types   _____

honeybees   _____

stingless bees   _____

bumblebees   _____

solitary bees   _____

live alone   _____

five main types   _____

carpenter bees   _____

leaf-cutter bees   _____

mining bees   _____

mason bees   _____

cuckoo bees   _____

Application

Name _____

The titles, main headings, and subheadings of two outlines are listed below in their proper order. Arrange these parts into two outlines. Be sure to follow the rules for labeling, indenting, and capitalizing the main headings and the subheadings.

parts of a flower • the calyx • consists of small, green sepals • prevents harmful insects from entering flower • the corolla • consists of colorful petals •attracts pollinating insects and birds • the stamen • consists of long, narrow filaments • produces pollen • the pistil • consists of stigma, style, and ovary • stigma: holds pollen • style: leads to ovary • ovary: produces seeds • reproduces flower

_____

_____

_____

_____

_____

_____

_____

_____

_____

_____

_____

_____

_____

_____

_____

_____

_____

_____

_____

_____

_____

record trips around the world • Ferdinand Magellan • Portuguese navigator • sailed around the world • three years • Nellie Bly • American newspaper reporter • took various transportation around the world • seventy-two days six hours eleven minutes • *Graf Zeppelin* • German airship • first airship flight around world • twenty-seven days seven hours thirty-four minutes • Wiley Post • American aviator • first solo flight around world • seven days eighteen hours forty-nine minutes • Yuri Gagarin • Soviet cosmonaut • first orbit of Earth in spacecraft • ninety minutes

_____

_____

_____

_____

_____

_____

_____

_____

_____

_____

_____

_____

_____

_____

_____

_____

_____

_____

_____

_____

_____

_____

_____

_____

_____

Name _____

Possible Score | 7 | My Score

A personal letter is any letter you might send to a friend or an acquaintance. It could be an invitation to a party, a thank-you note, or just a note to say "hello." The form of a personal letter is simple and informal. As you read the personal letter below, note the arrangement and indention of its parts.

Heading

> 2025 West Touhy Avenue
> Chicago, Illinois 60645
> July 3, 199—

Greeting

> Dear Michael,

Body

> Thank you for the beautiful alabaster paperweight you sent me from Florence. It arrived this morning in perfect condition. How nice to know you were thinking of me during your travels through Europe.
>
> I expect to be in Boston sometime later this fall. As soon as I'm sure of the exact dates, I'll let you know. I'm looking forward to hearing more about your adventures.

Closing

> Affectionately yours,

Signature

> Susan

A personal letter has five part: the *heading*, which includes the sender's street address, city and state, ZIP code, and the date; the *greeting*; the *body*; the *closing*; and the sender's *signature*. Notice, too, that a personal letter is usually written in the indented style—the first word in each paragraph is indented.

The envelope for a personal letter should include the address and the return address.

> Ms. Susan Salerno
> 2025 West Touhy Avenue
> Chicago, Illinois 60645
>
>
>   Mr. Michael O'Brien
>   80 Beacon Street
>   Boston, Massachusetts 02134

Practice 1

Write the following letter in the indented style. Use your own address and today's date in the heading. Be sure to include the proper punctuation in the greeting and the closing.

Dear Kim I'd love to visit you and your family on the farm the week of the eighteenth. As soon as I've made my travel arrangements, I'll let you know what time my flight arrives. And thanks for the invitation. I'm sure we're going to have a terrific time. Your friend Jill

_____

_____

_____

_____

_____

_____

_____

_____

_____

_____

_____

_____

Practice 2

Address an envelope for the letter from Jill Casey to Kim Potter. Be sure the return address matches the address you used in the heading of the letter. Address the letter to Kim Potter, Rural Route 5, Gilman, Illinois, 65712.

Name _____

Possible Score | 5 | My Score | [ ]

The form of a business letter is slightly different from that of a personal letter. As you read the following business letter, see if you can spot the differences.

Heading	4980 North Marine Drive Chicago, Illinois 60644 August 22, 199—
Inside Address	Ms. Renata Albin Educational Films Incorporated 65 East South Water Street Chicago, Illinois 60601
Greeting	Dear Ms. Albin:
Body	Please send me a copy of your latest catalog *Films in the Classroom.* I have enclosed a check to cover postage and handling. Also, will you send me any information you have on your classroom-speakers' program.
Closing	Sincerely,
Signature	*Robert R. Halsey* Robert R. Halsey

A business letter contains one more part than a personal letter—the *inside address.* The inside address contains the name and address of the person or firm to whom the letter is sent. It is written just above the greeting. Notice that the greeting in a business letter is followed by a colon, not a comma.

Notice, also, that none of the lines in the business letter above are indented. This is called the *block style.* A business letter may also be written in the semiblock style. In the semiblock style, the first word of each paragraph is indented. For letters written in the block or semiblock style, the block style is used in addressing the envelope.

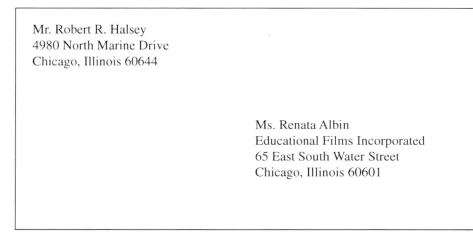

Mr. Robert R. Halsey
4980 North Marine Drive
Chicago, Illinois 60644

                     Ms. Renata Albin
                     Educational Films Incorporated
                     65 East South Water Street
                     Chicago, Illinois 60601

Turn the page.   **223**

Practice

Write the following letter either in the block style or in the semiblock style. Use your own address and today's date in the heading. Be sure to include the proper punctuation in the greeting and the closing.

Mr. Ronald Kirch The Pro Shop 825 West Main Street Evanston, Illinois 61102 Dear Mr. Kirch Three weeks ago, I sent you my application for employment at The Pro Shop. You advised me at that time to check back with you in a few weeks. Have you made a decision yet? Allow me to restate briefly my qualifications. I am a senior at Willard High School, where I am captain of the golf team. I have caddied at the Lakeview Country Club for the past three summers. I am also an experienced salesperson. Thank you for your consideration. I hope to hear from you soon. Sincerely Mary Ellen Peterson

Application

Name _____   Possible Score [17]   My Score [ ]

A. Read the following letter. Then, using the numbered lines, write the name of each part.

1. _____

2. _____

3. _____

4. _____

5. _____

6. _____

1. 4907 West Schubert
   Cedar Lake, Indiana 46303
   November 5, 199—

2. Ms. Cynthia Leonard
   Cynthia's Needlepoint
   180 West Randolph Street
   Chicago, Illinois 60601

3. Dear Ms. Leonard:

4. This letter is in response to your advertisement in today's *Chicago Tribune*. Please send me one copy of your book *Needlepoint and Relaxation*. I enclose a check for $14.95, which I understand also covers the cost of handling and mailing.

5. Sincerely,

   Ron Rutkowski

6. Ron Rutkowski

B. Write the following personal letter in the indented style.

   1150 Sutton Place Canton, Ohio 34102 December 1, 199— Dear Phillip I want to tell you what a great time I had at the concert last Saturday. Those groups were something else. And so were you, treating your sister's out-of-town visitor like an old friend. Thanks for a terrific weekend. Yours truly Margaret

_____

_____

_____

_____

_____

_____

_____

_____

_____

_____

_____

C. Write the following business letter in the semiblock style.

600 Market Street Boston, Massachusetts 02114 July 7, 199— Ms. Virginia Bauler The Common Fund 13 Reed Street Boston, Massachusetts 02134 Dear Ms. Bauler I am preparing a report on the future of the stock market for my senior business class. Since you are one of the leading financial analysts in our city, an interview with you would give my report added authority. May I interview you one day next week, between the hours of three and five o'clock? I will be happy to make an appointment with your secretary. Yours truly Robert Allenson

_____

_____

_____

_____

_____

_____

_____

_____

_____

_____

_____

_____

_____

_____

_____

_____

_____

_____

_____

_____

Name _____ Number Correct × 5 = ☐

Read the two partial paragraphs that follow and the sentences that come after them. Then, in the space provided, write the letter of the sentence that would make the best topic sentence for each paragraph. The topic sentence comes first in these paragraphs.

_____ 1. Some three hundred scripts are commissioned by the networks before the start of the season. Of these, only about sixty are made into pilots—filmed or taped test episodes. And only one in three pilots ever wins a slot on prime-time TV.

    A. Many new programs are planned for television.
    B. Most television programs aren't very good.
    C. To reach the television audience at all, a new program has to overcome many obstacles.
    D. Variety is the spice of life on television.

_____ 2. Now scientists have confirmed this belief. They have discovered that rainy days tend to make people moody. Sunshine, according to the scientists, lifts the spirit.

    A. Few people believe they can do anything about the weather.
    B. Nearly everybody believes that the weather has an effect on how a person feels.
    C. No one believes that the weather affects how a person feels.
    D. Many people are superstitious about the weather.

Read the two paragraphs that follow. Find the one sentence in each that does not support the topic sentence and that should thus be removed to give the paragraph unity. Then write the letter of this sentence in the space provided.

_____ 3. A. Some people actually believe that they can tell the age of most rattlesnakes by counting the number of rattle segments in their tails. B. But the facts prove otherwise. C. Although it is true that rattlesnakes usually grow one or two new rattle segments on their tails each year, the oldest segments fall off after only a few years. D. A rattlesnake rarely, if ever, carries more than ten rattle segments on its tail at one time. E. Rattlesnakes are most numerous in the southwestern United States.

_____ 4. A. Rocky Mountain National Park in Colorado is a mountainous haven for many different kinds of wildlife. B. Over two hundred varieties of birds have been spotted in this scenic, rugged section of the Rocky Mountains. C. Rocky Mountain National Park is also home to the Rocky Mountain bighorn sheep, as well as numerous elk and deer. D. And it has quite a large population of black bears. E. Rocky Mountain National Park has two entrances, one on the east side and the other on the west side of the park.

The following group of sentences can be used to make a paragraph. These sentences, however, are not in logical order. Read the sentences and put them in order by writing the letters A through F in the spaces provided.

_____ 5. A. Someting had apparently gone wrong with the guidance-control system.

_____ 6. B. Liftoff was perfect.

_____ 7. C. The rocket exploded in a ball of flame just seconds before it would have crashed.

_____ 8. D. The rocket rose straight up from the launchpad, trailing fire and smoke.

_____ 9. E. As the rocket nosed down toward the ground, an order was issued to destroy it.

_____ 10. F. Suddenly, the rocket began pitching from side to side.

Arrange the following sentences into a logical paragraph by writing the letters A through F in the spaces provided.

_____ 11. A. The diminishing winds and rain made the sailboat more manageable.

_____ 12. B. First, the wind, which had been blowing with gale force, began to die down.

_____ 13. C. As the sailboat struggled to remain afloat, two things happened.

_____ 14. D. We knew then that we would make it back to port safely.

_____ 15. E. We had nearly finished bailing out the boat when the sun peeked out from behind one of the storm clouds.

_____ 16. F. And second, the relentless downpour that had threatened to swamp the boat changed to a slight drizzle.

Find the word or phrase that best completes or answers each of the following four statements or questions and write its letter in the space provided.

_____ 17. In a topic outline, all —.

    A. the major headings are written as sentences

    B. the parts are written as words, phrases, or dependent clauses

    C. the subheadings are written as sentences

    D. the parts are written as sentences

_____ 18. Which of the following outlines has the correct form—A, B, or C?

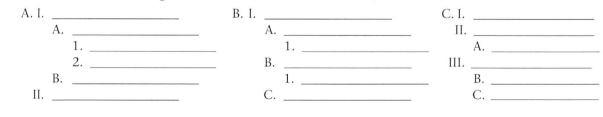

_____ 19. In a personal letter, the part that appears in the upper right-hand corner is called the —.

    A. body   C. heading

    B. inside address   D. closing

_____ 20. Which of the following greetings would you expect to find in a business letter?

    A. Dear Ms. Brisbane,   C. Dear Ms. Brisbane;

    B. Dear Ms. Brisbane.   D. Dear Ms. Brisbane:

COMBINING SENTENCES

Pretest

Name _____   Number Correct × 10 = ☐

Look at this sentence:

> The poem that I wrote will be published next week.

This sentence is the result of combining two shorter sentences:

> The poem will be published next week.
> I wrote the poem.

Each of the numbered sentences that follow is the result of combining two or more shorter sentences. Read each numbered sentence carefully. Then combine the sentences that follow it into a single sentence that is like the numbered sentence in structure.

1. The article that you mentioned was in yesterday's newspaper.
    The dog has been claimed by its owner.
    I found the dog.

    _____

    _____

    _____

2. Jupiter, which is the largest planet, is about forty-five times as big as Pluto, which is the smallest planet.
    Model railroads are not toys.
    Model railroads must be assembled by hand.
    Toys are purchased complete.

    _____

    _____

    _____

3. Stolen last year, our new car was never found.
    Jim was following us.
    Jim lost his way, too.

    _____

    _____

    _____

4. The diver broke the surface, gasping for air and holding a pearl in her hand.
    I had not expected to see him there.
    He was waiting on tables.
    He was taking orders.

    _____

    _____

    _____

5. Elaine Richmann, a member of the town council for years, was recently elected mayor.
   Our new mascot will go with us on the trip.
   Our new mascot is a goat.

   _____

   _____

   _____

6. To be first in everything was Rita's goal.
   He was always late.
   It was Fredrico's one great fault.

   _____

   _____

   _____

7. Julie's winning the golf tournament pleased her brother.
   Camilo enters every contest.
   It hasn't paid off yet.

   _____

   _____

   _____

8. Janina's disputing her bill upset the people at the store.
   Ralph practiced on the violin.
   It annoyed everyone.

   _____

   _____

   _____

9. That he wants another raise is no surprise at all.
   We can't agree on a solution.
   It is very unfortunate.

   _____

   _____

   _____

10. What you offer for this car will be acceptable.
    What will you name your cat?
    It's up to you.

    _____

    _____

    _____

Name _____ Possible Score [10] My Score [ ]

Suppose you were writing a report on Eskimo life, and you wrote these sentences:

> Most Eskimos live near the sea. The sea provides them with their food.

There's nothing wrong with these sentences. But you could combine them to avoid repeating yourself and to link the ideas they express more closely together.

> Most Eskimos live near the sea, **which provides them with their food.** [adjective clause]

Your second sentence has become an adjective clause in the first sentence. Adjective clauses are introduced by the word *which* when referring to things, like "the sea"; by *that* when referring to people and things; and by *who, whom,* and *whose* when referring to people.

When you combine sentences to form an adjective clause, place the adjective clause next to the word it modifies.

> My cousin asked me to visit her.
>
> My cousin's home is in Santa Fe.
>
> My cousin, **whose home is in Santa Fe,** asked me to visit her. [adjective clause]

You may combine more than two sentences. Here are three sentences that have been combined to form a single sentence with two adjective clauses.

> Tomatoes are a fruit.
>
> Tomatoes were once thought to be poisonous.
>
> Tomatoes originally came from South America.
>
> Tomatoes, **which were once thought to be poisonous,** are a fruit, **which originally came from South America.** [adjective clauses]

Note, also, that commas are used to set off nonessential adjective clauses.

Practice 1

Combine each of the following pairs of sentences to form a sentence with an adjective clause. Make the second sentence of each pair the adjective clause.

1. The number is incorrect. You dialed the number. _____

_____

_____

2. That woman is our new principal. That woman spoke to you. _____

_____

_____

3. Will the person please move it? The person's car is parked out front. _____

_____

_____

4. People shouldn't throw stones. People live in glass houses. _____

_____

5. I was looking for the man. The man fixed our computer. _____

_____

_____

6. Your friend called you earlier. I wrote down your friend's number. _____

_____

_____

7. The snow continued through the night. The snow began last evening. _____

_____

_____

8. The British built radar stations. The radar stations were for defense against sea and air attacks. _____

_____

_____

Practice 2

Combine each of the following sentence groups to form one sentence with two adjective clauses. Make the second and third sentences in each group into adjective clauses.

1. The banjo is a musical instrument. The banjo comes from Africa. The banjo first became popular here in the

nineteenth century. _____

_____

_____

_____

2. Alexander Hamilton favored a strong central government. Alexander Hamilton was the first secretary of the

treasury. The strong central government would be run by the elite. _____

_____

_____

_____

Name _____   Possible Score [11]   My Score [ ]

Look at these sentences:

> Tina will read us a story. The story was written by Joyce Carol Oates.

You know that these sentences can be combined to form a single sentence with an adjective clause.

> Tina will read us a story **that was written by Joyce Carol Oates.** [adjective clause]

Usually, you can make a sentence like this even briefer. You can reduce the adjective clause to a participial phrase.

> Tina will read us a story **written by Joyce Carol Oates.** [participial phrase]

The word *written* here is a participle and gives the phrase its name. *Written* is a past participle. The present participle is *writing*.

Now look at the next group of sentences to see how the sentences were combined to form a single sentence with two participial phrases:

> The blizzard swept across the Midwest.
>
> It closed roads.
>
> It brought business to a standstill.
>
> The blizzard swept across the Midwest, **closing roads and bringing business to a standstill.**
> [participial phrases]

Note that the verbs in the second and third sentences were changed to present participles when the three sentences were combined.

The position of the participial phrase in many sentences is up to you. Usually, you can place it where you think it sounds best.

> **Closing roads and bringing business to a standstill,** the blizzard swept across the Midwest.
> [participial phrases]

Practice 1

Combine each of the following pairs of sentences to form a single sentence with a participial phrase. Make the second sentence in each pair the participial phrase.

1. The president of the ad agency was a woman. The woman was named Mary Wells. _____

   _____

   _____

2. His was a record of distinguished service. It commanded our respect. _____

   _____

   _____

3. Juan walked briskly by the stereo equipment. He did not wish to spend any more money. _____

   _____

   _____

Practice 2

Combine each of the following pairs of sentences to form a single sentence with a participial phrase. Make the first sentence in each pair the participial phrase.

1. Fred was speeding in a school zone. Fred was arrested by the police. _____

_____

2. The child was bitten by a dog. The child was rushed to a hospital. _____

_____

3. Thomas tripped on the top step. Thomas tumbled down the stairs. _____

_____

4. The player crossed the goal line. The player did a little dance. _____

_____

5. The crowd fell on the purse snatcher. The crowd held him for the police. _____

_____

6. Cheryl burst through the door. Cheryl announced her engagement. _____

_____

Practice 3

Combine each of the following sentence groups to form one sentence with two participial phrases. Make the second and third sentences in each group into participial phrases.

1. At the end of the line stood Pilar. She was tapping her foot impatiently. She was looking at her watch.

_____

_____

_____

2. The boat pulled out of the harbor. It cut through the waves. It headed for the open sea.

_____

_____

_____

Application

UNIT 7   Combining Sentences

Name _____   Possible Score | 5 | My Score | |

Revise the following paragraph by combining the sentences to form new sentences having adjective clauses or participial phrases.

> There is a new kind of telephone booth. It is found in stores and restaurants from California to Wisconsin. It was invented by Mason Zelazny. The booth provides realistic background noise to bolster the excuses of people. The people are always late. A person selects one of the fourteen background tapes. A person inserts a dollar and makes his or her phone call. One tape, for example, provides a perfect background for the having-car-trouble excuse. This tape features service-station noises. It features horns honking. It features engines revving. It features a bell dinging every so often.

_____

_____

_____

_____

_____

_____

_____

_____

_____

_____

_____

_____

_____

_____

_____

_____

_____

_____

Producing Appositives

Name _____

One way to define or identify something is with a full sentence.

> The catamaran is used mainly for pleasure. **It is a boat with two hulls.** [sentence]

Another way is to combine sentences, turning one sentence into a clause in the other sentence.

> The catamaran, **which is a boat with two hulls,** is used mainly for pleasure. [adjective clause]

Still another way is to reduce the clause to an appositive. An appositive is a more compact and often a more effective way of expressing details.

> The catamaran, **a boat with two hulls,** is used mainly for pleasure. [appositive]

An appositive should be placed next to the word it identifies or defines. It usually follows a noun. But an appositive may sometimes appear before a noun.

> **A boat with two hulls,** the catamaran is used mainly for pleasure. [appositive]

Practice

Combine each of the following pairs of sentences to form a single sentence with an appositive. Make the second sentence of each pair the appositive.

1. Cathy sometimes gets seasick. Cathy is an experienced sailor. _____

   _____

   _____

2. Brian is always getting into trouble. Brian is the neighborhood practical joker. _____

   _____

   _____

3. Washington later became our first president. Washington was a skilled surveyor by the age of fifteen. _____

   _____

   _____

4. My friends are planning a camping trip to Utah. My friends are Luisa and Paloma. _____

   _____

5. Will the holder of the winning ticket please come forward? The winning ticket is number five. _____

   _____

6. Irene speaks three languages. Irene speaks English, French, and German. _____

   _____

Name _____ Possible Score [12] My Score [ ]

Look at this pair of sentences:

She studied chess problems all day. It was her idea of fun.

The word *it* in the second sentence refers to the whole idea of the first sentence. Both sentences are correct. But the ideas they express could be stated more precisely if the sentences were combined by making the first sentence into an infinitive phrase.

To study chess problems all day was her idea of fun. [infinitive phrase as subject]

Now look at the sentences that follow. The first two have been combined to produce the third and fourth sentences, both of which are acceptable.

I could phone her.

It would be a serious mistake.

To phone her would be a serious mistake. [infinitive phrase as subject]

A serious mistake would be **to phone her.** [infinitive phrase as complement]

There is another way you could combine these two pairs of sentences. You could make the first sentence of each pair into a gerund phrase.

Studying chess problems all day was her idea of fun. [gerund phrase as subject]

My phoning her would be a serious mistake. [gerund phrase as subject]

Note that when the subject of a gerund phrase is kept, it takes the possessive form, *my*. If the subject of this phrase were a noun—for example, *Mary*—then the form would be *Mary's*.

Infinitive and gerund phrases appear in sentences in places that are normally occupied by nouns. In four of the example sentences above, they appeared as subjects. However, they may also appear as objects and complements:

She likes **to study chess problems all day** for fun. [infinitive phrase as object]

She likes **studying chess problems all day** for fun. [gerund phrase as object]

Her idea of fun is **to study chess problems all day.** [infinitive phrase as complement]

Her idea of fun is **studying chess problems all day.** [gerund phrase as complement]

Practice 1

Combine each of the following pairs of sentences to form a sentence with an infinitive phrase. Make the first sentence of each pair into the infinitive phrase.

1. You could overlook his faults. It would be generous. _____

_____

_____

2. Herb would bowl a perfect game. It would take a miracle. _____

_____

_____

3. You did not vote. It means you're irresponsible. _____

_____

4. She was the best cellist in the orchestra. It was Fran's ambition. _____

_____

_____

5. You should see her. Irma is the person. _____

_____

_____

6. We should leave now. It would be a good idea. _____

_____

_____

Practice 2

Combine each of the following pairs of sentences to form a sentence with a gerund phrase. Make the first sentence of each pair into the gerund phrase.

1. He traced family histories. It was Norberto's hobby. _____

_____

_____

2. We could fly to San Francisco. It wouldn't cost too much. _____

_____

_____

3. He cheated on the test. It was a stupid thing to do. _____

_____

_____

4. The child whined. It disturbed the other passengers. _____

_____

_____

5. Bettina was late for her trumpet lesson. It really made her teacher mad. _____

_____

_____

6. She makes a lot of money. It is her goal. _____

_____

_____

Name _____

Possible Score | 15 | My Score | ☐

Look at these sentence:

> Geno never washes the dishes. It makes me mad.

Notice that the word *it* in the second sentence refers to the whole idea of the first sentence. You could combine these sentences, turning the first sentence into an infinitive or a gerund phrase. But you have still another choice. You could turn the first sentence into a noun clause.

> **That Geno never washes the dishes** makes me mad. [noun clause]

This noun clause is the subject of the combined sentences. And because a noun clause acts like a noun, it can appear as objects or complements, too.

> It makes me mad **that Geno never washes the dishes.** [noun clause as complement]

Both combined sentences have the same meaning. And in both, the noun clause is introduced by the word *that*. The difference between them is that the first sentence is more formal.

Noun clauses are also introduced by *wh-* words: *why, when, where, who, which, what,* and *how*. Here, for example, are three sentences. the first two have been combined to produce the third, a sentence with a noun clause beginning with *why*.

> I can't understand it. Why didn't you call at once?
> I can't understand **why you didn't call at once.** [noun clause as object]

Here are examples of two more combinations. Notice that the tense and punctuation of the noun clause will change when the sentences are combined.

> How did Rex find his way home? It's still a mystery.
> **How Rex found his way home** is still a mystery. [noun clause as subject]

> What did she say? I didn't hear it.
> I didn't hear **what she said.** [noun clause as object]

Practice

Combine each of the following pairs of sentences to produce a single sentence with a noun clause.

1. Ellen had a dentist appointment. Ellen forgot it. _____

   _____

2. Bill believes it. He has discovered a cheap substitute for gasoline. _____

   _____

3. Wisdom means knowing when to keep quiet. Latoria believes it. _____

   _____

4. Why did he steal the car? He could not explain it. _____

   _____

5. We know it. The earth's climate is changing more rapidly. _____

_____

_____

6. Louisiana once belonged to France. It's true. _____

_____

_____

7. When should he applaud? Moses never knows it. _____

_____

8. The temperature dropped below freezing. It was unusual for Mississippi. _____

_____

_____

9. Where will we find water? It is a serious problem. _____

_____

10. Which dress will you wear? It makes little difference. _____

_____

_____

11. Why did she quit? I don't understand it. _____

_____

_____

12. It is true. I spent the winter in San Diego. _____

_____

_____

13. How did Frank learn the truth? It is a story in itself. _____

_____

_____

14. What will he do after graduation? He has no idea of it. _____

_____

15. It is clear. Mr. Brandt will not cooperate. _____

_____

Application

Name _____

A. Combine each of the following pairs of sentences to produce a single sentence. Follow the directions given in parentheses.

1. She always looked on the bright side of things. It was her custom. (Make the first sentence into an infinitive

   phrase.) _____

   _____

   _____

2. Sheila cast her vote for Hansen. It discouraged us. (Make the first sentence into a gerund phrase.)

   _____

   _____

   _____

3. Robert Frost first achieved fame in England. Robert Frost was a fine American poet. (Make the second

   sentence into an appositive.) _____

   _____

   _____

4. Where had they gone? No one knew it. (Make the first sentence into a noun clause.)

   _____

   _____

   _____

5. I remembered it. Her birthday is today. (Make the second sentence into a noun clause.)

   _____

   _____

   _____

6. What's in the box? David wants to know it. (Make the first sentence into a noun clause.)

   _____

   _____

   _____

7. Joyce comes from a very small town. It is Polecat Creek, North Carolina. (Make the second sentence an

   appositive.) _____

   _____

   _____

8. He is very foolish. He gives anyone advice. (Make the second sentence an infinitive phrase.)

   _____

   _____

   _____

9. You contributed so much time. It made our program a success. (Make the first sentence a gerund phrase.)

   _____

   _____

   _____

B. Revise the following paragraph by combining the sentences to form new sentences having appositives, gerund and infinitive phrases, or noun clauses.

When should you give your plant a drink? You water plants in the morning. It is best. The water is warm, but not hot. Make sure it is. Some plants should never be allowed to dry out. Many ferns in particular should never be allowed to dry out. With other plants, it's just the opposite. You can water a cactus too often. You can damage the plant.

_____

_____

_____

_____

_____

_____

_____

_____

_____

_____

_____

_____

Name _____   Number Correct × 10 = ☐

Look at this sentence:

> The house that we rented has an ocean view.

This sentence is the result of combining two shorter sentences:

> The house has an ocean view.
> We rented the house.

Each of the numbered sentences that follow is the result of combining two or more shorter sentences. Read each numbered sentence carefully. Then combine the sentences that follow it into a single sentence that is like the numbered sentence in structure.

1. The petals of some flowers, which have a spicy taste, are used to flavor soup.
   The blood of insects does not carry oxygen.
   The blood of insects may be green, yellow, or colorless.

   _____

   _____

   _____

2. The French expression for a pseudonym is *nom de guerre*, which means "war name," and not *nom de plume*, which means "pen name."
   Football is as popular today in the U.S. as baseball.
   Football was based on the game of soccer.
   Baseball developed from the sport of cricket.

   _____

   _____

   _____

3. Working her way through college, Connie drove a taxi at night.
   Ralph was fishing in the lagoon.
   Ralph caught a seven-pound salmon.

   _____

   _____

4. Cancer is a disease marked by disordered growth of cells and occurring in plants as well as animals.
   The chamois is a shy animal.
   It is noted for its speed.
   It is sometimes called a goat-antelope.

   _____

   _____

5. The committee rejected Jim's plan, a hodgepodge of half-baked ideas.
   Dick discussed his career plans with Ms. McCarthy.
   Ms. McCarthy is the guidance counselor.

_____

_____

_____

6. To complain all the time is very foolish.
   You resent being overcharged.
   It is only human.

_____

_____

_____

7. His running again for office was a hopeless activity.
   We collected money for charity.
   It took a great deal of time.

_____

_____

_____

8. My mentioning the price was a mistake.
   You sent him a card.
   It was a thoughtful act.

_____

_____

_____

9. That the game will be canceled seems most likely.
   Truman won the election.
   It surprised many of the experts.

_____

_____

_____

10. Mark doesn't understand how this computer works.
    How did she lose her gloves?
    Natalia can't remember it.

_____

_____

_____

INDEX